Growing with Your Child

ELIN SCHOEN

GROWING
with
YOUR CHILD

Reflections
on Parent Development

DOUBLEDAY
New York
London
Toronto
Sydney
Auckland

PUBLISHED BY DOUBLEDAY
a division of Bantam Doubleday Dell Publishing Group, Inc.
1540 Broadway, New York, New York 10036

DOUBLEDAY and the portrayal of an anchor with a dolphin are trademarks
of Doubleday, a division of Bantam Doubleday Dell Publishing Group, Inc.

The author gratefully acknowledges permission to reprint from the following works:
C. Day Lewis, "The Newborn" from *The Complete Poems of Cecil Day Lewis.* Copyright © 1992. Reprinted by permission of Sinclair-Stevenson, Ltd.
"Living Proof." Lyrics by Bruce Springsteen. Copyright © 1992 by Bruce Springsteen ASCAP. Reprinted by permission.

Library of Congress Cataloging-in-Publication Data
Schoen, Elin.
    Growing with your child : reflections on parent development / Elin Schoen.
        p.   cm.
    1. Parenthood.   2. Parenting.   3. Parent and child.   I. Title.
    HQ755.8.S345   1995
    306.874—dc20   94-25715
                                                                                CIP

ISBN 0-385-42158-3
Copyright © 1995 by Elin Schoen
All Rights Reserved
Printed in the United States of America
January 1995
First Edition

10 9 8 7 6 5 4 3 2 1

For Herb, Jonathan, and Harry

Oh, Little Franklin! The look of happiness on his face when he saw me made my heart open and close like a sea anemone. I had never imagined I could love anyone so much . . . I . . . wished that in the welter of books about child development there was one about stages in parent development.

—LAURIE COLWIN, *Goodbye Without Leaving*

We are in this world to learn to become wiser, more compassionate, to grow. But if we know in advance how it will turn out in the end, how can we learn and how can we grow?

—ISAAC BASHEVIS SINGER, quoted by Nili Wachtel in her Postscript to *Meshugah*

Contents

Acknowledgments

The inextricability of the writing of this book from the living of my life was such that I came to call my deadline my "due date."

Therefore, when I think of all the people who have inspired and encouraged me throughout the two and a half years that it took for a nagging question—"Why, *precisely*, do I, and most other parents, feel parenthood is the greatest thing that ever happened to us?"—to develop into a manuscript, I think first, as I do in all other aspects of my life, of my immediate family.

When I married Herb, who was a widower, in 1985, I acquired another live-in relationship at the same time—with Harry, his thirteen-year-old son. Thirteen is not usually an easy period in any parent-child relationship. So my blundering into this thirteen-year-old child's life *in loco parentis*—without the early years of bonding, with no history together to cushion the shocks of adolescence—was fraught with difficulties for both of us.

From the beginning, Herb and I both felt that for me to try to function as a replacement for Harry's mother would be a mistake. And so I tried to be more like a mentor—and made a lot of mistakes, anyway. To a large extent, my relationship with Harry took place via Herb, who managed to create and sustain a nurturing context in which most of the friction that could have erupted between Harry and me dissipated.

But it wasn't until Jonathan was born, in 1987, that our family really jelled. I remember Harry's visit to my hospital room and his first encounter with his brother—and my delight at his joy at becoming a big brother. I felt, all of a sudden, much closer to him than I had before. And, through Harry's loving relationship with Jonathan, who worships him and has always called him "Bro," our closeness as a family has grown.

You will be reading quite a bit about Jonathan in this book, but not about Harry, who is now twenty-two and was not thrilled at the thought of my exploring our relationship in print. I'll settle for thanking him here for that relationship, which deepened my understanding of parenting and of the meaning of family—and a lot more.

Together, Jonathan, Harry, and Herb are my home base, my frame of reference, my proving ground, my starting point, my destination, my safety net—everything, in other words, that a family should be. As many times as they've kept me from stringing two thoughts together, they've fed my thoughts. As many times as they've intruded on my turf, they've expanded it. If it were not for them I never would have conceived of writing this book.

Which brings me to the people who facilitated my writing —the parents who let me into their lives and let me in on their family secrets. They are all exceedingly busy people. Parenthood and, for most of them, careers preclude their having much leftover time. Yet they somehow managed to give me the time I needed, and, during that time, the bulk of my material. In exchange for their candor, many of my interviewees requested anonymity. My gratitude to them, though off the record, is no less profound than my gratitude to those whose real names are used —Becka Moldover, Helene Sapadin, John Petaway, Stephanie Hickson, Rich Garner, Ruth Sack, Roberta Friedman, Stanley Friedman, Pamela R. Lopes, Frances Brent, Ron Koss, Ann Ruethling, Annette Streets, and Susan Millen—for their generosity and graciousness, for putting into words so many things that I never could have articulated without them.

But I would not have been able to make much out of what I heard from them without the help of some other exceedingly busy people. I came to this book with no training in psychology. My academic background is in art history. My professional background is in journalism. In order to get where I wanted to go, I needed knowledge that I did not have about how the human mind works, how families function, how individuals and the families they belong to interact with the societies in which they live.

A number of talented, dedicated people contributed to what amounted to my personal continuing education course. Edward F. Zigler, director of the Bush Center in Child Development and Social Policy at Yale University, gave me the opportunity to participate in the life of the Bush Center (which is a life force in educating policymakers in child development, and child developmentalists in the making of policy that affects families and children). This affiliation provided research sources as well as lectures and programs that sometimes suggested new avenues of research and that always proved enlightening and gave me the chance to meet people, exchange ideas—in short, to get out of the house and escape the isolation that is the biggest occupational hazard of writing.

I'm grateful to the entire Bush Center family for being there (for me and in general) and, in particular, to Rachel Chazan for orienting me in her field, transition to parenthood, and to Julia Denes, the assistant director, for her constant, thought-provoking interest in and input into my work-in-progress, as well as the finished product. Julia's insights and outlook always helped me to think in new directions and to clarify my ideas. And it was Julia who told me about Terry Eicher, a clinical psychologist in New Haven who explored, in his doctoral dissertation, the impact of daughters on their fathers' development.

The first time I met with Terry I came away with a shopping bag full of books and papers he thought might be useful to me. They were—especially Raymond Carver's essay "Fires." I also came away with the comforting feeling that I had found a kindred spirit, someone who truly understood what I was trying to do. And I was right. Terry has been unstinting in his support and enthusiasm. His abilities as a scholar and as a parent know no bounds. And neither does my gratitude to him.

I'm also deeply grateful to Jeffrey Lustman for his wisdom both professionally and as a parent, and to a number of other Yale University faculty members who were always helpful in giving me information I needed, as well as considerable inspiration: Donald J. Cohen, Albert J. Solnit, Steven R. Marans,

Frederick (Jerry) Streets, Sidney J. Blatt, William W. Hallo, and Peter Gay.

I'm greatly indebted to my perceptive, supportive editors at Doubleday, Casey Fuetsch and Lori Lipsky, and to others who have directly or indirectly enriched my work: Edith S. Hallo, Cis Serling, Jim Serling, David Gluzberg, Rosalie Streett, Joan Katz, Harriet Fidlow, Beth Stenger, Nathan Garland, David Millen, Robert LaCamera, Morris Wessel, Ben Schaefer, and my sister, Janet Ruhe. And special thanks to David Swinkin (without whom this book would still be in my computer), and to the incomparable Frances Apt.

Introduction

The joys of parents are secret, and so are their griefs and fears:
they cannot utter the one, nor they will not utter the other.
—FRANCIS BACON, "Of Parents and Children," circa 1625

Look, having a baby . . . overwhelms. Everything else is pea-
nuts.
—JACK NICHOLSON (from a 1992 profile in *Vanity Fair*)

WHAT I AM ABOUT TO SAY is totally unstartling, even
trite. Yet it surprises me and seems wholly original every
time I think of it: nothing I have ever done has been as fulfilling
as raising my child.

If someone had told me as recently as five years and eleven
months ago (as I write this, my son is a month away from his
sixth birthday) that I would feel this way, I would not have believed it.

Exactly five years and eleven months ago, when I managed

to drag myself and the two-week-overdue fetus I was carrying to a party, a close friend of mine, a professor of Assyriology, asked, with the same intense curiosity he lavishes on ancient tablets, how I felt about my impending metamorphosis into someone entitled to receive cards on Mother's Day.

The way he put it was: "Tell me, which do you think will be more satisfying, the books you've written or producing a baby?"

At that moment, forty pounds overweight, with tendinitis in my left foot (from lugging around all that weight), having just recovered from a root canal (attributable to my pregnancy only in my own mind), having recently realized that I would never be alone again, it was easy to answer the question. Definitely, writing a book was far more satisfying. You had to think to write, after all. Having a baby was not exactly an earthshaking achievement in my scheme of things at that moment. As Betty Friedan exploded, in *The Feminine Mystique* (in response to Margaret Mead's "glorification" of what she called "woman's biological career-line"): "One is inclined to say—so what? You're born. You're impregnated. You have a child. It grows."

A few days later, lying in the hospital with the newborn Jonathan gurgling in my arms, I thought of the professor and of his question and my answer—and of how ignorant I had been.

This is a book not about how to raise children, but about how raising children changes us, our attitudes, behavior, personality, goals, our views of ourselves and the world, subtly or dramatically, consciously and unconsciously. It is about how parenthood makes us grow, and even grow up, and how, through this process of maturation, we become better able to guide our children's development.

It is a by-product of my own growth, the result of exploring psychological terrain that I would not have known existed were it not for my son's existence.

Not that parenthood has been uncharted. It's been charted, all right. In academic journals, magazines and newspapers, in books of nonfiction and fiction, in television news shows, in TV series, and in the movies, parenthood—its triumphs, failures, history, future, norms, aberrations—has been investigated and illustrated by writers and scientists, many of whom are parents themselves. One might think that by now every nuance of parenthood had been uncovered, examined, explained, even dramatized. That's what I thought—until I tried to find out about what was happening to me as the result of having become a parent. And what turned up was surprisingly little hard evidence that anything was happening to me at all.

Most of the scientific and journalistic literature about parenthood focuses on the impact parents have on their children. And most fiction about parents and children either turns the child's lens on the parent or, again, describes the effects of the parent on the child. One exception to this orientation is the abundance of research on the biological changes wrought by motherhood. But the subject I was really looking for, which could be squeezed, I suppose, into a heading like "Parenthood as a Force in Adult Development," proved so elusive that each discovery seemed like a sighting of the Loch Ness monster.

One such "sighting" was particularly valuable: the weighty and splendid volume *Parenthood: Its Psychology and Psychopathology*, edited by E. James Anthony and Therese Benedek. Glancing through the table of contents, I found chapters entitled "Parenthood During the Life Cycle," "The Reactions of Parents to the Oedipal Child," "The Effect on Parents of the Child's Transition into and out of Latency." "Aha," I thought, "the mother *and* father lode!" That's exactly what it is. When it was published, in 1970, it was unprecedented. And it is still one of a kind, the primary source of information on parenthood from the parents' perspective.

But dealing as it does mainly with theory, it left me with as many questions as answers. (Where was the practical, hands-on, everyday stuff? Did anyone ever capture these theories in action? Where were the feelings, reactions, observations, experiences of mothers and fathers themselves?)

In the classic studies of adult development, George E. Vaillant's *Adaptation to Life*, Daniel J. Levinson's *Seasons of a Man's Life*, and *Passages*, by Gail Sheehy, parenthood is barely a blip on the screen. This, despite the fact that all three books were published after the Anthony and Benedek volume, which quite convincingly established that, in the words of Therese Benedek, "being a parent is in the center of a normal parent's self concept" and "each child in a different way . . . enlarges the scope of [his parents'] personalities, enhances their sense of identity."

It was, not surprisingly, in fiction that I found some small but tantalizing glimpses into the essence of parenthood. I remember my excitement on realizing that in Avery Corman's novel *Kramer vs. Kramer* the dominant theme, far overshadowing the custody battle, is Ted Kramer's coming of age not just as a parent but as a person, through singlehandedly having to care for Billy, his four-year-old son, after his wife abandons them. She feels she has to be on her own in order to find herself, but it is through being with Billy that Ted finds *himself*.

"He believed he had grown because of the child," Corman wrote. "He had become more loving because of the child, more open because of the child, stronger because of the child, kinder because of the child, and had experienced more of what life had to offer—because of the child."

There it is, pure and unbelievably complex, a statement of the power of parenthood to change us, to widen the dimensions of our existence, to deepen our understanding of ourselves and others.

But where were the real-life Ted Kramers (and their female counterparts)? Where were their detailed descriptions of the ways in which a child can make us more loving, more open, stronger, kinder, and more receptive to what life has to offer?

I knew that the vast repository of insights that I was after did exist, but it evidently remained locked up in the minds and hearts of millions of parents who had never learned to look profoundly and steadily into themselves in that role.

How is it, I wondered, if the parental journey is as lifealtering, as intrinsic to our being and to our becoming as I knew that it was from my own, still embryonic experience, how is it that getting into the nitty-gritty of "parenthood as a force in adult development" is so difficult?

·   ·   ·   ·

Looking back on the first year of Jonathan's life, of my new life as his mother—or rather, sifting through some notes I took during that year—I found part of an explanation for the great parental reticence I was encountering.

My notes were contained in *Baby's Journal*, which offered plenty of space beneath drawings evocative of a Victorian children's storybook for "mother and father" to record everything a new parent might possibly want to remember.

I liked that little attempt to nudge fathers to participate in the undertaking. The two truisms of baby diaries—that in most families the first child gets far more coverage than the second, third, and later children, and that this is usually women's work —still seem to apply. My husband contributed one line to "our" documentation of Jonathan's earliest months: "This is truly a child without hair."

But getting back to the format of my *Baby's Journal*: its page headings, beginning with "Waiting for Baby," are both open-ended and specific, both practical and fanciful ("Baby's First Silliness"), designed to jog the parents' imaginations as well as their more mundane preoccupations ("What Christmas Brought"). But nowhere are the parents encouraged to open up about what this baby has awakened within them, how they are reacting to parenthood. A parental reaction, in this baby book as in others I've looked at since, means parental observation and analysis of what is going on with baby at any given moment.

Of course, given all the perfectly blank pages, some parents might be moved to describe the ways in which their new child is shaping far more than their sleep patterns or financial priorities. But that is not the expectation or design of baby books any more than introspection on how Mommy or Daddy grows is society's expectation or design. And social norms do not come from nowhere; they grow out of the concerns, beliefs, behavior —the psychological norms of the individuals who make up the society.

What Wordsworth intuited—"The Child is father of the Man"; in other words, we are all, men and women, the products of our childhood—became conventional wisdom through the work of a Victorian father of six named Sigmund Freud. Although Freudian theory was debated and disputed during his lifetime and since, it remains the bedrock of modern psychoanalysis. And psychoanalysis has powerfully influenced every school of psychological thought. Fundamental to Freudian theory is the belief that the personality is formed in early childhood. How long the formative period lasts is still controversial, but not the basic premise.

Therefore, childhood has always been the major focus in research on human development. Even in literature exploring the interpersonal dynamics of the parent-child relationship the direction of the influence is predominantly parent-on-child rather than child-on-parent. And in the investigation of adult development, the resonance of childhood experience is sacrosanct. The emphasis is more on the influence of the child within each of us than on the influence of any children who happen to live with us.

Yet, as we'll see, Freud himself did speculate, from time to time and from both a personal and universal standpoint, about the psychological impact of parenthood, about some of the ways in which having and rearing children change us. He did not place parenthood in a theoretical framework, but Therese Benedek and her co-contributors to *Parenthood: Its Psychology and Psychopathology* did. So did Erik Erikson, whose elegant schema showing the potential for psychological growth and maturation from birth through senescence was the wellspring of the field of adult development.

But although Erikson clearly considered parenthood a vital source of personal growth, this particular insight was, for the most part, left behind as the field evolved.

Erikson's writings certainly illustrate, with unsurpassed contextual breadth, that we never completely outgrow our childhood. At the same time, however, he was deeply aware, and tried to make his readers aware, of "how much the older generation needs the younger one," as Robert Coles wrote in *Erik H. Erikson: The Growth of His Work*, and of the fact that "the child's 'dependency' is only half the story of human relatedness and need."

In formulating his theories about the way an individual's

identity progresses or regresses, expands or contracts, becomes richer or more bereft, flourishes or withers over the years, Erikson coined the word "generativity" to describe a way of being that he viewed as essential to psychological health in adulthood. Generativity, he wrote, "concerns parenthood . . . the establishment (by way of genitality and genes) of the next generation . . . the interest in establishing and guiding the next generation."[1]

What qualities, exactly, characterize the "generative" person, in what ways generativity fosters the development of "integrity," the "fruit" of Erikson's vision of the life journey, he doesn't say. But it is obvious from his sketch of what happens in the absence of generativity—"a pervading sense of stagnation and interpersonal impoverishment"—that generativity must encompass some degree of selflessness, the ability to put the needs of another above one's own, a sense of responsibility toward others and toward society, and that this orientation outward beams inward, feeding into what all human beings ultimately seek—the seeking of which, in fact, has become a fetish in modern times—namely, feeling whole, possessing self-esteem, important components of what Erikson simply called mental health.

Erikson did make a point of adding that the rewards of generativity are not limited to those who are parents. "There are people," he wrote, "who, through misfortune or because of special and genuine gifts in other directions, do not apply this drive to offspring but to other forms of altruistic concern and of creativity, which may absorb their kind of parental responsibility."[2]

It was, ironically, this qualification, this acknowledgment of the potential for generativity in everyone, on which some of the leading theorists of adult development, people who followed but were not necessarily followers of Erikson, based their interpretations of generativity. Therefore, in both the academic and popular literature on adult development, this term became identified more with "mentoring" than with parenting.

How is it possible that the benefits of mentoring should have excited so much more interest than the benefits of parenting, which is obviously the original model of mentoring, the paradigm for all "forms of altruistic concern and creativity?"

I believe that the explanation lies in the existence of cultural blinders that were in place earlier in recent history than we may think. In 1950, addressing the Midcentury White House Conference on Children and Youth, Dr. Benjamin Spock worried about education focusing "so largely on the world outside the home (commerce, science, technology, the arts, communication, politics) that it is difficult for a girl not to get the idea that the only contribution the world respects is in these fields. For boys, too, our education neglects, out of all proportion, the importance and the satisfaction of human relations, of family living, of rearing fine children."[3]

Despite the lip service that both men and women have always paid to the joys of bringing up children, when it comes right down to the ways in which society takes the measure of a man or woman parenthood pales by comparison to work; what is accomplished in the course of our private lives takes a back seat to how we make our livings.

And when we discard society's yardstick and try to take our own measure? Then, it seems, the dominance of the work ethic is accompanied by something else, something more elusive and sometimes downright ethereal, something variously sought in romantic love, in expressions of creativity (painting, crafts), in efforts at self-improvement (jogging, studying), in attempts to escape or transcend our stressful environment (meditation, yoga, travel).

Self-fulfillment. That's what we're after. Although parenthood seems to fit in with these private pursuits of happiness, it doesn't, really, for a surprising number of people. If anything, the self-sacrifice and constant interruptions and disruptions of parenthood are often seen as hindrances to what Therese Benedek called "high individuation," finding out who you truly are and being that person—which manifests itself, in the language of the generation that gave it cultlike status, as "doing your own thing."

The process of achieving "high individuation," of creating and defining and fulfilling one's self as extensively as possible, is widely regarded by both women and men today as something that takes place either inside the person or outside the home.

Nowhere has this view been more passionately or intelligently expressed than in Betty Friedan's *The Feminine Mystique*, particularly in the author's explication of Abraham Maslow's theory of personality development, which culminates in the achievement of "self-actualization," as a psychological backbone for her argument that the role of housewife–mother–sex object stunted women's growth. In the thirty years since *The Feminine Mystique* was published, the idea that self-actualization, unlike charity, does not begin at home has become so intrinsic to the way we see ourselves, both women and men (who, in any case, had been freed of any notion of self-definition-through-domesticity with the Industrial Revolution), that Friedan's *The Second Stage*, in which she surveyed the bleak, family-unfriendly economic and political landscape of the early eighties and contended that, yes, parenthood and homemaking could be self-actualizing if "freely chosen" (for men, too!) met with a tepid-to-hostile reception. "I don't like Betty Friedan anymore," claimed a sixty-year-old Connecticut woman whose frustration at not having reached some sort of professional nirvana was as palpable as her satisfaction with having raised two highly productive children—productive both procreatively and professionally. "She sold out."

Even my son, Jonathan, recognizes that parenthood ranks low in the hierarchy of self-actualizing pursuits. He once asked a friend of mine, Becka Moldover, what her "job" was.

"I'm a mother," Becka answered, to which Jonathan, the product of nonsexist childrearing and nonsexist day care, promptly responded, "No. I mean, what's your *real* job?"

Ironically, Abraham Maslow, unlike Friedan in her feminine mystique period, did not, in considering the contexts in which self-actualization might occur, declare the home (or rather the work one does to maintain it or the childrearing that takes place in it) off-limits or, for that matter, inevitably limiting.

When exploring "creativity in self-actualizing people," for example, he admitted that "unconsciously I had assumed that creativeness was the prerogative solely of certain professionals." But some of his "subjects" convinced him otherwise.

One woman he singled out was "uneducated, poor, a full-time housewife and mother [who] did none of [the] conventionally creative things and yet was a marvelous cook, mother, wife and homemaker. With little money, her home was somehow always beautiful. She was a perfect hostess. Her meals were banquets. Her taste in linens, silver, glass, crockery, and furniture was impeccable. She was in all these areas original, novel, ingenious, unexpected, inventive. I just *had* to call her creative. I learned from her and others like her that a first-rate soup is more creative than a second-rate painting, and that, generally, cooking or parenthood or making a home could be creative while poetry need not be; it could be uncreative."[4]

In 1968, two years before his death, Maslow told a *Psychology Today* interviewer: "The great educational experiences of my life . . . taught me what kind of a person I was. These were experiences that drew me out and strengthened me. Psychoanalysis was a big thing for me. And getting married. Marriage is a school itself. Also, having children. Becoming a father changed my whole life. It taught me as if by revelation."[5]

This book evolved from, and revolves around, the stories, ideas, and wisdom of the many men and women who struggled to define their parental selves for me and to explain how becoming, being, and developing as parents transformed their larger selves. Most of them live in Connecticut, where I live. I would have liked to travel elsewhere and talk to parents in a wider variety of settings. But one major effect of parenthood on my life that I noticed immediately on setting out on my research was that I was not willing to go too far geographically.

Just as my son provided the impetus for this book, he defined its boundaries. Parenthood is like that, expanding us at the same time as it limits us. I've always loved the old Spanish proverb "*La vida es corta pero ancha.*" Life is short but wide. Now, having added parenthood to my own mix, I'd change "wide" to "deep."

But the more parents I talked with, the less the lack of

geographical distribution seemed to matter. The area I really wanted to explore—"the nurturing domain," as Kyle Pruett so beautifully put it in his groundbreaking book *The Nurturing Father*—seemed to be common ground.

Just to be sure, I asked Rosalie Streett, the head of Parent Action, who is constantly on the road and on the phone addressing parental concerns. She finds they are the same from coast to coast—especially, she told me, the need for more of four things: time, money, information ("They're always worried, 'Did I ask the right questions when I was trying to find good day care?' 'Did I do toilet training right?' "), and "something I call 'inspiration,' which they would get if the media, schools, society as a whole respected the role of 'parent' more."

Within the nurturing domain socio-economic, geographic, educational, religious, and ethnic boundaries melt away. I remember that one of the techniques Barbara Walters disclosed in her book *How to Talk with Practically Everyone About Practically Everything*, which was published in the early seventies, was to ask people about their children. And it works. It always has and always will. No matter what the level of the discussion, logistical or existential, no matter that the two people holding the discussion come from opposite ends of the political or cultural spectrum, if they are parents, then parenthood will bring them together. Parenthood is the universal bonding experience.

My subjects may not come from many different parts of the country, but they do come from different socio-economic levels, professions, races, and religions. I talked with mothers and fathers, with married couples and single parents, and with biological and adoptive parents. What they all had in common going in, apart from the mere fact of parenthood and before even considering what they might share psychologically as parents, is that they are raising their children as well as they can. They are functioning, not dysfunctional. They are as invested in their children as they are in their jobs, often more so. For them, parenthood is definitely a source of personal fulfillment, even if they are not always conscious of it, even if their feelings during the average day are more the result of stress than contentment. In short, they are (to borrow a phrase from Bruno Bettelheim, who borrowed it from the British psychoanalyst D. W. Winnicott), "good enough" parents. Not flawless, but good enough. And good enough according to their own criteria, not mine or anyone else's.

So there will be no bad news on these pages. No mothers and fathers whose responses to parenthood were destructive or even primarily negative, no heads of families in which carelessness, to paraphrase Sue Miller, outweighs love.

The tendency of scientists, journalists, novelists, and filmmakers to focus on the abnormal, on everything that can possibly go wrong for parents and their children, can often obscure that a lot is going right. Millions of parents are trying to do the best they can. Their childrearing and their children's development stay well within the "normal" range.

It is the reactions of those parents to parenthood that have interested me. Studies of abnormal psychology and behavior *often* enlighten us about human psychology and behavior in general. Studies of the normal, which are undertaken far less frequently, *always* do. Looking into the lives of people who function well (for instance, trying to account for the resilience of some survivors of war or disaster rather than for the vulnerability of others) often suggests approaches to helping those who have trouble functioning.

The great Jewish philosopher Abraham Joshua Heschel once wrote that the arena for measuring the quality of a culture should not be its "expression" (its books, universities, artistic accomplishments, and scientific discoveries) but "existence itself" (the daily life of "a whole people, not only individuals").[6] For every individual struggling to raise children well, parenthood is, and always has been, at the center of "existence itself."

But all too many people are barred from becoming good enough parents not because they don't care or don't try but because society fails to support their efforts. This failure will continue as long as we don't have good enough day care, afterschool care, parental leave plans, health care, all the services that keep parents and children from falling behind, available for our "whole people, not only individuals." It will continue as long as teachers, day care providers, pediatricians, and most others whose work concerns children are underpaid and therefore undervalued. (An exception is people who manufacture toys, entertainment, and other products for children. There are big bucks to be made in this market!) It will continue as long as our society places a higher priority on what we produce in the marketplace than on what we produce in our daily lives.

Through exploring the meaning of parenthood, the changes that have taken place in good enough mothers and fathers over the course of their lives as parents, I have seen that real success over the long haul for individuals, and for our society, depends on our ability to value our quiet achievements in ordinary life as much as our more obvious and easily measurable achievements in the world, to celebrate what we *know* is most precious to us and live according to the directions in which it takes us.

Steven Marans, a talented child psychoanalyst, once told me that in order to understand small children's behavior, parents should "learn to listen to the music, not the words." I think that if we want to understand ourselves better as parents, we have to reverse the emphasis. We already know the music. But we need to put words to it. This book is an attempt to begin that process.

Growing with Your Child

I

Beyond Jonathan's Lunchbox

Motherhood and Fatherhood as Equal Opportunities for Development

I'm not gonna wax loquacious on the subject of my own children but . . . when I told my granddad that my wife was pregnant, he said, "Boy, you haven't lived till you've had a family." And I thought, What does he know? He's just a broke-down old cowboy, and I'm a very sophisticated actor. And as always, he knew more about me than I did.
—TOMMY LEE JONES, *GQ*, March 1994

OVER THE SOFA in Terry Eicher's living room hangs a large print of Vincent Van Gogh's *The First Steps*. This painting is a centerpiece of his doctoral dissertation, too, an image he refers to over and over, a symbol of the power of visual images to take us where language does not easily reach yet encourage us to reach for language adequate to express what we find.

In *The First Steps*, a tiny girl in a sunbonnet has just emerged from the protective arms of her mother and is about to toddle toward her father, who is kneeling several yards away. The father apparently has been working in the garden. But not anymore. This is his child's big moment. He leans toward her, arms outstretched, encouraging.

What is the father feeling? What does the sight of his little girl—her half-smile asking, Is this really me doing this?—mean to him? The only clues that Van Gogh gives are in the man's welcoming posture and in his idle spade and wheelbarrow, which represent work ignored as he concentrates on his family. But the father's back is to the viewer. We cannot see his face; we can only guess at his feelings.

Terry Eicher, himself the father of two daughters, did more than guess. Woven through his dissertation, an exploration of the ways in which men change and grow as the result of parenting girls, is an attempt to "see" the expression on the face of the gardener, to reveal precisely how, as this father "coaxes his daughter to take her first steps . . . he is the one, really, who will be coaxed out by her."[1]

Terry Eicher grew up wherever his father's work as a geologist took the family—Saudi Arabia, France, Italy, England, Texas, New York, and Egypt, which they fled during the Suez crisis. But now the drama in Terry's life is of a subtler sort, the drama of what he calls "the dailiness of life." He is "rooted in the real stuff," as one of his subjects put it, both in his work as a clinical psychologist and in the preoccupation that takes emotional precedence over his work, in fatherhood, being a father, and observing other fathers.

Long before settling on the topic of his dissertation, Terry had been aware of his daughters' impact on his life, "not in any sophisticated, profound way. I'd noticed at the level of just sheer pleasure how nothing in the world seemed so important, nothing gave me as much satisfaction, carried as much meaning. When I was at work, I'd wish I were at home with my kids. I'd think about them a lot. I noticed how much I loved brushing their hair, learning to put barrettes in their hair, making their lunches in the morning. In just a million little nitty-gritty ways like that I was just fairly preoccupied with these kids.

"So I wasn't really thinking about my personality changing

or anything like that. It was really just that my life spun around having daughters. And then if I tried to think what kind of difference they made to me as a person, in those days I could have pointed only to things at the surface of my life, to changing the way I dressed in very tiny ways. They'd encourage me to wear a purple shirt or a sweater that was more hip or more interesting."

At that time, had anyone asked Terry about the deeper impact of fatherhood, his answer would have been more or less like that of the first man he interviewed for his thesis, a psychologist who was amazed at the notion that his daughter might have had some influence on him: "That never occurred to me. I've always been so worried about my effect on her. Am I messing her up in some way? What neuroses am I burdening her with?"

It was partly concerns of this sort that led Terry to the topic of his dissertation. But he was also inspired by something much simpler, an everyday experience—reading to his daughter Caitlin, who was then six years old. Both he and Caitlin especially loved the *Little House on the Prairie* books.

"There was a part of me," he recalled, "that was just enthralled and enchanted with this life on the prairie, the homey routines, smoking the venison, making the candles. I'd grown up in some ways always wishing that my family had been peasants or something, that we hadn't moved around so much, that we'd spent more time in fewer places and really settled in those places. And I identified so much with the kids. Then, somewhere along the line, the focus changed."

In his dissertation Terry described this change as "the rather startled realization that I identified more with Pa than with his children." And he went on to "hazard the hypothesis that this shift in identification [itself] signals an enormous effect of parenthood."[2]

But revelations of this sort are usually not unprecedented. In Terry's case, the psychological groundwork began in his very first moments of fatherhood, when his older daughter, Jessica, was born. He can talk about it now with a fluency he could not have summoned then. "I was twenty-four and a half years old, just a kid. And I think that the day after she was born, I went from being a kid to being an adult. The world got turned on its ear at that point. Until then, everything had been relative. But this wasn't. This was just right at the center of my heart and at the center of my life in a way that nothing had been or that I thought anything could ever be. With my daughter, with this child, with this baby, there was no irony. There was no distance, no detachment. This was it. This was really it. Nothing intellectual about it at all. It was all feeling."

Listening to Terry, I was amazed at something that also struck me as I read his dissertation and, later, as I read *Fathers and Daughters: Portraits in Fiction*, the collection of short stories that he edited with Jesse Geller; that is, the extent to which I, the mother of a son, identified with so many of the emotions and experiences described by Terry and the other fathers of daughters.

At first, the connection seemed evident. Mother-son. Father-daughter. Of course. There's something pretty singular going on when parent and child are of different genders, a special bond. According to Freud, "the most perfect, easily the most ambivalence-free of all human relationships" is the one between mother and son, because it is "undisturbed by later rivalry." Peter Gay, having quoted this observation in *Freud: A Life for Our Time*, commented that "this sounds more like a wish than a sober inference from clinical material." And, in the same spirit, I have to say that after reading Terry Eicher one could easily draw the same conclusion about the father-daughter relationship.

But I was responding to something less rarefied. I was surprised that so much of what I had assumed to be the emotional turf of mothers was claimed by fathers as well.

This was not the first time it had occurred to me that when it comes to nurturing children, men and women may be more alike than different. My own husband, after all, had easily and joyfully fallen into the "night shift" when Jonathan was an infant, pacing with him, soothing him, singing to him for hours. Jonathan, from the beginning, bonded with his father as strongly as he did with me.

It was enormously moving to see what I thought of as maternal qualities in Herb—and in other men, men I had photographed with their children, men I had asked about fatherhood, male friends, even fictional characters like Ted Kramer. These were exceptional men, I thought. And perhaps each glimpse of a man nurturing a child was all the more touching and memorable because I did view it as exceptional.

But if my husband and Ted Kramer and Terry Eicher are exceptional, it is not because they managed to overcome a handicap that has always prevented men from nurturing but because their innate potential to nurture somehow flourished despite society's expectation that they would not be nurturers.

In recent years the literature on the ways in which fathers influence their children's development has grown measurably. The emotional package of empathy, compassion, and self-sacrifice that has always been labeled "maternal" can as easily be "paternal." It can be considered, in other words, simply "parental."

But this psychological reality is still not widely reflected in the home front and workplace.

According to the latest Labor Department statistics, women outnumber men in "nurturing" occupations, thereby making those jobs still "women's work": 97.7 percent of nursery school and kindergarten teachers are women, and 97.2 percent of child care workers in private homes are women. (The overwhelming female presence on these jobs has more to do with attitudes—"What's *he* doing here?" a young mother asked on seeing the young man who had just been hired to teach at my son's day care—than salaries, which are, on the average, only slightly lower for women than for men.)

In social policy concerning the workplace, parental leave for the most part means—or is, through the workers' application of it—maternity leave. Although fathers are becoming more of a presence in parenting magazines, which used to reach out almost exclusively to the female part of the parent population, it is striking that there is not one magazine on the market (at least as of this writing) called *Fathering* or *Working Father* or *Father and Child*. It does seem that if a publication called *Cigar*

Aficionado can find an audience, so could a magazine for men interested in fatherhood; surely they outnumber aficionados of cigars.

And in our private lives? The proliferation of TV commercials showing happily nurturing fathers, and the emphasis in TV sitcom fathers on tender paternal behavior, are welcome signs of change that is taking place, however slowly. But what many of us applaud in principle we do not necessarily put into practice.

In my conversations with other parents and in my own home, evidence keeps turning up that men have trouble coming to terms with their nurturing selves and that women have trouble relinquishing chunks of what has so long been their turf.

In our household, for instance, Jonathan's lunchbox has come to symbolize the little tug-of-war between my husband and me that underlies our fairly equal division of labor and love where Jonathan is concerned. Usually, Herb gets Jonathan up and dressed and takes him to school. I make breakfast and pack lunch. But one recent morning Herb let me sleep and did everything—and at the last minute, I came downstairs to say goodbye. I also checked to see what Herb put in Jonathan's lunchbox.

Why did I feel the need to check the lunchbox? Don't I trust Herb to pack a nutritionally correct lunch? That's what he thinks, and on reflection I realized he was right. Somewhere in me is the atavistic presumption that moms have the lunch gene. Accompanying it is the issue of territorial prerogative: lunch is my job. And on top of *that*, I felt guilty for not having done my job that morning.

Herb expressed his annoyance by grabbing the lunchbox (before I could add a single carrot) and Jonathan and fleeing. Later he admitted that, although he resented my "spying" in and of itself, he had already felt put-upon. He had acted that morning out of what he thought was pure generosity—he knew I was tired and he wanted to give me a break—but there was in his attitude an element of look-at-me-going-above-and-beyond-fatherly-duty. He was experiencing feelings that several women have told me they've noticed in their husbands. "Why is it," goes the refrain, "that there are all these things that we just do without thinking about it, but whenever a man does it, he thinks he deserves a medal?" Herb did expect at least a pat on the back. Instead, I had questioned his competence.

Herb and I consider ourselves accomplished in both male-female role-dropping and intergender communication, but is anyone really all that enlightened in these matters?

All of us need to be reminded now and then that the capacity to be a successful parent is not primarily determined by gender. The route to accepting this liberating fact lies, I think, in understanding that successful bonding and childrearing has as much to do with what we allow parenthood to bring to us and to bring out in us as with what we bring to parenthood.

Therefore, although the paternal *style* of parenting typically differs from the maternal (as established through studies of parent-child interaction), the emotions that sustain the care giving and the benefits reaped by both parent and child are pretty much the same whether the parent is a man or a woman. Nurturing can come as naturally and spontaneously to men as to women—as Joanne Marks discovered through observing her husband evolve as a father.

I met Joanne Marks at a restaurant where I was having lunch with a close friend. When the subject of parenthood came up, my friend's and mine, I noticed that the woman at the next table was listening—or trying to, since she was also coping with her talkative little girl and her very young baby.

In no time at all my friend and I had admired the children and Joanne Marks had introduced herself and Zoe, age four, and told us that baby Cara was just two and a half months old. Soon we learned that Joanne was on maternity leave—she teaches music in a local elementary school—and that time was running out. "I don't know if it's the hormones kicking in, but I've been crying for three days. I love my job, but what I really want to do is stay home and hold the baby. She's probably the last baby I'll have. I'm closer to forty than thirty."

Like so many other parents, Joanne and her husband, Kevin, both need to work—Kevin's field is computers—to provide for Zoe and Cara. And so they feel that it is also up to both of them to make sure the children are nurtured adequately.

It was little Zoe who first mentioned her father's substantial presence in her life. "My daddy hangs out with me," she announced, "and usually . . ."

"Usually you make projects, right?" said Joanne.

"Right! Usually, I make my bed and we make books, too."

"Her dad helped her make a book about the new baby and her, Xeroxed some of the pictures we have, and put a story in it," Joanne explained. "And you and your daddy make great messes, too, right?"

"Right!"

"Kevin and Zoe get into these projects," Joanne told me, "and they'll just trash the whole house. One time—I had started taking a class after work, and the first time I went, I came home and found blankets over all the furniture in the living room, and every marker we owned was on the floor and every crayon and every book, and there was tons of paper all over. Zoe was running all over the place, and Kevin was sleeping. They had had so much fun. She totally wore him out.

"Now the first thing that occurred to me was, Did Kevin give her dinner? And of course he hadn't. They'd built these massive tents with the blankets strung all around. They'd built houses and had pretend people in some of them and they'd been in some of the tents. But it never occurred to him to feed her. So Zoe and I had dinner at eight o'clock—Kevin had totally conked out. Then I spent about an hour picking up markers and crayons and blankets. But Zoe had had a great time. They both did.

"You know, Kevin always teases me. He tells me I give him instructions on how to do everything, as if he can't figure out how to do it. He just does things his way. It may not be my way, but it usually works out pretty well.

"Now here's something interesting that Kevin did. When Zoe was about a year old I went to a workshop for teachers one Saturday afternoon, and when I came back I said, 'Where are Zoe's bottles?' And he said, 'I put them up in the attic. She can drink from a cup. She can drink whole milk now. She's not eating enough solid food. So, you know, what's the point?' He had just made that decision; he'd packed up all the bottles. I said, 'Well, did she eat lunch?' And he said, 'Yeah, she ate more than I've ever seen her eat.' And that was it; she never had another bottle.

"I think a lot of why Kevin is so good with kids is that his own father was very nurturing, first of all. After his father died, his mother went back to work, and every day after school Kevin took care of his little sister. So he got into his fathering role when he was about fourteen. He kind of raised his sister."

Watching Kevin fathering Zoe and Cara, Joanne was sometimes reminded of her own father, who was more of a "worrier" than her mother. When Joanne was about thirteen she fell on a stick, severely gashing her wrist. "The nurse next door came over and put a butterfly on it and my father wouldn't let me move from the kitchen table for two and a half hours till my mother came home. What my mother seemed mainly freaked out about was that I had come running into the living room and nobody had thought to wash the blood off the floor, so it was setting in the carpet. And shouldn't we clean it up? Daddy's concern was entirely about me.

"One time when I came home at a very early hour from sleeping at a friend's house I found my father sitting up in my sister's room. She had broken her arm, and he was sitting on a dining room chair kind of dozing. He had sat by her bed all night. And she was nineteen years old! A nineteen-year-old with a broken arm, and my father would not leave. My mother was fast asleep."

As Joanne reminisced about her father I was reminded of Atticus Finch, the widowed, small-town attorney in Harper Lee's *To Kill A Mockingbird* whose devotion to justice was matched only by his devotion to his young son and daughter, Jem and Scout. The novel, written in Scout's voice, ends after the children are rescued by their mysterious neighbor from an attack by a man seeking revenge on Atticus. Jem, who was knocked unconscious, is going to be all right. And Scout, who maintains that she wasn't scared, is reluctant to go to sleep. Finally, Atticus manages to get her to bed. The story closes with her unforgettable words: "His hands were under my chin, pulling up the cover, tucking it around me . . . He turned out the light and went into Jem's room. He would be there all night, and he would be there when Jem waked up in the morning."

I thought, too, about that other great, gritty novel of childhood, Marjorie Kinnan Rawlings's *The Yearling*, in which the father, having fought off a bear that was viciously attacking his son's dog, decides that both he and the dog will spend the night in the boy's room. The boy lies in bed, shivering, still frightened, and his father says, " 'Move close, son, I'll warm you' . . . His father was the core of safety . . . A sense of snugness came over him and he dropped asleep. He awakened once, disturbed. [His father] was crouched in the corner in the moonlight, ministering to the hound."

For all the indications that many people still think men are about 99 percent more likely than women to define and develop themselves through work rather than fatherhood—as a recent Gitano jeans commercial summed it up: "When you educate a man you educate a person; when you educate a woman you educate a family"—there have been consistent hints in both fiction and nonfiction that even the most stereotypically authoritarian father figures were getting a lot more out of the experience than they let on. Even in the characters of Clarence Day and Archie Bunker we saw glimpses of the fathers they could have been—if only . . .

That they cared for their children, were moved by their children, and perhaps even progressed emotionally to some extent because they had children was shown through the occasional action, gesture, facial expression that made them, finally, sympathetic characters rather than caricatures. We did occasionally feel for them, for their emotional isolation in the midst of their bustling family life, for their inability to verbalize the love they obviously felt, for the fact that their fatherly feelings were always trapped on what Terry Eicher described as "the frontiers of the inexpressible."[3]

Some fathers of the authoritarian mold managed to give us more than a hint of their children's impact on their lives.

Sigmund Freud's letters to his close friend Wilhelm Fliess, for example, provide stunning documentation of, among other things, Freud as a passionately involved parent.[4]

As one reads the letters, it is impossible to forget that Freud was not only the father of psychoanalysis; he was also the father of Mathilde, Sophie, Ernst, Martin, Oliver, and Anna. He frequently interrupted his ruminations to provide charming and zestful bulletins on "the little ones," also known as "the rascals," "my troop," "my brood," "the worms," and "the little sheep," and by affectionate nicknames (Annerl, Mathildchen, Oli, and so forth).

Although Freud evidently did not immerse himself in the hands-on care of his "brood"—right after Anna's birth he wrote that she was "guzzling" milk and "is said to accommodate satisfactorily to all demands," although "I scarcely see her"—he was obviously smitten with his children, fascinated by them, very much present in their daily lives, very much under their influence.

He worried, boasted, exulted, suffered, pondered, marveled, and endured like any concerned parent. In documenting their ailments (remarkable not only for their frequency but for their variety—colds, tonsillitis, chickenpox, measles, scarlet fever, diarrhea, mumps, influenza, something called albuminuria), he went beyond symptoms and sympathy to confess his own concerns, even his fear.

Once, when Martin came down with possible diphtheria (it turned out to be a bad sore throat), Freud wrote, "I was shaken . . . now we had to be prepared for [the other children] taking turns, but would they all survive?" Later he confided, "Much joy could be had from the little ones if there were not also so much fright."

But Freud did get "much joy" from them. He regularly reported on their new teeth, their birthdays, their naughtiness (which he tended to find "charming"), their clever remarks, and their attractiveness. ("The loveliest part of the wedding, by the way, was our Sopherl—with curled hair and a wreath of forget-me-nots on her.")

He was at his most expansive—and expressive—after the

birth of his first child (as are most parents!), beginning one letter with the request that Fliess "kindly predate" its receipt. "I should have written it long ago, but did not get to it, what with work, fatigue, and playing with my daughter." Later he wrote, "When our little Mathilde laughs, we imagine that hearing her laugh is the most beautiful thing that could happen to us, and in other respects we are not ambitious and not very industrious."

According to Peter Gay, Freud did not tend to "parade" his tender feelings—"but in my family," Freud wrote in a 1929 letter, "they know better." "The tokens of Freud's affection," Gay concluded, "the subtle clues his bearing conveyed to his children sufficed to create an emotional environment of warmth and substantial trust."[5]

That Freud deeply felt and appreciated his children's influence on him is evident not only in his letters to Fliess and elsewhere in his correspondence but in his work itself, as we'll see later.

In the traditional scheme of parenthood, mothers nurture and fathers provide. But nowadays fewer fathers would say of their newborns, as Freud did of Anna, his youngest, "I scarcely see her." And fewer contemporary mothers would be unable to identify with Freud's recurrent worries about not earning enough to support his children. (At one point, having run into some theoretical snags, he wrote to Fliess that his dream of "eternal fame" was on the back burner and, with it, the delightful prospect of "lifting the children above the severe worries that robbed me of my youth.")

In the early seventies, when Therese Benedek contributed to *Parenthood: Its Psychology and Psychopathology* a pair of essays that took a fresh look at the innermost workings of motherhood and one of the first looks into the psychology of fatherhood, mothers were already providing as never before, although the stay-at-home or even openly nurturing father was, for the record and probably for the most part, still a thing of the future.

That Benedek was aware of this cultural shift and the impact it would surely have on individual psychology, on parenthood, and on the family may not have been apparent from the titles of her essays—"Motherhood and Nurturing" and "Fatherhood and Providing." But it is more than implicit in her message: that "motherliness" is not only biological or instinctive in origin but is created through the nurturing process itself, and that fatherhood is not, at bottom, a culturally created *role* but is driven by a real and provable paternal instinct.

In Benedek's scheme, motherhood and fatherhood are separate but are equally motivated by instinct, activated through nurturing, and catalytic in adult development.

Fatherhood originates biologically, according to Benedek, in the drive for survival. This drive is played out both in the wish to produce offspring and in the need to provide for them. Therefore, supporting one's family is not "a culturally imposed burden" on men but "nature's order." Nor does she see this urge in men as dissimilar to that of males of other species who contribute "according to an instinctually preformed pattern" to the physical sustenance of their young, bringing them food, protecting the family turf—and sometimes going beyond providing, sometimes exhibiting behavior that could accurately be described as nurturing.

It is often when men are deprived of the chance to be with their children, Benedek wrote, that the instinctual component of fatherhood becomes most clear. For soldiers during World War II, for example, the pain and fear of leaving wives and children, perhaps for good, often was mitigated by the sense of paternal responsibility (they had to return; they needed to support their children) and paternal identity (should the worst happen, their lives would continue in their children). In fact, this reason for being—paternity—may literally have saved lives. Many soldiers wrote home that their thoughts and dreams about their children enabled them not only to endure the deprivations of war but to surmount real danger.

And when thoughts and dreams become everyday routine? Then, Benedek suggested, what is motivated by instinct gains momentum through nurturing behavior itself. Nurturing, she emphasized, means not only the exclusively maternal function of breast feeding, but bottle feeding (and, later, spoon feeding), rocking, dressing and undressing, hugging, bathing, diapering, playing, reading, teaching, toilet training, disciplining, instilling values, all the caring acts of which both mothers and fathers are equally capable.

As the mother nurtures the child, building the child's confidence (or, in Erik Erikson's lexicon, "trust") in her, the child's responses build her confidence in herself as a mother. Likewise the father, nurturing the child, receives, through the infant's gratification, the satisfying, confidence-building confirmation of his competence—and the foundation of his commitment—as a father.

John Updike's description of a father taking his first child in his arms for the first time fleshes out Benedek's construct: "In even the smallest infant there was an adhesive force, a something that actively fit your arms and hands . . . *We're in this together, Dad,* the baby's body had assured him, *and we'll both get through it.*"[6]

So parents are not born but made, through the actual interactive process of parenting. "The hook," as Kyle Pruett put it, is "the sense that important, meaningful, real, and intimate things (are) happening and growing . . . setting down taproots, here, now, for tomorrow."[7]

"The primary source of development through fatherhood," according to Benedek, "is the same as for development through motherhood."[8] Children activate parental development. It is through responding to and caring for the child that an adult takes the first steps into parental selfhood. The bonding experience, the initial interaction in which the baby elicits the parent's response, stirring into being parental commitment—and more —is the template for the process that continues, if we're lucky, if we let it, throughout parenthood.

Loving and nurturing our children is a transforming process that builds our parental identity and devotion in a geometric crescendo: we do something for the child, the child responds, this response evokes emotion in us, from this emotion comes another nurturing act, and so forth. And from this process emerges and re-emerges the parental self, which, as we're about to see, can radiate outward in many different directions, profoundly influencing the evolution of the person as a whole.

II

Not Just from Caterpillar to Butterfly

The Process of Development Through Parenthood

It is as true to say that babies control and bring up their families as it is to say the converse. A family can bring up a baby only by being brought up by him.
—ERIK H. ERIKSON, *Identity and the Life Cycle*

BEFORE ERIK ERIKSON divided the life cycle into five stages of childhood and three stages of adulthood, Jaques, in Shakespeare's *As You Like It*, described the "seven ages" of man, each step in the individual's voyage from "mewling . . . puking" infant to the "second childishness" of senility.

Long before Shakespeare, the Hebrew "Sayings of the Fathers" divided "the days of our years" into fourteen landmark ages, beginning with five (when one is fit to study Scripture) and ending with a hundred (when one is as good as dead). And long before the Hebrews, an Akkadian scribe impressed on a clay tablet his (or her) breakdown of life which, interestingly, begins at forty.

The urge to see distinct periods in the course of life, to carve it into neat, sequential, logical parts to comprehend it in its entirety, could almost be said to be instinctual.

It was only natural, therefore, for Therese Benedek, at the 1958 meeting of the American Psychoanalytic Association, to declare parenthood a "developmental *phase.*" It is indeed tempting to think of parenthood as a fixed period that one goes through on the way to the next time slot in one's life.

But when does this period begin? In real life, people become parents at any age from the onset of puberty until the close of fertility. Furthermore, parenthood never ends, not even after our children move out of our homes and into their own. The intensity of our involvement with our children waxes and wanes; but once a parent, always a parent.

By 1974, Benedek, again addressing her colleagues, felt it necessary to point out that she long since had revised her definition of parenthood. It is a developmental *process*, she said, not a phase.

Much of the time, this process goes on without our acknowledging or even recognizing it. Parents do not usually brim over with awareness that their children are making significant contributions to their lives. On the average day, in fact, faced with a toddler gone haywire or a six-year-old who insists that we repair every one of his armless and legless plastic figures at the exact moment when all we want to do is collapse with the newspaper; on the average day, it may seem as if the yield from our investment in parenthood is pretty meager.

But there are plenty of moments when, if we're not too busy preserving them on videotape, our pride in our children and gratitude for their existence hits us full force. And then we may catch hold of the sustaining thread that enables us to calm the raging toddler, put down the newspaper, and fix the plastic figures—and that later in life may lead us to say, as did one young grandmother, "I cannot imagine what I would have been like had I not had children."

That sustaining thread is our parental identity, which rises or falls according to how well we connect with our children.

Our children can enrich us only to the extent that we are open to their influence.

Each of us comes to parenthood prepared—or not prepared—by our personal history, our experience of being parented, of growing up, of contending with adult life. And our response to parenthood is determined not only by our past but by our present, by how old we are, what we do for a living, by our economic status, and by other personal and social facts of our lives that make us who we are.

Some of us come to parenthood longing for a child; some of us are taken by surprise and either welcome the pregnancy or are overcome by trepidation, or both. Some of us, shaped by the history of being nurtured, are "natural" nurturers; others, never having been or felt nurtured, aren't. In a two-parent family the mix is complicated and enriched by the addition of the other partner's entire past and present and by the nature and quality of the parent-parent relationship.

But however well or poorly prepared we are to be parents, however positive or negative our attitude toward parenthood, whatever our economic status or educational background, whatever the state of our marital union, the final and strongest influence on us and the way we develop through and throughout parenthood is our children themselves.

The secret garden at the heart of Frances Hodgson Burnett's novel of that title symbolizes that influence. Two long-neglected, lonely children find each other and the garden, and, through making the withered garden flourish, find renewal. But then the garden's "magic" is transmitted through the children to Archibald Craven, the bitter, self-absorbed man who is the uninvolved, unevolved father of one of them and guardian of the other. They draw him into the garden, into childhood, and he too experiences rebirth. He falls in love with his son, and in discovering fatherhood he gets, as they say, a life.

Our children, each in his or her own way, are like the secret garden. As we cultivate them, they cultivate us.

As Jeffrey Lustman, a psychiatrist with a teenage daughter and a preteenage son, told me, "Parenting is a lot about whether you're capable of responding to the invitations your children tender by way of eliciting from you a different way of acting with each new chapter in their development.

"My daughter, for instance, teases things out of me when she's ready for them, and then the ball's in my court. Am I capable of responding? With each stage I discover a new person in her that allows me to be very different with her. And what happens then between us is just that much more rich and complex. It's like going from caterpillar to butterfly to caterpillar to butterfly. It's not just the chrysalis and then the butterfly and that's it."

Altruism and Self-Discovery

Developmental theorists of different psychological persuasions have echoed in their own terminology Freud's concept of human growth as having to do with "the interaction between two urges . . . 'egoistic' and . . . 'altruistic' . . . the one towards personal happiness and the other towards union with other human beings."[1]

The successful balance of our need for autonomy, on the one hand, and connectedness, on the other, is the cornerstone of mental health and, when we fall in love and get married or live together, the primary determinant of a healthy relationship. In fact, Benedek went so far as to say that "it is not the passion of love or its blindness that is at fault in the bankruptcy of many marriages, but the immaturity of . . . one or both partners who did not develop to the level in which gratifications could be postponed and aims and responsibilities could be shared."[2]

For Erikson the first phase of adult development is the ability, having "become oneself" or established one's identity to a substantial degree, "to develop a true and mutual psychological intimacy with another person . . . a true twoness." (Or, as the psychoanalyst George Klein once suggested, a "wego."[3])

Erikson wrote that "it pays to ponder" Freud's deceptively simple statement that the two things people should do well are "to love and to work." He went on to propose that, to Freud, love went beyond self-gratification to encompass "the expansiveness of generosity," and that work, important though it is, should not be so consuming as to usurp the individual's "right or capacity" to love.[4]

Both Erikson and Benedek set up the establishment of a mature relationship—that is, one that supports the further development of the "wego" as well as each partner's ego—as a prerequisite for the couple's gratification of their "wish (if indeed developments wait for the express wish) to combine their personalities and energies in the production and care of common offspring."[5] Both Erikson and Benedek also acknowledged that in real life things often don't happen this way.

This is the point where Benedek took a speculative leap beyond Erikson to suggest that even if things don't happen this way, if, say, two immature people get married and have children "prematurely," "the transactional processes of marriage and parenthood" can themselves promote personal and mutual development. In a marriage, Benedek wrote, "each of the partners, stimulated by the ongoing psychodynamic interactions with each other, [can achieve] another level of integration of his or her personality." She added, "The process of maturation gains another dimension through parenthood."[6] A dimension of immense proportions, as it turns out.

Parenthood is one force among many that influences our development as adults, but it is one of perhaps unmatched potential, because nothing merges the egoistic and altruistic sides of our personalities like parenthood.

The dictionary definition of altruism—"the unselfish concern for or devotion to the welfare of others"—could as well be a definition of parenthood. What the dictionary doesn't tell us about altruism—that it's never entirely unselfish, that within even the noblest do-gooder is some degree of self-interest (the Talmudic rationale for performing good deeds is that in so doing we enhance ourselves)—is also true of parenthood. In spades.

With parenthood, normally, comes a major shift in focus from the self to the other, the child. This shift in itself represents a significant change in the parent's self view—an enlargement of it, in effect. The child, more than any other person whom the parent may have loved to the point of selflessness (including the other parent!), represents an extension of the parent's self. What we perceive as getting out of ourselves, pouring so much of ourselves into our children, actually gets us into ourselves more deeply and in more ways than ever before.

When parents say, as they often do, that they "see themselves" in their children or that their children are their future, they are not just waxing sentimental; they're reaffirming, consciously or not, Freud's observation that children revive in us the narcissism of our own childhood.

In identifying with our children, we identify with our selves in a more profound and far-reaching way than we do with any other person or through any undertaking, even that which is generative (altruistic, creative). It is in this identification—or identifications, since our children lead us more deeply into ourselves in several ways—that we find the key to change.

Change Through Resolving Childhood Conflicts

Normal development—the movement of our personalities toward sophistication and coherence—unfolds in childhood through the "weathering," as Erikson put it, of internal and external conflicts primarily involving our parents and resulting in many instances of our identifying with them (incorporating aspects of them into our selves) and separating from them (differentiating ourselves from them).

Needless to say, we do not emerge fully formed into adulthood, with no psychological loose ends. As Erikson emphasized, our attempts to deal with unresolved childhood issues not only continue, but help keep us "psychologically alive," developing as adults, moving toward whatever we, and the people important to us, define as maturity.

While many of us encounter opportunities to work on resolving aspects of our past before becoming parents or without raising children, nothing brings it all back like the moment-to-moment experience of parenting. Our children, because of the intensity of our involvement and our identification with them, revive our personal histories with unprecedented clarity and power. "It happens all the time," a young mother told me. "My son does something I did at his age, and all of a sudden I'm him and at the same time I'm my parents, reacting, and I'm feeling the same friction in the situation between me and my son that was between me and my parents."

In the last chapter I described how parental selfhood for both men and women begins to take shape through the nurturing process; how the parent is not only the giver but a recipient; how the famous "bond" goes two ways so that even as the infant's confidence grows through the parent's care giving, the parent's confidence grows through the infant's gratified response to this care.

What happens is that the parent acquires new self-esteem. It may be restricted to the parent-child interaction, or, as we'll see later, it may become enhanced by subsequent triumphs and spill over into other areas—into the parent's career, for instance, or into a creative endeavor.

But to get back to the nurturing process, focusing on the mother's experience for the moment: what the mother receives from the infant, what nourishes her self-esteem, derives in part from the satisfaction of supplying someone who needs her more than anyone has ever needed her with comfort, warmth, nourishment, and security.

But there's more to the story. The mother's trust in herself reflects the child's trust in her, and something even deeper, something from long ago that is buried within her psyche and that surfaces now, though not all the way up to the level of conscious memory. It reflects, Benedek wrote, "the confidence which the mother herself . . . incorporated into her mental structure while receiving from her own mother" when she was an infant.[7]

And what about fathers? The self-esteem that a man derives from successful nurturing also comes from gratifying the needs of this touchingly dependent, vulnerable little creature. But his transformation, too, like the woman's, is driven mainly by the access his infant gives him to his own infancy.

"Each man's earliest security," Benedek wrote, "as well as his earliest orientation to his world, has been learned through identification with his mother."[8] Later, of course—and not much later—boys focus more on their fathers as role models. The passionate connection with their mothers, their identification with the maternal role, no longer dominates their being; it becomes, in the normal course of unconscious events, repressed.

Until they become fathers. Then, according to Benedek, an infant's gestures, sounds, and expressions in response to the father's care giving and affection stir up in the father the resonance of how it felt to be nurtured, of having been on the receiving end of "motherliness" (although it could as well be "fatherliness"). This may be, as Terry Eicher put it, "the crux, the central effect of children on their fathers."[9] It is the initial re-introduction to our earliest selves, as we bond with our babies, that is the archetype for a developmental process that continues for both men and women throughout the course of parenthood.

"I propose," wrote Benedek, "that in each 'critical period' the child revives in the parent his related developmental conflicts. This brings about either pathologic manifestations in the parent, or by resolution of the conflict it achieves a new level of integration in the parent."[10] She is careful to point out that "the father, like the mother, repeats with each child, in a different way, the steps of his own development, and under fortunate circumstances achieves further resolution of his conflicts."[11]

Over and over, as I talked with them, parents gave me reason to recall this "proposal" of Benedek's and to marvel at its accuracy and its universal applicability. Certainly it is not the only explanation of the way parents can progress on the developmental continuum. As we shall see, parents move toward greater "integration" in their personalities and in their lives by routes other than the psychological battlegrounds of childhood. But the idea that our children provide us, as they grow, with successive opportunities that we might not otherwise have had for working through conflicts dating from when we were growing up, and thereby moving on in our personal growth, is probably as close as anyone has come to formulating a real psychodynamic of parenthood.

At first, when our children are infants, the "memories" of

our own earliest months elicited through our interaction with them take place on an unconscious level. We do not actually think, as we soothe and comfort our babies, about the way we felt when we ourselves were soothed and comforted by our parents. But after our children reach the age at which our conscious memories begin, we may become aware of the process of associating what our children are going through with our experiences when we were at that stage of development—and of our development as adults being influenced through that process.

Jennie Gruman, who became a mother for the first time when she was thirty-nine, found herself "blowing up" at her five-year-old son every time she tried to help him read. He'd short-circuit in the middle of C-A-T, say, and into her mind would rush, "What's wrong with him? Is he stupid?" Out of her mouth, through gritted teeth, would come, "Stop being so lazy! I hate laziness!" Or "I know you know this word. You just read it yesterday. Why are you pretending not to know it?"

The child, of course, would burst into tears, wailing, "I really don't know it! I forget!" Then Jennie would apologize, hugging and kissing her little boy, ashamed and bewildered, not knowing "what had come over me."

Until one day it dawned on her that reading and her general schooling had been "the be-all and end-all of existence" for her parents, and that she, now the parent, was browbeating her child to do well just as her parents had browbeaten her. Her child's protests and tears brought back her feelings of "being stupid," her frustration at her parents' demands. Suddenly she knew how her child felt. Not wanting him to feel pressured to learn and possibly grow to hate studying, as she had, she was able to work on becoming more relaxed about the "reading issue," to help, not hinder, his efforts. Her self-esteem rose a notch as a result.

The good feelings that flow through us when we improve ourselves in some area of parenting often have a cumulative effect—even though we do not succeed in resolving each conflict dredged up from our past—and can lead us to feel better about ourselves in general. But working through childhood conflicts may have a more specific effect, too. Jennie, for instance, felt that her conquering the "reading issue" contributed to a less perfectionistic attitude toward raising her son and toward her work and her marriage. The resolution of these conflicts can lead to improvement in our mental, emotional, or even physical health.

Change Through Empathy

What, exactly, accounts for Jennie's "sudden" memory of herself as a child, suffering the outrage of her demanding parents? What caused the shift from her unconscious identification with them to her conscious link with her child's conflict, wanting both to resist and please?

Holding her child, wiping away his tears, trying to erase the frustration she had caused him, Jennie felt to the core of her being his eagerness to please, his disappointment at failing to do so, his rage at being misunderstood—and, more than that, his helplessness in the face of this formidable task: trying to make sense out of what to him was alphabet soup, to decipher these mind-boggling things called words.

It's hard to learn to read; Jennie had forgotten all about that. Now, moved by her son, drawn by him into this painful moment of childhood, Jennie found herself on his wavelength. And remembered. And identified.

"If only we could remember our own struggles [as children]," wrote Bruno Bettelheim in *A Good Enough Parent,* "then we and our children would be much better off."

Well, many parents, sensitive to nuances of their children's behavior and attuned to the possible reasons for that behavior, do remember. It is their efforts to understand what is going on within their children that leads them to remember not just events, scenes from their own early years, but how it felt back then, what it's like to be small but sometimes wanting to be big, vulnerable but sometimes wanting to be in control, dependent but sometimes wanting to be independent.

Parental empathy—the emotional and intellectual equivalent of getting down on one's knees to talk to a small child—benefits both the child and the parent. Let's consider what might happen when a hypothetical father, who, unlike Jennie, was not pushed and prodded to excel academically, finds himself up against his child's reluctance to read. The father, his memory jogged by his child's tears and protests, might simply remember how formidable the task of sounding out words seemed when he himself first tried it. Period. No dredging up of conflict. Just the memory of being a little kid with a big job in front of him. And, filled with the feelings that "job" engendered, identifying with his child, who is now filled with those feelings, he guides the child patiently. The child progresses. This progress is an accomplishment both for the child and for the father. The father's feelings of accomplishment are incorporated into his self view just as his child's are. Both of them have progressed.

In my discussions with parents I found that children foster our development not only through sparking the revival and resolution of our childhood conflicts that correspond to theirs but through another dynamic as well. Many parents described the profound effect of the access their children gave them to childhood in general. They described the ways in which their children pulled and prodded them into empathizing with childhood in a broad sense, into experiencing once again the state of being a child.

Many parents found, for instance, that a child's tacit invitation to share in discovering the world one blade of grass at a time became a chance for them to rediscover the world. And through this revival of what Abraham Joshua Heschel called "radical amazement" (which comes so naturally to children, which came so naturally to us as children), they recovered or expanded or discovered in a conscious way their spiritual selves.

Our openness to this intimate contact and connection with childhood can also reshape our creative efforts. It can alter the way we work, even the nature of our work. It can lead to permanent changes in our behavior, attitudes, and interests.

Jennie benefited from her empathetic response to her son's frustration by becoming more patient (in order to help him), feeling more self-esteem (having succeeded in helping him), and eventually being able to defuse some of the pressure to perform with which she had always tortured herself (and him!).

But helping her child with reading could, like any other type of parent-child interaction, prove fertile ground for a number of changes in a parent—in Jennie. The patience honed over months of reading lessons could become ingrained in Jennie's personality and improve her relations with her fellow workers.

Her eagerness to teach her son may spark her imagination; perhaps she'll invent reading games or projects for him and derive satisfaction from this vein of creativity within herself. And —this may sound far-fetched but it's certainly been known to happen—she may go on to market her methods, reaping more satisfaction not only from helping other parents but from the extra income!

Furthermore, reading with her son may stimulate Jennie's curiosity about subjects she had considered boring or off-limits. Maybe she was brought up to think herself "not good at" science. Now, scrambling for books to foster her son's love of reading, she discovers herself fascinated by astronomy, geology, biology—enough so that she begins to read science books for her own pleasure and enlightenment.

Maybe—again, with her son's best interests in mind—Jennie becomes interested in reading about education, and her new knowledge feeds her son's intellectual development as well as her own.

Or, by introducing her son to books she had loved, and buoyed by the waves of nostalgia these stories and pictures evoke, she may plunge into a serious exploration of children's literature. Perhaps she'll become a collector of antique children's books or try writing children's books. Even if they never make it into the bookstores, even if they make it only as far as her son's classroom or, for that matter, his bedroom, her newfound creative outlet will give her a sense of accomplishment heightened by her son's (and possibly his friends') appreciation of her efforts.

As the boy gets older, Jennie's interest in his education— joining a parent-teacher group, volunteering for classroom duty, and so forth—may lead to an expansion of her social network, to lasting friendships with other parents. Through her activities in the school she may become involved in the community at large, may support a particular candidate for the school board.

And for the first time in her life, Jennie, who has always been shy, may find in herself a new feistiness. Let's say she strongly disagrees with a certain teacher's approach to a subject. She takes on the teacher; the teacher refuses to back down. So she takes on the principal. This new ability to express her opinion in order to get what she wants—again, for her son—can spread beyond her parental life, helping her become more effective on the job, for instance.

It's clear that Jennie, spoken of right here as a hypothetical mother, has gained as much from reading with her son as he has. Her learning and maturation parallel his. He is shaping her just as—and because—she is shaping him.

Of course, a single issue in parenting doesn't usually change a mother or father in so many ways. But the story shows the myriad *possibilities* for change in just this one area of interaction. If we consider the transformative potential of the innumerable other areas in which each parent's life is touched by each child, we begin to grasp the vast and growing influence of parenthood on us as the weeks, months, and years pass.

Change Through Hope

In his dissertation on fathers and daughters, Terry Eicher wrote that "few questions seemed to prompt fathers to such a torrent of words as the question of their fantasies about their daughters' future, about what they imagined their child will be and what they wish for her."[12]

Much of the enthusiasm sprang from the fathers' strong personal identification with their daughters—all the more remarkable because these are fathers talking about daughters, not fathers talking about sons or mothers talking about daughters— and was mostly implicit in their remarks. But one father couldn't have been more explicit. He said he wanted his ten-year-old daughter to be "some feminine version of me, only better!"[13]

Forty percent of the fathers in Terry's study expressed their hope that their daughters would in some way follow in their footsteps, perhaps improving on their accomplishments, or take another path entirely, perhaps one they wished they had taken. "The father who imagines funding his daughter's biological research in New Guinea," Terry wrote, "is not himself a biologist, but is at every opportunity an awed and passionate naturalist." Another father "is not himself particularly active politically but feels this neglect occasionally nagging at him and wishes his daughters, as it were, to scratch that itch." A man whose "roots in community activism stretch back to scarcely broken commitments of the 1960s and 70s . . . wishes keenly for his daughters to remain similarly attuned to moral and political struggles around them."[14]

Our identification with our children often includes projecting onto them the optimism, the hopes, the feeling of omnipotence we once had ourselves—in different form, perhaps, but with the same result: they represent a clean slate, limitless potential, our second chance, lost dreams reborn—incarnate.

In "On Narcissism," Freud wrote that parents "are impelled to ascribe to the child all manner of perfections which sober observation would not confirm." Furthermore, they make him "the center and heart of creation, 'His Majesty the Baby,' " as the parents, of course, thought they were when they were children. His life will be an improvement on their lives. They project onto him the expectations they themselves haven't brought to fruition.

Of course, the parent whose *modus operandi* truly reflects this model of Freud's is far from the model parent. Living entirely or largely through our children is unhealthy for both the older and younger generations. At the opposite psychopathological extreme are parents who cling to their infantile narcissism as if it were a Linus blanket and are unable ever to give to, or receive from, their children. Most parents, however, manage to achieve a balance between living their own lives and helping their children live theirs.

The forty-eight-year-old father of two boys, one twenty and the other six, told me he doesn't believe that his children have to accomplish what he was never able to accomplish or to "live out my life more fully. In fact, when I think about their future, I feel a little uncertainty. I'm afraid for them. I don't expect them to be better off than I am. I worry that they won't be happy. I worry about them going into a world of AIDS, famine, more cutthroat competition than I ever had to deal with. Their lives are much more complicated than mine ever was. When I was twenty, I didn't have the foggiest notion of what I was going to be, and it didn't matter. But for my twenty-year-old son, who is also in limbo, it matters. It's killing him.

"In some ways I wish they could've grown up in the fifties like me; everything was so much saner, easier. So, no, I don't feel they're going to continue where I left off or anything like that. But I do have a sense of legacy because of them—that because I was here, I gave life to future life. I'll be leaving life, two lives, after I'm gone. And that's a good feeling."

This is a replay of the "good feeling" this man had had in childhood, when, like any child, he had enjoyed the soothing belief that he would live forever. Now, in the harsh light of adulthood, he knows the truth. But he achieves a great degree of comfort, of accomplishment, from having two children who will, in the normal course of things, survive him and will have their own children.

As our sense of "immortality . . . is so relentlessly assailed by reality," Freud wrote, "security is achieved by fleeing to the child."

When our children bring back for us moments of our childhood, we savor again the innocent assurance that we are immortal and the expectation of our limitless possibilities. When we were really children, these expectations were fantasies. Now, as adults, we have made them real by becoming parents. The phantom hopes of childhood are now flesh and blood. Our dream of immortality has been realized in our children. Whether or not we consciously view them as extensions of ourselves into the future, they are our link to the future; their existence means we have more of a future than we had before.

This sort of wishful thinking is an important component of the parental self. It is also a powerful catalyst for change in the parent's outlook and personality.

Our "hope and expectation of self-realization through the child" can motivate us to alter our behavior and attitudes in any number of ways, all of them geared toward facilitating the child's eventual emergence from the parental cocoon as "some . . . version of me, only better!"

Merely getting out of ourselves to the extent that we now invest so much of our energies in someone else broadens us as human beings; we may become more altruistic in general, more generous, more compassionate.

Many parents see successful parenting (as opposed to other forms of success) as their "real job." They are able to relax their total focus on "getting ahead" in a material or professional sense, and they find that their professional loss is their personal gain (again, as one mother put it, in terms of becoming "a warmer, more unselfish, caring, responsive, responsible, complete person").

Other parents push themselves harder, sometimes taking on more than one job, in order to give their children opportunities they missed (travel, summer camp, lessons, classes, a first-rate college education). And the time consumed by work and by parenthood leaves far less time for themselves, their old selves— but they find that they prefer their new selves.

Some parents, even while admitting that their children consume much of the energy they used to pour into their marital relationships, say that they do not view the sacrifice as an entirely bad thing. "Looking at it from the outside," a young father of four told me, "our relationship may appear to have suffered. But I find that although the time my wife and I now manage to find for each other is far shorter, it's also far sweeter."

When I asked Barbara Orlov whether she and her husband considered their two children their "real job," their major preoccupation, she confirmed the impression I had already received from her home, the décor of which could be described as Early Parenthood, starting in the small front yard, where a yellow plastic swing dangled from the maple tree, and continuing into the living room, where baby pictures covered the surface of the baby grand piano and the walls were a gallery documenting the art of family life.

Barbara works three days a week as a physical therapist; her husband, Sam, is a manufacturer's representative. Her days off are mostly devoted to being with her two-year-old son and fund raising to supplement the scholarship that enables her five-year-old daughter to attend an expensive—but essential, Barbara believes—parochial school.

For Barbara, "time to myself" means the half hour each week she spends at the osteopath's office getting therapy for her back. Time with her husband has been pretty much eaten up by their preoccupation with their kids. "It's hurt our relationship," she told me, "but we're working on it. It takes a lot of work."

Barbara is frustrated, too, by the pressure to "scrimp and save, scrimp and save" that has come with parenthood. Her parents had always provided well for her in material things; and she had done well for herself and her husband before the kids came along, working her way up to a top job in health care management, "even without having had business training."

Parenthood has pushed her back into the less fulfilling, less lucrative "physical end" of her business. It has made her days longer and harder. It has diminished her wardrobe and, at times, her sex life. It keeps her from getting to the gym to work off the weight she gained as a result of all the stress. But she is happier about herself and within herself than she has ever been.

Barbara's parents gave her a lot of things, but self-esteem was not one of them. Her mother demeaned her constantly; her father didn't defend her. "Just one example of what my mother did to me," she said, her voice tense, "is when I went away to school and got a D in a course—and I'd always got all A's in high school—my mother stopped calling me by my name for a long time. She called me 'Dummy.' That pretty well sums it up."

Even Barbara's professional success did not compensate for her mother's confidence-breaking influence, which, she believes, her mother learned from *her* parents, who possibly picked it up from *their* parents, and so on back into her family history. "When I called my mother to tell her I got this big management job," Barbara recalled, "she made some cutting remark so I couldn't even feel good about that."

But the tide turned when Barbara became a parent. "Having kids has made me stronger. For the first time, I know I've accomplished something. I don't need approval from anyone else anymore. I have a feeling inside me that I've accomplished something that I really didn't think I could from so many years of being told I was a lousy person.

"I look at my kids and I know *they're* not lousy. They're good kids. They have confidence I never had. And I know I am partly responsible for that. It makes me proud; it actually gives me a little confidence. I have stopped a cycle, a generational cycle. I'm making happy, healthy kids who will someday produce another generation of happy, healthy kids instead of dysfunctional ones.

"I feel I'm a pivotal person. And I feel good about myself, having been able to gather up enough strength in myself to change this tradition of putting down, always putting down kids, not building them up, that had been passed from generation to generation in my family. Now I think, because of me, my children's future will be better, and so will the future of generations after them. And because of my children, because they've given me this opportunity to accomplish something so important and to feel so accomplished, maybe my future will be better, too."

Not long ago, in a secondhand book store, I came across a copy of a story by Frances Hodgson Burnett that I had never heard of —*Editha's Burglar*. This little book, sixty-four pages in all, was published in 1888 and apparently has never been republished. I was immediately charmed by the gilt-edged cameo of the heroine on the cover (not to mention the melodramatic lithographs that give the book the air of a Victorian documentary), and intrigued by the idea of well-known author and unknown book.

But the biggest thrill came from discovering that *Editha's Burglar* may have been a trial run for Burnett, perhaps her first attempt to weave a story from the theme that blossoms so fully in *The Secret Garden:* the power of children to bring adults to higher ground.

Editha is "only seven—and a little over," a sweet and serious child who is "left to herself a good many hours in the day" in her parents' opulent London home. Her father is consumed with the books he writes and the newspaper he edits—just how consumed becomes apparent when, in the middle of a rare talk with his daughter, he asks her how old she is.

Editha's mother is "gentle and loving" but thoroughly taken up with her clothes, her social life, herself. Still, the little girl adores her papa and is "very, very fond of her mamma, and very proud of her," as well as protective. She never disturbs her when she is sleeping, which is much of the time, and she helps her to dress, "bringing her things to her, buttoning her little shoes and gloves, putting the perfume on her handkerchiefs, and holding her wraps."

Like many a lonely child, Editha reads "perhaps . . . more than [is] quite good for her," even newspapers, in which she learns about an occupation that both worries and intrigues her: robbery. What if burglars break into her house? On the other hand, she feels sorry for people who have to earn their living stealing other people's things. "I suppose no one ever taught them any better," she thinks.

Then a neighbor's house is robbed. Editha's mother is frightened. Since she's "not a very wise little mamma" and is given to thoughtlessness, she tells her daughter that, in the event of a burglary, she should never scream or resist; it's better to have one's things taken than to be killed. This advice, of course, sound though it may be, would hardly reassure the average child. But Editha is not the average child. She reassures her mother that if a burglar should come, she, Editha, will protect her. And, sure enough, one comes and she does.

Editha goes to bed that night feeling all the more responsible for her nervous mother because her father has had to rush to Scotland on a business trip. When she hears noises, she slips downstairs, curious as Mary Lennox in *The Secret Garden* and fearful only that the intruder will awaken and alarm her mother, and confronts a truly astonished burglar.

"Well, I'll be blowed!" he says. Editha suggests that he should say "blown." "I'm sure it isn't correct to say you'll be blowed." Then she proceeds to question him—"Are you educated?" "Is your business a good one?"—while persuading him to take her own little treasures, which she goes upstairs to get for him, rather than her parents'.

As he leaves, via the window, she thinks that "if he had had advantages, he might have been a very nice man."

In the end, Editha gets her trinkets back; the burglar, now in custody, returns them, along with a large and obviously hot silver watch on which he has scratched an affectionate greeting.

As for her parents, they are overwhelmed when Editha tells them what happened, concluding with, "He knew I was not going to scream, Mamma. And he knew I was too little to hurt him. I told him so." At this point the fairly precious text becomes as melodramatic as the accompanying lithograph of Papa and Mamma engulfing their little girl. "I have left her too much to herself," the mother says, weeping. "I will be a better mother to her, after this, and take care of her more."

But old-fashioned though the book's style may be, its message will never be dated. It is Editha's generosity, the courage that could come only from her naïve belief in the goodness of others, her abundant concern for her parents—it is everything that makes Editha herself, a child, that shows her mother and father the way out of their preoccupation with themselves and into a genuine rapport with that child, *their* child.

They, like Archibald Craven in *The Secret Garden*, illustrate the truth of what Terry Eicher said of Van Gogh's paternal gardener, urging his baby daughter to take her first steps: "He is the one, really, who will be coaxed out by her."

The parental self can begin to grow with the child's first breath or the child's first steps. Or it can begin to grow later, even much later. As we learn from *Editha's Burglar* and *The Secret Garden*, it is never too late.

III

The Spiritual Nature of Parenthood

". . . on a summer night in a dusky room
Come a little piece of the Lord's undying light
Crying like he swallowed the fiery moon . . .
In his mother's arms it was all the beauty I could take
Like the missing words to some prayer that I could never
    make."
—BRUCE SPRINGSTEEN, "Living Proof"

THINK BACK to the time when your first child was born. Many parents experience a kind of rebirth on witnessing the miracle of the new life they have produced—so many parents, in fact, that this sense of revelation is built into the idioms for "giving birth" in several languages ("to give to the light"—*dare alla luce*—in Italian, for instance, or "to bring to light"—*proizvesti na svyet*—in Russian).

Some parents, regardless of the language they speak, further express this awakening by describing a sensitivity (heretofore dormant or nonexistent) to the beauty and wonder of the natural world. Some men and women, going into parenthood, may already have a strong affiliation with a religion, a sense of their religious identity, a spiritual core. But others recall, as one mother put it, a "spiritually deprived childhood." Often, children inspire their parents to intensify their religious affiliation or to set down religious roots for the first time. As the world spins ever more out of control, many people find that religion or a strong cultural tradition gives them control, at least where it counts most: in their personal lives.

Many parents feel a need to create this safe haven for their children and themselves, to nest and provide in a nonmaterial sense. And so they find themselves moving in the direction Anna Freud once recommended to a young man who had written to her from the depths of his depression. "I agree with you wholeheartedly," she wrote, "that things are not as we would like them to be. However, my feeling is that there is only one way to deal with it, namely, to try and be all right oneself, and to create around one at least a small circle where matters are arranged as one wants them to be."[1]

The impulse—and then the commitment—to create a meaningful context for a child is often stimulated by the parent's initial experience of the child as pure, fresh, unspoiled, precious, vulnerable; each parent has his or her own words to describe this personal yet common perception.

Then, as the child develops, parents often become aware of their child as a spiritual being, and notice that the nature of childhood is profoundly spiritual. Faith, so perfectly defined in the Epistle of Saint Paul to the Hebrews as "the substance of things hoped for, the evidence of things not seen," comes naturally to small children. Their hopes and dreams flourish, unfettered by the skepticism that experience brings; for them, the invisible is viable.

And what they see, they see head-on; their vision is unprejudiced by perspective. (This is concretized in their drawings.) So much that enters their line of vision mesmerizes them. I remember watching Jonathan, as a toddler, discovering moss on the ground, sitting and bouncing on it, patting it—soft!, patting a tree—hard!, the moss again—and his face said, "Hey, I was right; it is different!" Then he hugged the tree and put his ear to it as if listening to what it had to say.

And I was mesmerized. I tried to imagine what the moss and the tree meant to him—or, for that matter, what a leaf meant, a sudden flash of sunlight, something moving that had been still before, all the things that I wouldn't notice but that were huge discoveries to him.

Often, watching their children explore, parents realize that they have lost the capacity for one-on-one communication with the universe, or their capacity for faith, or both. Often they find themselves longing to retrieve those qualities through, with, and for the sake of their children.

Parenthood can be in many ways, not all of them religious, a spiritual quest. When parents, for example, make the effort to observe traditional holidays and ceremonies, this can be ritual by rote, to be sure; but for some people it can be much more. It can connect them to their childhood memories and therefore to the childhood of their children now unfolding; it can connect their children to their ancient tradition; and it can connect the family to its own community and to its unique, strong identity in the world.

The spiritual dimension of parenthood is what parents often refer to when they talk of the meaning that parenthood gives to their lives. It is, for many of us, an important subtext of a statement like "Parenthood changed my life."

Discovering the Sacred in the Mundane

My conversation with Kate Robicheau was winding down. She was slumped in a corner of the sofa, obviously exhausted. Her sons, age thirteen and six, had kept her going all weekend. And now she was wilting from two hours of trying to pin down for me exactly how the boys—who also had kept her up too late the night before—enhanced her life. It was time to end the interview.

But just as I got up to leave, Kate started talking again. "I can remember the moment after Ben was born when suddenly I felt passionately connected to him," she said. "I think it was about a day and a half after he was born. It was around midnight, and I started getting a little antsy, and I called for him and the nurse brought him to me all wrapped up in his little blue blanket and he was steamy from just having come from his bath. I was very anxious for him to get there and it was like, Ah, that's the one, that's mine! You know, *That's* the one I want! Yes, you brought the right one in! It was very strong."

Kate's voice had become stronger as she talked. She sat up and leaned forward, her face and voice becoming more animated, the words tumbling out. "And when Tom was born, it happened much, much faster. It took maybe just about an hour, and I had an incredible sense that it's this one and no other and being passionately linked to him.

"The thing is, this time around, with Tom, because I had experienced it with Ben, I knew even before giving birth that I was going to feel that way. I remember thinking that I would be passionately loving this little creature very soon but not yet because I didn't know him yet. I hadn't seen him, I hadn't held him in my arms, but sure enough this was going to happen. It was weird; it was like knowing that you're going to fall in love right before you do—a strange feeling, almost astonishing."

It never seems to happen the same way twice. And sadly, it doesn't always happen. But when it does, the bond between parent and child is the wellspring of the relationship those two people will share for the rest of their lives. And, as we've seen, through this psychological umbilical cord the nourishment flows both ways.

Often, from the parent's perspective, the fusion with another human being who is totally dependent goes beyond biological instinct, beyond the assumption of responsibility, beyond scientific explanations. Often, the bond for the parent is not only with the child but also, through the child, with something larger, with things more easily felt than said. One mother recalled how, although she is "very unphotogenic," in every photo taken during her daughter's first year she looked beautiful. Another mother, describing how she had bonded with the photo of her adopted baby, broke down in sobs as she struggled to describe holding him for the first time. When she recovered, the word she used to describe the moment was "heavenly."

I was not surprised by the number of parents who, grasping for words adequate to encompass these overwhelming sensations, seized on religious terminology. My own husband, after all, always recalls my reaction to the newborn Jonathan as a "conversion." (That this analogy may come more naturally to him than to the average person—he is a rabbi—doesn't alter the fact that no other term is more accurate.)

There is a page in Terry Eicher's dissertation on fathers of daughters that builds to the emotional pitch of "Amazing Grace" ("I once was lost but now am found/Was blind but now I see") as he evokes the language of men "converted" by fathering girls: "We heard their thirst slaked . . . We heard them with a stake in the world . . . entering a fourth dimension . . . blessed with felicitous immortality . . . saved."[2] Indeed, one man did say he was "blind and now able to see." Then Terry pointed out how the catalyst for one of the most famous conversions of all time—Saint Augustine's—was the voice of a child. Boy or girl, Saint Augustine didn't say. (Terry, of course, thought it must have been a girl.)

I have heard parents speak of "miracles," of their "awe," their "wonder," of "ineffable joy." Not that these folks were necessarily religious. This is the language of transcendence, rather, of being transformed, of moving from one sphere into another, and it is refreshing to hear in this age when child care experts routinely rely on the language of business school (for example, "the adult management team" for a child's circle of grown-ups). It is the ethereal version of a friend of mine's "being a mommy is so big!" or of the wonderful phrase that one of Terry's subjects came up with: "rooted in the real stuff."

But wait a minute. Couldn't "real stuff" refer also to the all-nighters, the tantrums, the daily grind and grunge of parenthood, the side of parental experience that has become great material for the Dave Barrys of the world? (As in this exchange from Barry's "How to Talk to New Parents," which appeared in *Glamour* magazine: " 'She had one today,' " the mother, a stockbroker, will report in the concerned, thoughtful tone that people normally use to discuss the Middle East. 'It was runny and sort of yellow.' 'Huh!' replies the father, a very creative advertising executive, 'I thought it looked a little yellow yesterday, too!' ")

Nothing ethereal there! As Barry observed: "Taking care of a newborn baby means devoting yourself, body and soul, twenty-four hours a day, to the welfare of someone whose major response, by way of positive reinforcement, is to throw up on you." It's true. Nothing can reduce our routines or preoccupations to their lowest common denominator like parenthood. Yet no experience can be as sublime.

Listen to Norman Mailer, ruminating in his preferred third person on the summer he spent tending to five of his six kids: "Six good hardworking mindless weeks . . . his brain full of menus and shopping lists and projects and outings. [He] had not contemplated his ego in weeks . . . he now possessed an operative definition of remarkable banalities. 'The children almost drove me mad' was rich in context to him, and he could hardly have done without the lament of the truly wasted, 'I didn't have a thought to myself all day.' They were clichés. They were also paving blocks at the crossroads of existence. Who could deny after an experience like his own that all the big questions might just as well originate here?"[3]

Starting with: What accounts for this paradox? Is it a paradox? Terry Eicher doesn't think so. "Having children," he says, "is participating in something so fundamental to the cycle of life in the world. Reproduction! We try to connect with this through a lot of channels—art, mostly; a love relationship with another adult. But these are all representational. Parenthood is the real thing. That's it. It's my connection to the cycle that begins with reproduction. It's my connection to the miracle of life. It's the only direct connection to all of that."

The ethereal and earthy aspects of parenthood are, in Terry's view, yin and yang. Sometimes one is in ascendance; sometimes the other. But they work together, joining each parent to the essence of creating and cultivating life, to the heart of the matter, the heart of everything that matters, the heart of matter itself—to what it means to be human. As parents, we step into the flow of history, become part of the endless process of creation, become partners with all those millions of human beings, past and present, in ensuring a future for the human race. As parents, we truly claim "a stake in the world."

But sometimes the very universality of this achievement can diminish it. When parenthood is devalued, as it so often is, in the hierarchy of human accomplishments, it is because of the belief, which is widespread, that virtually anyone, with health, luck, perseverence, can achieve parenthood, and that only a few of us can create a skyscraper or a life-saving medication or a movie or a poem.

The fact is, although childbirth is common, universal, everyday, the arrival of this child, my child, now, is unprecedented, never to be replicated. When each of us becomes part of the continuum of act upon act upon act of creation, our contribution is like no one else's. We, having made or having welcomed into our lives this particular original human being, have become even more distinguishable from anyone else, even more ourselves.

The singularity of each and every baby is one of the world's most remarked-upon phenomena (thus the cliché "unique as a thumbprint on a baby's hand"). But what of the parent? Think of what each parent brings to the making and rearing of a child.

Our behavior as parents, who we are as parents, is determined by how old we are when our child is born, who our own parents are or were and how they raised us, what our work is and how we feel about it, our socio-economic status, whether we are married or cohabitating or single, whether (if we are married or cohabitating) our partner works, whether (if our partner works) he or she finds work satisfying or not, our personality, our partner's personality, our health, our partner's health, whether or not the two of us have a good relationship, whether we have other children or stepchildren.

In short, we are shaped as parents before the baby arrives not only by our genes and psychology but by all the cultural and social, even historical, contributions to our identity and by the meshing of all that has gone into us with the totality of our partner's being.

And then, once the baby is here, we are further shaped by the child itself, its position in the hierarchy of siblings, if there are any, by whether it is a boy or girl, by its unfolding personality, health, and appearance, by the kind of support we have in caring for the baby, by our spouse's reaction to the baby. And the list of variables contributing to our uniqueness as parents expands throughout our interaction with each child in all of his or her singularity.[4]

Talk about unique! We always find, when we get together with other parents, common ground. But deep down each of us is one of a kind, and this is among the first things we learn from our children.

One father said that he saw "so much born in my kids that comes from my wife, from me, from our parents, from our grandparents. They're so innocent, but there's something in them also that's almost—old."

Another man explained that "just as the bond that's formed between the mother and newborn during nursing is purely physical and emotional, not intellectual, I felt the same thing as a father. Call it a massive amount of love for this being who just came into existence and continued to unite my wife and me every time I thought of him, every time I looked at him. The feeling was one of awe—this being is part of us."

"A massive amount of love." The love that this father feels for his child—for both of his children—is not quantifiable. It is not like love for another adult, which one expects to have returned in kind. An infant can't possibly return our love in kind, and the emergent child doesn't always want to! And so, for the first time, the new parent may experience a love that expects no rewards except for the privilege of feeling this way. Many parents told me they did not believe they had the potential for this kind of love—until it happened.

Jeffrey Lustman, remembering the birth of his first child, said, "I watched my wife, who in pregnancy was daily communing with this experience, already having it. For me, I was just waiting. I tried hard and had my version of her pregnancy, but I was basically spinning my wheels, thinking about having a child, and she was falling in love with this visceral thing that was happening. Not just a thought; a visceral, body thing. I'm not saying she loved pregnancy, but she was bouncing off an experience, interacting with a kind of rock of experience. I didn't have any rock to react to. What I had was this question: Will I be able to love? Because I don't love all kids. I thought, What if I don't love my kid? Holy shit! Am I going to pretend for thirty years?

"And then she was born, and it was like an off-on switch. From the very first day of my daughter's life I discovered the capacity to love that I had not known existed. I mean, I've loved deeply, many people, but not the way I love her. That kind of love is just different, more full."

Diane Foster was able to explain "that kind of love," at least as it has transformed her own life, with the fluency of one who has actively looked for the answers to, as Mailer put it, "all the big questions." Diane's childhood was a varied landscape both geographically and spiritually. Because of her father's career, she grew up on three continents. But it was the places her father's internal restlessness took them—"I went with him to everything from Christian Science churches to Self-Realization Fellowship; you name it, we did it"—that determined the direction of her life more than anything else. Like her father, Diane was always searching for "something, anything, everything that might help." And the search took on an almost desperate urgency when she was in college after a devastating automobile accident left her confined to a wheelchair.

"I just fell apart," Diane recalls. "It was like the little cartoon figure who walks off the cliff and then goes 'Blaaagh!' Everything was called into question, from the most basic ideas. Like: What is a self? Where does it exist, really? I was pretty heavily involved in Christianity when I was in college, but the Christian method, prayer, dialogue with God, didn't make any sense to me anymore. I thought I needed a technique, a tool, that's more fundamental.

"When I could walk again, I went to Japan on a pilgrimage, and at one point I was sitting on some stone steps way out in the countryside and all of a sudden a shadow was cast across the path and it was a Buddhist monk. He was wearing sandals and his feet were all lacerated. For some reason, I suddenly remembered my father telling me when I was a little kid that doing Zen meditation had helped him more than anything else, and if I'm ever really stuck, I should remember that. And I thought, I'm really stuck."

Diane went to a town south of Tokyo known, on the one hand, for its tourist attractions and, all the way on the other hand, for a temple with a renowned Zen master. She ended up studying with him for eight years. She met her husband there. "He had finished medical school," she explained, "and, after his residency, he took a trip to Japan. When he got off the plane at the Tokyo airport, he went to the tourist bureau to find out where he could do Zen meditation, and they sent him to the master I was studying with, and we met. We decided to come back here to get married, and then we returned to Japan for two and a half years. Sophia was born there."

The first time I talked with Diane, who has been working on her doctoral dissertation on Buddhism for most of Sophia's six years, she was happily preoccupied with material matters. She and her husband and Sophia were about to move to a new house. Her mind was filled with floor plans, shopping lists, and the impending arrival of a woman from the real estate agency who would tell her what she could do to make her present house more marketable. But all of this dropped away as she described the meaning of Sophia, recalling how motherhood finally established her comfortably, made her at home on the more exalted plane of existence she had reached through meditation.

"Having a child was like being an instrument of some higher force for me," she said. "It was as if I'd never experienced love like that in my life, never even imagined it. I guess that's the central experience of being a parent, that I've almost become a channel for something so much greater than myself. And feeling that much love for someone else changed my entire world view, my perspective, everything. At first it was all-consuming and over the years it's become less so—but it's something I have to think about and I can feel it. It's always something to go back to. And one thing, in terms of me personally, is that I can never really feel lonely again in a profound way, because I think loneliness is wanting to feel that kind of love from somebody else. I developed a certain peace of mind that can never go away. Even when Sophia grows up, it will never change."

But there was still more to this picture, and it did not emerge until later in the conversation, when I brought up an effect of parenthood that I thought belonged to the psychological rather than the spiritual realm. I asked Diane whether, since becoming a mother, she had, like many parents, become more fearful, less inclined to take even garden-variety risks, such as traveling by plane. Her answer astounded me. It took us right back to her concept of parental love, expanding it dramatically.

"I think I'm less fearful now," she said. "I used to go on an airplane and if I wasn't heavily sedated I'd have panic attacks. Now I feel I've been a part of life, and it's different. In other words, if I die now, I feel I'll have participated so deeply in what life is, having had Sophia. I've given life. I've created some life. So if I disappear now it would be okay. Do you know what I mean? It's not that death is something I'm ready for, but I no longer fear it. I've done a lot. I've had a child."

Secular Spirituality: How Children Make Everything Old Seem New Again

When Selma Fraiberg named the period from birth to age five "the magic years," she was referring to the quality of the young child's thinking. Her book of that title focuses on giving parents a profound appreciation of the child's view of things, the better for them to understand and deal with their children's behavior. But, as Fraiberg must have been aware, "the magic years" also captures the way many mothers and fathers think of this stage of their children's lives.

Although it is, of course, a mistake to think of babies and young children as innocent creatures, psychologically speaking, there is an air of innocence about them as they drink in everything that is new. It is magical to watch this happen, to realize that everything *is* new to them. As we watch and guide them, and try to interpret and explain, we are able to feel their enchantment, their curiosity, their surprise, at times their fear.

Through our children we can rediscover the child's eye view of the world. We can become more keenly attuned to our own nature, the child's nature, and nature itself. We can escape the "unreasonable world," as Sinclair Lewis put it in 1917, which "sacrific[es] bird-song and tranquil dusk and high golden noons to selling junk—yet it rules us. And life lives there."[5]

Our children, more surely than any other influence, convince us that that is not, in fact, where life lives!

The young mother of a two-year-old, only days away from the delivery date of her second child, told me that for all the pleasure she derives from "translating the world" for her daughter, she finds it equally exciting when, as often happens, her daughter sharpens her perceptions. "She slows me down. I used to rush, so that going through the day I could be walking down the street, for instance, and wouldn't notice anything. That's very unfortunate! I always thought, when I was younger, what a terrible thing, to walk and not really see anything. She makes me see. That's one of the greatest things she's given me. All the exploration. It's like exploring the world again—her discovery of the ground, her discovery of a blade of grass. It's wonderful. Although it can also be very frustrating, when you want to get to the park and it takes forty minutes because she stops to look at every puddle and ant and flower!"

"We're stuck until we have children in our own minds," said Frances Brent, who is a poet, a short story writer, an editor, a teacher, and the mother of two sons, nineteen and two, and a six-month-old daughter. "With children," she told me, "you see things in a way that you don't as an adult because you see them new and you see them up close and you see the ways they can be used that as a dumb adult you didn't. The furniture, for instance. When you have a child, you get to be intimately familiar with the furniture in your house. You see the bottom sides. You see the grain. You discover the noises it makes when it's hit with something; you hear it. You discover how delightful everything is in a way that adults don't ordinarily notice."

A new perspective on furniture came up in my discussions

with other parents, too. Becka Moldover mentioned how her children showed her that "furniture is a tool to be used and not an intrinsic thing in its own right, so my concept of what furniture actually is expanded. We adults may want to think of a chair as something to sit on, or something we'd like to last for generations. But suddenly we become aware of it as something to climb, to explore, to jump onto and off—so we modify our expectations of its longevity. Maybe with luck it'll last till next year!"

Becka also remarked on how inspiring sofas and beds can be to the imagination; how they can be forts and fortresses, palaces, caves, pirate ships, battlefields, hide-outs, launching pads for myriad adventures, sometimes literally launching pads. In fact, Becka went on to say, children alter one's view of all kinds of objects; pots and pans become musical instruments, paper bags become masks, and, as every parent of a little boy knows, anything, *anything*, even a peanut butter sandwich chewed just so, can become a gun.

Talking with Becka reminded me of a children's book that is so true to the from-under-the-furniture perspective that I'm always a little shocked, and more than a little impressed, on remembering that it was written by a grown-up, William Kotzwinkle. *The World Is Big and I'm So Small* takes us along with a young rabbit as he makes up his day, turning his high chair into a rough-riding vehicle, a pot into a crown, some cartons in the back yard into a castle, himself into a knight, and, finally, his father into "the King"—all rendered even truer to the child's-eye view through Joe Servello's illustrations, which have a wide-angle quality, as if we're looking up at them, being "so small" ourselves.

When our children draw us into their fantasies, as the little bunny did his father (who, after making sure he ate his carrots, carried him "up the mountainside" to bed), when they stir and expand our appreciation of our surroundings, sometimes they also renew long-forgotten tastes, smells, sensations that, flooding back, remind us who we were as children and put us more in touch with who we still essentially are.

I had one of these gratifying flashbacks while walking with

Jonathan late one February afternoon. A light snow was falling, and the icy residue of the last snow laced the frozen lawns. Jonathan kept veering from the sidewalk and stomping across the lawns, relishing the crunching sounds his feet made as they smashed the islands of ice. And I remembered relishing the sound of ice patches breaking under my feet when I was his age and found myself joining him, to his delight and mine. Moments like this, in bringing us closer to our own heyday of pure joy and magical thinking, bring us still closer to our children. It feels good to be on their wavelength. We may feel relief, too, at this evidence that our years of adulthood have not eroded our capacity to do what comes naturally to children.

"Through my kids," said a father of four, "I remember what I lost as I got older, the way I used to notice and think about the wonders of nature. With them, I'm able to recapture that, and I find that happening even more now as they get older and are able to express more of what they're feeling and thinking."

Discovering What We Truly Believe

As children become more verbal, parents may find themselves under a different but no less magical kind of spell. Now the questions start. The tough questions. The questions about death and God and how things grow and how they come to be in the first place. The questions for which we sometimes—no, often—do not have answers. The questions that greater minds than ours have been grappling with since the beginning of time. The questions that make us laugh because they are so charmingly naïve, that make us proud of having produced a little Socrates (or, at the very least, our own private spin-off of "Kids Say the Darndest Things"). The questions we write down so that we can repeat them to relatives and friends. The questions that illuminate for us our children's struggle out of magical and into objective thinking and that, in so doing, make us see our children as all the more magical, since they make us contemplate what we believe about any number of things, and why.

"Sometimes she asks things that hit me to the core," a

mother said of her four-year-old daughter. "I mean, this sounds silly, but the power company came to trim some branches from the trees recently, and they really butchered this one tree. My daughter asked me, 'Does a tree hurt from that?' It was such a good question. And it made me think we take so many things for granted, and children remind us that maybe we shouldn't. Does a tree feel? Who knows? But maybe we should act as if it does, respect it, not destroy it. I thought and thought about this."

I was stymied recently when Jonathan wondered whether God has feet or "does he come to a little white point at the bottom like a ghost?" "What do you think?" I asked. Jonathan came down on the side of the little white point. He couldn't conceive of God going into a store and buying shoes.

When the subject of God came up again, as I knew it would ("Is there anyone else in the world named God?" Jonathan wanted to know), I had on hand a couple of those books which help parents explain to their children things that they themselves find inexplicable. They were useful. But what was more useful was turning on myself the question I always asked Jonathan: "What do *you* think?" Because of Jonathan, because he needs me to give him answers (or, better yet, a foundation for what I hope will be a lifetime of asking questions), I began trying to figure out what I think and feel about matters of transcendence.

Before Jonathan, I felt much as the mother of one of Jonathan's classmates did before parenthood. "While I wasn't exactly a nonbeliever," she said, "there was no heart in it. My spiritual life was shut down, turned off, not addressed." For this woman and for me, it was our children who, as she put it, "opened it up."

Kate Robicheau, too, found that her children's curiosity has nudged her into closer examination of her beliefs—to her satisfaction. She can actually trace the growth of her confidence in expressing her beliefs from one child to the next. When her older son, Ben, began questioning her about God and Jesus, her open-mindedness (she was "interested in religion but not necessarily Christianity"), paired with her husband's strong suspicion of religion, led her to take the approach of "Well, some people think this and when you grow up you can decide for yourself." It didn't feel right to her. Ben became an adamant atheist, touting evolution as his religion even in elementary school.

By the time Tom came along, "I explained things very differently. I told him, yes, there is a God, definitely. It isn't like a person sitting up on a cloud, but it is what made the earth. We don't really know all the details, but we call that God. And you know I was much clearer about it. I went more with my gut feeling of there being some higher order and meaning and beauty in the universe versus the objective scientific outlook.

"I had always been interested in what the religious life was all about, how a person could be attracted to it and why, and who lives the religious life; it makes a lot of sense to me. I don't think I've necessarily incorporated religion into my own life very well, but it does come out with the kids. I've been having to deal with it a lot more strenuously because I'm a mother.

"We were in the Southwest last summer, up in Mesa Verde, where the Anasazi Indians lived in cliff dwellings seven hundred years ago. And that has got to be a sacred place if any place is. It's incredible. Ben felt it, too. We had this wonderful discussion about Native American religions. Ben said he thought they made a lot of sense because they're about the natural life cycle and the seasons and how nature fits together and how beautifully things are made. He feels there's not enough about nature in the Christian church. And I agree with him. It's not outside enough; it's not physical enough.

"Whatever's now at the core of my sense of connection with the world and my spiritual reckoning, my children have brought it up and brought it out. I have these moments of incredible appreciation—not every single day, but they happen. They add up."

As the distance between a child's birth and present reality gets longer, as our children become less our own and more themselves, our awe and wonder may dissipate. As Diane Foster told me, "Of course, I don't go around in this state of perfect love all the time." But there are always the moments when the connection to the spiritual side of ourselves is revived by direct confrontation with our children's awe and wonder. By responding to our children, by trying to find answers to their questions, we often find answers for ourselves.

Discovering Our Religious Identity

Not long before our conversation, Kate told me, she had had a dream. "It was about the church in my childhood, in Walnut Creek, California. In my dream I go into the sanctuary and see what I used to see when I sang in the choir—the wood beams that I used to look up at; the families I knew. It's like going back to a loved, special, treasured place, everything about it, even the parking lot, the hot asphalt. I've had several of these dreams about going back to this church. It must have been very important to me."

Recently in her waking hours, too, Kate has felt the sense of belonging, the pleasures of church life, rekindled. Ben, who has a lovely voice, was recruited for a church-sponsored boys' choir and agreed to join despite his atheism. So now, Kate says, she's in the church basement a lot, cooking meals with the parents of other choir members. "I love church basements and back rooms and church kitchens; I really do. And the church that Ben sings in is beautiful, with lots of old wood and signs of many people caring for it for many years. It has a welcoming feel.

"As a choir parent I can be there and be part of things without having to make clear statements about what I believe and don't believe. I've joined a book group there. I even went to one meeting of something called the Inquirers' Group or something. You know, they're exploring what is it to be Episcopalian? What is it to be Christian? I feel like going again to find out more."

Establishing a religious identity, which is what Kate seems to be doing, can play a vital role in the interplay of separation from and identification with our own parents and our own childhood that guides the process of growing up. Nothing, according to the majority of parents I've talked with, jogs the need for religious identity quite like the desire to "do what's best" for our children or to be our best for them.

Sometimes, thus motivated, we run from our religious past. I did not have to go far to find an example of this. My sister, turned off by the lack of spirituality that she found within the synagogue of our youth, became a Baha'i at the age of nineteen and deepened her affiliation because of and on behalf of her children, who "in very concrete ways have reinforced my commitment, my quest, and my faith."

Sometimes, we run toward our religious past. A single woman who, at the age of forty-two, adopted a baby girl, told me of her joy whenever she uses the special holiday tablecloth that has been in her family for three generations and is now hers and her daughter's. Just seeing it, touching it, brings wonderful memories and reminds her that she is transmitting her family's cultural tradition to her daughter. Although she had been fairly observant before adopting her child, she now finds deeper satisfaction in prayer and feels more a part of her religious community.

Other parents join houses of worship solely because they want their children to be part of a religious community. Typically, the search for a house of worship in which the family can feel at home starts when a child approaches "Sunday school age," which tends to be the age when a parent started Sunday school. Or when the child starts asking existential questions. Or when all the child's friends begin attending Sunday school.

Often, even when men and women have been unaffiliated since their own Sunday school days, they find that they want their children to have the religious context that they had when they were young or that their spouse had or that one or both of them didn't have or didn't have enough of or didn't have in the right way. In the case of mixed marriages, it usually isn't until children come along that differences in religious traditions and beliefs surface and need to be resolved.

Often, the earnest effort to find the right religious environment for their children, a place where their children will develop the religious identity that many parents feel can serve as an internal line of defense for their children in a world that revolves around material more than spiritual values—often, this search ends up benefiting the parents, too.

One father said that now, instead of feeling "afloat" in his community, he has "ties." His wife recalled the time, before they had children, that they decided to join a synagogue. "We went there, and everyone was very welcoming, but we didn't feel a part of it. Then, with the kids, we wanted to join because it was important for it to be a part of their lives. And I guess because we now had them as a motivation, this time we did feel connected."

Sometimes this connection leads to the development of a genuine and lasting religious identity, one that never existed in the first place or, as was the case with Melinda Stern, one that grew from roots that had never taken hold.

I noticed the photograph right away, a formal family portrait— from the turn of the century, I guessed, and probably from Russia. The men and boys were wearing yarmulkes. In the modern suburban split level where Melinda Stern lives with her husband, Jerry, and four-year-old Amanda and six-month-old Libby this photo seemed to be the only reference to family history—Jerry's family's history, Melinda told me. Her parents had not been big on preserving memories or tradition. They were devoutly nonobservant Jews, to the point that Melinda's father talked her brother out of having a bar mitzvah. The idea of a bat mitzvah for Melinda never occurred to anyone.

She remembers feeling "excluded" when Jewish friends at school had their bar mitzvah ceremonies, when they discussed happenings at the temple to which her family did not belong. She remembers being mystified when a fifth-grade classmate talked about Pesach. "I asked her what it was, and she said, 'You don't know? That's Passover!' And I felt terrible."

But she also remembers feeling "some sort of spiritual stirrings" from a very early age. Not long ago, when a friend of hers who grew up Catholic described what she called "a faith experience," Melinda could recall having had similar feelings during her own childhood.

But it wasn't until Amanda was born that Melinda's "repressed spirituality" started to surface. "When I looked at this baby I was holding, this new baby, it was a miracle. Really, it was beyond words. I couldn't get over it. I'm still astonished— here's this creation of a whole new life."

But she was not "into Judaism," she remembers. "A rabbi stopped by to see me in the hospital and I thought it was a pain. Even though I was awed by the miracle of my baby, I was definitely uncomfortable with the whole Jewish thing. I just wanted that rabbi to go away."

Melinda and Jerry joined a synagogue soon after Amanda's birth, "but it was a perfunctory thing" until, through a chain of emotionally charged events that included conversations with her husband and with a therapist as well as a lot of "soul searching" on her own, she allowed herself "to do things differently from my parents so that I would be able to give my children everything that my parents didn't give me."

Melinda enrolled Amanda, at eighteen months, in a parent-toddler program at the synagogue. "I was learning right along with her! The kids would have a snack, challah, and they'd say the blessing over it, and I'd learn it. This class really was, for me, *parents* and toddlers. I hadn't known this stuff; I actually did learn."

Melinda began taking books about Judaism from the library. She joined the Saturday morning Bible study class. "After class, a lot of the time the rabbi would do a bar or bat mitzvah, and I began crashing the ceremonies. There I'd be, not even knowing these kids or their families, and it was still so moving.

"One thing I always liked was when the rabbi invited the parents and grandparents up on the *bima* [dais] and took the Torah out of the ark. I don't remember his exact words, but he would explain that the idea, in Judaism, was that no individual or generation stands alone. The past and future are an intrinsic part of each of us. And he'd say that that's what is symbolized as we hand the Torah *l'dor v'dor*, that is, from generation to generation, until it reaches the hands and, it's hoped, into the heart of the bar or bat mitzvah. Then he'd hand the Torah to the oldest person, who would hand it to the next oldest person, and so on down to the boy or girl.

"And the rabbi would always say something like this: 'It is said that when a grandparent witnesses the bar or bat mitzvah of a grandchild it's like being at Mount Sinai all over again.' I really liked that—the idea that someday my little girl will be up on the *bima* and I'll pass all that tradition, all that faith and history down to her, embodied in the Torah. I liked that image. When I was a child none of this was transmitted to me. I missed out, and it was a loss. I didn't want that to happen to my girls.

"But just knowing that when they are bat mitzvah there will be this great symbol of the Torah being handed to them wasn't enough. I didn't want it to be just a symbol for them. I felt I had to have the knowledge and the feeling and the love of it myself so that I can give them not just the symbol but the substance."

Melinda began attending services regularly, lighting the Sabbath candles at home, praying on her own, and studying Torah, Talmud, and Hebrew. Finally, in the fall of 1991, she joined her temple's adult bar and bat mitzvah class.

"I did it for my kids," Melinda told me, "but I've been so enriched by it myself. First of all, knowing I'm now able to really hand down to them the Jewish identity that's so important gives me a great deal of satisfaction. And having found my own identity, having added this spiritual content to my life, it's as if I've filled in a big blank. But in a way that's for them, too. If I'm a better person, then I'm a better parent. By being a better parent, I become a still better person."

When Libby was born two years after Melinda began studying to become bat mitzvah, "I was so different from when I had had Amanda. I had memorized two blessings that I wanted to say when she was born. And I did, right when she was born. I said the *shehecheyanu* and another one that I found in Anita Diamant's *The Jewish Baby Book:* 'God is good and creates good things.' I liked that."

Libby was just short of ten weeks old when her mother stood on the *bima* with her fellow members of "the Class of 5753,"[6] as they enjoyed calling themselves, "to publicly affirm my identity and responsibility as a Jew." Melinda looked out into the congregation and saw Jerry's parents and her own fa-

ther and her mother (who has since begun her own Jewish studies—inspired by her daughter). Snuggled next to Melinda's
mother was Amanda. And through the open doors to the hall-
way, Melinda could see Jerry, pacing back and forth with Libby.
She could hear Libby crying.

By the time Melinda got up to give her speech, Amanda
was sound asleep. Libby was still crying. Melinda, who was
nursing, became conscious of "that letdown effect." Suddenly
she felt overwhelmed by fresh gratitude for the beautiful, hand-
embroidered prayer shawl she was wearing for the first time. If
she leaked, no one would know.

"This is a sweet moment," Melinda began, looking at the
peaceful Amanda, one of her reasons for being there, and listening to the howls of Libby, her other reason for being there.
L'dor v'dor. From generation to generation.

IV

The Healing Nature
of Parenthood

My daughter . . . came into the hospital room. Obviously, I
couldn't move and I'm totally paralyzed. And she comes in, with
her little doctor's kit, and she climbs up on the bed, and she
takes care of her daddy.
    —DENNIS BYRD, who was seriously injured while playing de-
      fense end for the New York Jets, in a 1993 *Prime Time Live*
      interview

IN THE LAST PAGES of *The Secret Garden*, fatherhood
cures one of the worst cases of depression in literary history
(at least, in the history of children's literature). Archibald Craven's recovery was dramatic indeed. There he was, wandering
through the "far-away beautiful places" in which he sought but
always failed to find escape from the bitterness that had plagued
him since his wife had died in childbirth, leaving him with a
sickly infant, Colin, whose care he had left to servants and doc-

tors and who had grown, predictably, into a child whose very misery repelled his father.

Archibald Craven "had not meant to be a bad father," Frances Hodgson Burnett wrote, "but he had not felt like a father at all." He had hidden in his room. He had fled into foreign landscapes—until one day, resting by a stream in an Austrian valley, he suddenly was moved by his magnificent surroundings. "It was as if a sweet clear spring had begun to rise in a stagnant pool and had risen and risen until at last it swept the dark water away . . . 'What is it?' he said, almost in a whisper . . . 'I almost feel as if—I were alive!' "

"It" was, of course, the magic of the walled-in garden back home at Misselthwaite Manor reaching out to him, all the way to the banks of that Austrian stream. The garden had been his wife's. Since her death it had withered, locked up—like him, like his son. But now, without Craven's knowledge, his orphaned niece Mary Lennox and her exuberant friend Dickon had brought the garden to life again. And through the magic of the garden's rebirth, through the magic of childhood itself, as well as through the nurturing friendship of Mary and Dickon, Colin had come to life again, too.

Without the enchanting image of that garden, Burnett's book probably would not have remained in print for fifty-five years and been made into a film in 1949 that became a classic and, recently, into a TV special, another feature film, and a Broadway musical. But without Colin, there would have been no magic for Archibald Craven. He would have forever remained a heartsick Yorkshire recluse.

It is, finally, Colin's need for his father that propels the garden's magic, as Burnett would have us believe, across the English Channel and halfway across Europe to bring the father to life, to make him function as a father, to heal him, to bring him home.

When I first read *The Secret Garden* at the age of eleven or twelve, it was Mary Lennox's story that captivated me. Mary immediately became my closest fictional friend; *The Secret Garden* was my favorite childhood book. It is now, so many years into my adulthood, still among my favorite books, partly because I never outgrew my bond with Mary, but mostly because the magic of parenthood in my own life brought into high relief for me the story's deepest message: parenthood in and of itself can be therapeutic.

If we think of parenthood and therapy at the same time it is usually in terms of the parent requiring therapy to work through some of the problems that childrearing has raised for him or her. Or of the parent thinking that a child who is exhibiting disturbing behavior may be disturbed and in need of therapy.

But what proved true for Archibald Craven has proved true for many real life parents in many different ways. In my own case, the healing process took place over weeks and months, apparently on an unconscious level, until one day I became aware that something important had happened. I can't pinpoint the moment of this awareness or the reason it came to light; I simply recognized that I had become reconciled to my mother's death—or, more precisely, that I had stopped mourning her absence and had begun feeling that much of her is still present within me as Jonathan's mother.

Jonathan was born eight years after my mother died. One of the first things I remember thinking after he was born was— with a great thud of sorrow—if only she were here. How unlucky Jonathan was to have missed out on having her as his grandma!

His arrival did not have a therapeutic effect on me. Happy though I was, as much as I loved him, his very existence made me miss my mother more than ever. But it wasn't long before his existence became a balm. I was so proud of him. (And wasn't this the pride I always knew my mother felt in me?) I was so passionately bound to him that I would hear his cries, for instance, inside my head while I was taking a shower, even when he wasn't crying. (And wasn't this, undoubtedly, the way my mother had felt about me? As if I were almost physically a part of her?)

When I sang to Jonathan, I heard my mother's less than mellifluous voice (which I inherit) singing old tunes and lyrics I hadn't heard or thought of in years. Yet there they were. I hadn't forgotten a word or a note. I had heard them so many times from my mother that they had been stored somewhere in my being. And at the right time, they came forward, intact. Reading to my baby produced sensory memories that were equally soothing. So did feeding, bathing, changing, comforting, appreciating him—and delighting in the first signs that he appreciated me.

It was not, of course, as if I were walking around exclaiming to myself, "I am my mother; she is in me. The void has been filled. I have now stopped grieving and can move on." It was nothing as conscious as that. But it did seem, after a certain point, that through mothering I had revived a sense of my own experiences of being mothered, a sense of my mother's nurturing me. In replaying this—now as the mother—I was indeed preserving the essence of who and what my mother was and of my relationship with her. It came down to thinking of myself as carrying on for my mother, continuing her "tradition." And that notion strengthened me and continues to strengthen me.

At the same time, I've found, like any parent, that the therapeutic value of parenthood is not an across-the-board phenomenon. Parenthood tends to create as many wounds as it heals. It stirs up, with amazing frequency, both old and new conflicts and problems. But that's just it. In persistently bringing to our attention so much of ourselves, present and past, our children may disturb, annoy, confuse, unnerve, infuriate, and worry us—and make us feel guilty. But they also give us an unparalleled opportunity to work through serious issues we otherwise might never have recognized or faced.

"I don't know if it's this way for other people," Melinda Stern is saying, "but having kids brings up so many things from my childhood." We are sitting in the spacious playroom that adjoins the kitchen–dining area of Melinda's home. Four-year-old Amanda, having just climbed down from the sofa where she was admiring my earrings, is making music—clattering pots and screaming with joy. Libby, almost six months old, snuggles in her mother's arms, busy with a project of her own—manipulating with both hands and both feet an antimacassar she has snatched from the sofa, trying to figure out how to smush the whole thing into her mouth.

Melinda, attending to what is going on around her (hushing Amanda, discouraging Libby's oral adventure) while telling me what is going on within her, acts out what she is describing at the moment: "I'm living in the present, but I'm still often working my way through the past at the same time."

I have come here to discuss one aspect of Melinda's reworking of her past—her embrace of the Jewish tradition that her parents had rejected. But it turns out that the story is more complex than I thought. That Melinda's house is practically devoid of pictures and other tangible memories signifies something other than a lack of tradition or sentiment. There is a family secret. It is something Melinda's parents never discussed with her, hardly mentioned.

It is something Melinda has consciously avoided thinking about until recently, and it comes out in our conversation almost as an aside—as a possible explanation, Melinda thinks, for her parents' distaste for religion. "I'll tell you something very sad that happened to my parents," she says. "When I was three months old, my parents' four-year-old daughter died of a respiratory infection, something that nowadays wouldn't have been any problem to treat. I always wondered if that had something to do with it, with my father and mother thinking that religion was ridiculous."

Melinda is still wondering about this because she has not yet reached the point where she can ask her parents if the loss of that child, her sister, caused them to lose their faith. But the reason she feels that she is approaching that moment is that she is now a parent, too.

"Before I became a mother," she tells me, "I never understood much about my parents losing a daughter. It sounds stupid now, but I always thought, 'Oh, that's so sad.' I didn't really understand. I hadn't known my sister. I didn't even know her full name, her middle name. That's how much we didn't talk about it."

Now, however, Melinda thinks of her sister often. "And I think about her from the point of view of a parent. I'm thinking about her as a four-year-old; Amanda is my four-year-old. And I'm thinking, What if she'd been my daughter? I don't know how my parents survived that. Now I have a great deal more sympathy for what my parents must have gone through."

Melinda's understanding and the forgiveness that came with it—for her parents' "unhealthy" silence about her sister's death, for the religious void that may have opened in the wake of that loss—did not appear overnight. When Amanda was born, Melinda remembers, "it never occurred to me to name her after my sister. We named her after my father's father." It was only after weeks, then months and years, of nurturing her own child that Melinda's comprehension of her own parents' tragedy began to grow.

When Libby was born, "it was so meaningful for me that she was a girl," Melinda says; "in a way it was as if my sister was being reborn. My sister's name was Elizabeth, and Libby is a nickname for Elizabeth."

At this point Libby, frustrated because her mother has taken away the delicious-looking antimacassar, begins to fidget. Melinda stands up and walks her back and forth, comforting her as she talks. "I don't think my parents knew what to say when I told them I was naming the baby after my sister," she says. "I thought it would make them feel good, but they weren't effusive. It was just—that's very nice, what an honor. But I know inside that it meant something to them. I don't think they ever got over her death. I think it's affected all of our lives much more than I was ever aware. I don't think they're truly over it now."

Neither is Melinda, she admits. Three months ago she realized, with a jolt of horror, that Libby and Amanda were the exact ages she and her sister had been when her sister died. No sooner did the thought come than she banished it. "It's so uncomfortable, so painful . . ."

But at least, she says, she has brought the secret that dominated her childhood into the open, where it has helped her understand much about how her parents were when she was a child and why some elements of her own childhood were bitter and sad. It has brought her closer to her parents, she thinks, and closer to understanding certain essential things about herself.

A lot of the memories that our children awaken are pleasurable. Melinda mentioned the thrill of opening a fresh can of Play-Doh for Amanda. She hadn't smelled Play-Doh since she was around Amanda's age, and its unmistakable, earthy-sweet scent brought back the joy of that time in a rush.

Another young mother had a similar flashback the first time she saw her toddler take a swig of his bath water. Suddenly the memory of sipping warm, soapy water while being immersed in it washed over her, and she was able for a moment to enjoy her own childlike sensuality, thanks to her child.

Such moments put us in touch with the source of our selves and in tune with our children's experience of the world. They can be immensely satisfying.

So can some memories of our parents in our childhood that arise from time to time as we care for our children. Often these memories are reflections of our parents in ourselves. Kate Robicheau recalls, with some amusement, "this certain way my mother used to stand"—she jumps up to demonstrate, hands on emphatically slanted hips—"and point"—she points. "It's very characteristic and it comes down in the family and every now and then I find myself doing it when I'm lecturing my kids."

Kate, whose mother died three months after the birth of Kate's older son, takes comfort in her almost automatic recreation of her mother's household habits and rituals. "I've been making the boys tea in special cups since they were babies and they do find it soothing. That was one bit of special attention I got from my mother, through tea. And I plant marigolds every year, and my kids know my mother did that, and that I plant them for her. She loved the smell of marigolds; the stinkier, the better."

Joanne Marks, the elementary school music teacher and mother of two little girls who spontaneously told me about her nurturing husband and her nurturing father when we first met, is periodically shocked and bemused when, looking at her hands, "I see my mother's hands."

Joanne frequently finds her mother's words coming out of her mouth. "One of her favorite sayings was 'Be kind and sweet to everyone you meet.' I hear myself saying it to Zoe, and other things my mother and my father told me over and over a thousand times."

Recently, when Zoe began pleading for a Barbie doll, Joanne felt her mother's old resistance to Barbie welling up inside her. "When I deal with issues like this," she said, "I can hear my mother inside my head. My values come from her values so much." And Joanne also encounters her father, who died several years ago, in her parenting. "He used to read to us a great deal," she says. "Now, when I'm reading Zoe some Pooh poems out of *Now We Are Six*, it's as if he's there. I don't think you ever get rid of your parents."

This, of course, was Therese Benedek's bottom line, of Freudian lineage. In 1975, fifteen years after Benedek first mapped out the power of parenthood to help us resolve conflicts from our own childhood, Selma Fraiberg cast the process in a therapeutic mold in a paper titled "Ghosts in the Nursery."

"The ghosts," she wrote, "represent the repetition of the past in the present."[1] Often these spirits are benign, causing us to imitate our parents' admirable traits and habits, comforting and even healing us by helping us maintain for ourselves and our children the warmth of family tradition. Like Kate Robicheau and Joanne Marks, we welcome these ghosts and encourage them to stick around.

But just as often the ghosts in a nursery can be of an entirely different ilk. Mischievous, even malicious, revenants from a partially or wholly troubled past, they "take up residence" in our parental selves, making us repeat our parents' sins of omission as well as those they committed.

It was these unfriendly ghosts, the troublemakers, with whom Fraiberg's patients contended. Her paper documented two cases of young mothers whose "emotional starvation" of their babies eerily echoed their parents' maltreatment of them. Both mothers could remember the nightmarish events of their childhoods. But it was what they had repressed—their feelings of pain, fear, and shame—that materialized as "ghosts," blocking their ability to form the most rudimentary bonds with their babies. Through extensive psychotherapy these women were finally able to experience again the agony of their childhood and, in an attempt to keep their children from suffering as they had, to banish the ghosts.

"The key to our ghost story," Fraiberg concluded, is that "access to childhood pain becomes a powerful deterrent against repetition in parenting." For many parents, as Fraiberg was careful to point out, it doesn't take psychotherapy to achieve this "access." "If history predicted with fidelity," she wrote, "the human family itself would have long ago been drowned in its own oppressive past. The race improves. And this may be because the largest number of men and women who have known suffering find renewal and the healing of childhood pain in the experience of bringing a child into the world. In the simplest terms—we have heard it often from parents—the parent says, 'I want something better for my child than I have had.' And he brings something better to his child."

Instead of replaying the past, these parents, brought to full consciousness—through identification with their own children —of their parents' failings and their own suffering, set out to improve upon the past, to correct it.

From what I've heard and read, it is a rare parent whose dealings with his or her past amount to total rejection of it and departure from it. Even in the worst cases, the memories are not entirely bleak. As E. James Anthony has reminded us, family histories have a romantic edge. "There is no such thing as 'real' parents," he wrote. "They are always amalgamations of fact, fantasy, and folklore."[2]

Even if there are ways we want to bring "something better" to our children than our parents brought to us, there are also ways in which we want to emulate our parents. The process of parenting usually reflects, in all its ambivalence, the process of development in childhood.

Most of us continue identifying with as well as separating from our parents throughout our lives. And both our attempts to emulate and our attempts to be different from our parents can be healing.

The relief Kate Robicheau finds in the ways she reflects her mother—her mimicry of her mother's posture, her continuing her mother's practice of nurturing through tea—go hand in hand with a conscious effort "to improve on my mother."

"I'm aware of inadequate parenting in my own childhood," she told me, "a lack of real attention from my mother. She was depressed a lot. Also, I was one of four children, I don't think I got as much attention and nurturing as I needed. It's been extremely satisfying to give that to my children in sitting and hugging them more than I was hugged, in a lot of ways."

Greg Weber, like Kate, felt emotionally short-changed as a child. But when he says his father "wasn't there," he means it literally. Greg is forty-three, a computer programmer and analyst and the father of two adopted sons, Jeremy, who is in second grade, and Zachary, who is in kindergarten. In talking about his father, Greg did bring up one positive thing his father did, but in most of his recollections, his father, who was constantly away on business, hardly figures at all.

"He would take us with him sometimes," Greg told me, "during Christmas vacations, and particularly I remember summer trips that lasted up to six weeks, in fact, traveling out West. During the day he'd be off doing business and my mother would take us sightseeing and then we'd all meet for dinner." But apart from this obviously pleasurable memory, Greg's paternal past represents a classic example of negative parental behavior handed down not just from parent to child but through more than one generation of parents and children. Greg knew that his father's obliviousness of his paternal role was an echo of Greg's grandfather's abdication of that role.

"My father was raised almost as an orphan," Greg told me. "Did you ever see the movie *Awakenings?* It was a true story. My father's father came down with encephalitis in that same epidemic, and ten years later he started to deteriorate physically, then mentally. My father never talked about it. It was like a horrible secret, but you got bits and pieces. My grandfather behaved bizarrely, and the family couldn't cope. They didn't understand; so he was kicked out of the house and ended up dying alone in a rooming house. Which in the book *Awakenings* they say happened to thousands of those people.

"My father's mother worked in sweatshops six days a week, so my father was raised by aunts and uncles. Then, when I was growing up, my father didn't know what he was supposed to do and how to do it, so he wasn't there for me." Because of this history, Greg was afraid that he "wasn't going to be a particularly adept father."

In "Ghosts in the Nursery" Selma Fraiberg described a pivotal moment in the therapy of "Mrs. March" after she has finally begun to bond with her baby. "The baby herself was ensuring those bonds. For every gesture of love from her mother, Mary [the baby] gave generous rewards of love. Mrs. March, we thought, may have felt cherished for the first time in her life."[3]

Although it took long sessions of psychotherapy for Mrs. March to recover and confront the misery of her own childhood and to gain confidence in her ability to depart from her awful history and be a loving mother, ultimately it was her child who, responding to Mrs. March's efforts to nurture, nourished her budding confidence. In fact, as Fraiberg pointed out, the therapist "did everything within her capacity . . . as a developmental psychologist to promote the emerging attachment" that was so crucial to Mrs. March's recovery. "When Mary rewarded her mother with a beautiful and special smile, [the therapist] commented on it . . . When a crying Mary began to seek her mother's comfort and found relief in her mother's arms, [the therapist] spoke for Mary. 'It feels so good when mother knows what you want.' And Mrs. March herself smiled shyly, but with pride."

Greg Weber's pride in not following in his father's and grandfather's footsteps is also palpable. At the time he and his wife, Sheila, went to South America to adopt their first child, he was more self-assured than he had been when they started the seemingly endless adoption procedure. He had got himself to the point where he thought, "Okay, there's going to be a strange kid in the house and it's going to take months to learn to relate to this child."

He was shocked when it took "about an hour" to feel close to little Jeremy. Warmed and encouraged by the feelings that he tentatively acknowledged as fatherly, feelings that were stirred merely by holding this baby, knowing that this was his baby, he was able to make the leap into active, hands-on fathering. And, as with "Mrs. March," his eagerness to break the defective parental mold he had inherited was reinforced by his baby's enthusiastic responses to him.

About a month before Greg and Sheila had gone to South America to pick up Jeremy, Greg's father died. "The year before that," Greg recalled, "my father had had triple bypass surgery and I was too busy with work to go see him. He knew we were going to adopt a baby and he was very excited about it. And we had gotten a picture of the baby; they send you a picture to hang on to while they hold up the adoption process.

"When I told my father we had this picture, he asked me to send it to him. I put it off and put it off and then finally sent it. After he died and I went to collect his effects, I found the envelope unopened. It had arrived right after he died. He never saw the picture of the baby, his grandson.

"This whole experience—putting off and not seeing him or sending the picture in time—gave me the sense of what it was like when I was a child and my father was gone. I didn't want to do that. I wanted to be a good parent."

But along with Greg's determination to be different from his father came an understanding of and identification with his father. Greg now knew what it was like to be limited in his ability to be with his family by the very responsibility of supporting his family. He saw that "once my father had committed himself to a certain path, there was no escape from it. He had to do what he had to do, which was take products out on the road, find dealers to carry the merchandise."

Greg felt similarly trapped by the pressure of his work. He often found himself thinking, on the job, that he'd rather be with his family. "Working all those hours, sometimes I felt I *was* my father," he told me.

Greg's admission not only moved me but made me wonder

whether his new empathy with his father signified more. I guess I was hoping he'd tell me that parenthood had indeed been a miracle cure for him, erasing forever the insecurity caused by his father's chronic absence, leading to some kind of posthumous reconciliation with his father.

"When you found yourself having to work long hours," I said, "and feeling trapped like your father and missing your kids —did that make you wonder whether your father had missed you, and maybe wished he was home with you, all those years?"

"I don't know," Greg said. "I'm not sure. I know what mistakes my father made."

"Well, what if you'd asked him, 'Dad, did you ever wish, when you were on the road working, that you could've been home with us?'"

"I'm not sure I would've gained any additional insights from him."

"He might've said that he did miss you."

Greg thought for a minute. "I know he enjoyed his work and he made his choices. He was a very bright guy, but in terms of personal insight, I don't know that that was really his strong suit. What I've been thinking is more the sense of, gee, wouldn't it have been nice if he had gotten to see the kids, and how sad it is that he missed that."

It is possible that, had Greg's father lived, Greg might have arrived at a firmer resolution of his feelings through seeing his father as a grandfather. "If he were still alive," Greg said, "maybe we would have gotten to compare notes."

Therese Benedek was, I think, generalizing a bit when she wrote that grandparents, free of the day-to-day frustrations of motherhood and fatherhood, seem to get more enjoyment from their grandchildren than they did from their own children. But it does seem that our children can give our parents a new lease on life, and that this might loosen tensions, bringing about a renaissance in our interactions with our parents. Parenthood can heal our relationships with our parents in the present as well as banish the ghosts from the past.

"I was always terrified of becoming a mother," Diane Foster told me, "because I'd had a horrible relationship with my mother—to the point that it became physical. She'd hit me. And when I got older, I'd hit her back. I disliked her intensely."

But Diane's becoming a mother changed her attitude toward her mother. "I still dislike her; I mean, I can't get rid of my resentment. I feel that she wasn't a good mother. But I now handle all this differently. I don't think of her in terms of what she didn't give me. I think of her as a person who had limited capabilities and was doing the best she could. And there's no point in punishing her for it. I was very close to my father. He was great. I don't know what I would've done without him."

In fact, Diane's adoration of her father was a sore point for her mother. "They used to fight constantly about me. They had a terrible relationship." Her mother was "rather unstable," she thinks. "Probably having three kids was too much for her; she couldn't cope with it very well. She's someone who needs absolute stability to function. And she had a hard life. We were always moving from country to country, so she never had even the geographical stability she needed; and the friction with my father put her further off balance."

When Sophia came along, she almost immediately became "a mediator" between Diane and her mother. "When I take Sophia over, there's a softer side of my mother that can come out with Sophia. She can show a lot more affection toward Sophia than she could toward me, or can now. And she does things with Sophia that she never did with me.

"And people don't stay the same. She's not the same person at sixty that she was at thirty-five. I'll see her catching herself. Sophia will say, 'I want to do this,' and my mother will say, 'Oh, no, no, no, no, you can't do that,' and then she'll stop herself and say, 'Oh, okay, what's the harm in it?'

"This makes my relationship with her easier. It doesn't make me any less resentful that she wasn't that way with me, but it makes it possible to have some other relationship with her than just 'I'm so angry at you because you were so mean to me.' It's a new relationship that doesn't have too much to do with the old one."

But it is not only the appreciation of the way age and

grandmotherhood have mellowed her mother that has proved therapeutic for Diane. "When I find myself spontaneously telling Sophia how much I love her or how wonderful she is or admiring things about her, I think, 'How in the world could my mother never have told me these things?' I never remember her telling me that she loved me or that I was wonderful or anything of the kind, or being at all interested in what I was doing or thinking or seeing. It's unimaginable to me now that she could have been like that. But I needed the perspective that came from being a mother myself, and loving my child so much, for it to be unimaginable. Before, I thought that's just the way it was."

"So your saying these things to Sophia," I said, "and realizing that your mother's not saying them was abnormal for a mother, enabled you to . . ."

"It gave me a normal frame of reference."

"Then you knew that it was your mother's behavior that was not normal? And that there was nothing wrong with you?"

"Exactly."

"As a child, you may have thought your mother was not loving and affectionate because you didn't deserve love and affection?"

"Right. That's the bottom line. That's exactly right."

Because of Sophia, who is now six years old, Diane has stopped blaming herself for her mother's lack of affection toward her. She has even entertained the thought that her mother's inability to show affection was just that, an emotional block, not evidence that her mother didn't love her.

Tanya Landau credits her two-year-old daughter, Brett, with having brought about a rapport with her own mother that never before existed. Tanya, who is twenty-seven and temporarily "retired" from her academic career to be a full-time mother, grew up with three brothers and a sister in the Midwestern college town where her parents still live, two thousand miles from the New England college town where Tanya and her husband, Jake, live. But Tanya's new role as a mother has eclipsed the distance, geographical and otherwise, between her and her mother.

Tanya's father taught history and her mother worked "very much out of necessity" as a nurse. "She worked a lot, and she enjoyed nursing, but I never got the sense that she was fulfilled by her job. And I feel that even more so now, now that I know her better. We talk about it and I know she would've preferred to work less and spend more time with us if she'd been able to. She's just thrilled that I'm able to stay home with Brett and she thinks it's wonderful and she would've loved to do that.

"My mother and I have become much closer since Brett was born. There's a whole new world that's opened up between us. It's Brett-oriented, child-oriented. We hadn't been close. We didn't have conflicts, but she wasn't a close friend or a confidante. And I wouldn't say we had that much in common in our interests. In that sense, I had more in common with my father. There wasn't a lot of intellectual interaction with my mother. But after Brett was born, that opened up a whole realm of possibilities for discussion.

"I've always felt that my mother was a good mother. She was nonintrusive, not at all overbearing. I recognize those as good qualities, and now I learn from her. She's the person I always turn to for advice. I call her. Brett has a splinter, what should I do? She says it'll come out in the bath—and it does.

"I learn more and more about her, about who she is, through these discussions about Brett—about her life before us and what it was like bringing up five children, things I never heard before. It's opened up a whole new world."

Going into my interviews, armed with the insights of Therese Benedek and Selma Fraiberg, I expected to hear a lot about parenthood proving therapeutic in terms of the parents' pasts. I was also aware of what could be called the Archibald Craven factor—parenthood as a means of recovering from illnesses, psychological disorders, or tragic events that occurred *in adulthood* (although, in the case of psychological disorders, the roots may have been in childhood). I had experienced this myself when motherhood turned out to be the only means through which I was able to reconcile myself to my mother's death.

But I had no idea how widespread or varied the Archibald

Craven factor was until some parents spontaneously told me that their children had been instrumental in their weathering present-tense traumas.

Tanya Landau, for instance, was in the middle of talking about her new, "Brett-oriented" relationship with her mother when her focus shifted to her father. She was describing her daily phone conversations with her mother, which both exemplify and facilitate their new closeness. But then she stopped and after a thoughtful moment said that it hadn't only been Brett's birth that had launched this long-distance dialogue. "After Brett it really intensified," she said. But the constant calling back and forth had started with her father's accident.

In 1987, two weeks before Tanya and Jake's wedding, Tanya's father was in an automobile accident that left him almost entirely paralyzed. "After that," Tanya said, "we all started calling my mother more."

Tanya had always adored her father, who was deeply involved in his children's lives. His passion for travel and learning made their childhood an adventure and made them grow up to be adventurous. Tanya's experiences in Europe, in the Middle East, and in India took on an extra dimension when she shared them with her father. "Since his accident, his being able to live via our experiences has been the one thing that's let him have any sanity. Because of his condition you might expect that he wouldn't want us to leave or to go far. And on one level, he doesn't. But on another level he still has this in him, to encourage us to go places—because he somehow, while we're away, lives through us, through our letters and the excitement of what we bring back and our experiences. He's able to live that.

"And now, through Brett, his first grandchild, he's able to relive parenthood."

For Tanya, giving her father this opportunity, and watching the relationship between her father and Brett flourish, has provided a substantial antidote to her own emotional devastation following the accident. "Brett's been like a new lease on life for him. He finds it worth living just to see her. We visit him whenever we can, at least every three months. It's getting better and better for him because she's beginning to interact with him more, and she's very sweet to him. I guess because at a very early age she was exposed to the ventilator and all the equipment around him, she isn't scared of anything and she accepts how he is, sitting in his chair, and recognizes the things that belong to him, and she's very, very protective of him.

"It's sweet to watch. If the nurse comes close to him, she says, 'Don't touch, don't touch.' If he's sleeping, she says, 'Shhh, sleeping.' And she also—I can't imagine how difficult it is for him, really, because he can't return her hugs and kisses— she also tries to give him kisses and hugs. But she's very tender, because she knows it can be uncomfortable for him. It's just amazing to me to see how much children understand, how much they sense. And how much they can give us, how much she's helped all of us."

For Laura Cerciello, parenthood proved therapeutic in that it finally motivated her to seek the therapy she had avoided for years and to stick with it. I met Laura in the office of the non-profit organization that she manages, and our conversation naturally turned to our children. She showed me a picture of Beth, her eight-year-old daughter. And although she indulged in some griping about the *Sturm und Drang* of single motherhood (she was divorced five years ago, and her former husband is in the picture only part time), she was coping well enough with the pressure to joke about it.

Since time was a problem for Laura, I asked if she'd mind jotting down some of her observations about what parenthood has meant to her. That way, when we did get to talk at length, I could focus on issues that she has found important.

To my surprise, the next time I saw Laura she handed me a five-page, single-spaced essay. Even more surprising—jarring, in fact—were her opening lines: "Parenthood has been a literally sobering experience for me. I am a recovering alcoholic, now sober for the better part of six and a half years." Throughout her narrative, Laura identified her ex-husband and her daughter with initials rather than names, which brought to mind certain works of nineteenth-century Russian fiction, as did the bleakness of her story.

Laura and her husband never thought they were "fit material for parenthood." Laura came from "generations of alcoholics" and was thoroughly "in the grip of the addiction." Her husband's nemesis was depression. The pregnancy was "an accident," but a welcome one, Laura wrote. "Our denial permitted us to believe that somehow we would both change by having the child." Unfortunately this did not happen.

With the help of her doctor, who knew about her "condition," Laura managed to cut down on her drinking during the pregnancy. Beth was born "on the small side, but seemingly normal." Laura's joy was enhanced by her mother's presence before, during, and after the delivery. "Her visit brought a tremendous sense of linkage and continuity. I enjoyed a closeness with her I had not heretofore felt."

But the same week that Beth was born, Laura's husband lost his job and sank into a six-month depression that kept him from being able to "connect" with the baby and crumbled Laura's vow, silently conceived in the euphoria of new motherhood, to give up drinking. She adored her baby and took care of her "as best I could, despite the drinking." And she hated herself. "It was easy to fall into blaming circumstances and my husband for my drinking, but deep down I knew the onus was on me and I felt like a criminal."

When her husband finally found work in "a seaside town," Laura thought their situation would improve. Her delight in taking Beth to the beach and on long strolls through the lovely streets, and in watching the baby "thrive much the way the hardy geraniums on our terrace did," led to a renewed determination to stop drinking. Once again, she "cut down"—until her husband decided they had to move again, to a city Laura disliked, where they were saddled with a responsibility she felt incapable of handling, the care of an ailing relative.

Six months of "alcoholic hell" later, Laura wrote, "I was on a plane with Beth heading for the sanitarium where I would get the help I so desperately needed."

Now, nearly seven alcohol-free years later, Laura is confident that she will never take another drink. But she does not think she will get over the guilt she feels. She is sure that the "mild developmental delays" Beth has experienced are a direct result of her drinking during her pregnancy, or of Beth's separation from her while she was in treatment (Laura's brother and sister-in-law cared for Beth, who was then only one and a half) or of both.

Doctors have reassured Laura that Beth's problems are not necessarily related either to fetal alcohol syndrome or to that early separation, but Laura still feels responsible. She worries that someday when she tells Beth her story—as she knows she'll feel obliged to do—"she'll hate me, and with good reason.

"So from time to time, I do feel very bad," Laura told me. But for the most part, she enjoys her closeness with Beth and Beth's closeness with her. Beth, who is thriving now—"an intelligent, intuitive, spirited, warm, and very loving girl"—keeps Laura going in this "new life," just as she got her started in it.

"I always knew that I loved her," Laura told me, "but when I was drinking it was as if I were with her but not really with her. I know this because of the way I feel now and the way I didn't feel then. For an addict, the addiction is the most important thing. Whether you like it or not, it is, because you care more about attending to that; it's your priority. And really, it's something that stands in the way of you and your relationship with anyone else. It's like something that is quite solidly there.

"So, you know, I was feeding her and changing her and taking her out for her walk, but I wasn't connecting with her in the way that I wanted to."

Now, at the Alcoholics Anonymous meetings that Laura attends, she hears parents talking about such things as passing out in the parking lots of their children's schools. "It was never that way for me," she says. "It's probably true that sometimes I was not all there because I was woozy from alcohol, but mainly it was psychological. It was that the child was not the main thing. And then you feel so rotten about it that the rottenness itself is something that thickens the veil between you and the other person. I knew this all the time.

"Now on the whole I feel much better with myself. I can be good with her. Even for the average parent, there are days when you feel crummy about yourself and are not wholly connected with your child. I have days like that, too, but when I was drinking it was always like that. Now I feel that I'm with her. I'm present. I'm present for the parenting."

In a case I heard about from a psychologist, a little girl not much older than Beth provided a "therapeutic experience" for her father that was similar to the support the babies in "Ghosts in the Nursery" gave their mothers. Without the child's "help," the psychologist said, the "work" the man was doing in his office five times a week would not have proved nearly as effective.

"This patient came to me in a state of profound depression," the psychologist told me. "He was a talented and accomplished guy, but he could never allow himself any satisfaction or enjoyment from his considerable accomplishments or his marriage or his child. His daughter was about two years old, a marvelous toddler, as best I could tell from his descriptions—ebullient, outgoing, and very much involved in trying to get his attention, as young girls tend to do.

"But he related to this child when he started treatment as an object to be observed. He couldn't allow himself to be affectionate with her. He would remain aloof and would observe her from an intellectual vantage point. His occupation was of such a nature that he could study aspects of the child's development in a professional way, but he never had any warmth or closeness with her.

"And what happened in the treatment was, as he was working through why he couldn't get pleasure in his work, why he couldn't allow himself to feel accomplished, why he couldn't allow himself to enjoy his relationship with his wife or his daughter—his daughter began to blossom.

"At the same time that he was working through his inability to enjoy his life, he began to be more engaged with his child. He found he was beginning to feel pleasure and delight with her, and not only in his engagement with the child but in his identification with the child's exploration of the world.

"For his entire adulthood he had worked hard and achieved because it was a job to be done and he wanted status, but there had never been any joy in it. Now, through engaging with his robust, healthy child and identifying with her joy, he blossomed along with her.

"It was a marvelous thing to see and was a compelling experience for me. I actually saw *him* as this young girl blossoming and discovering the world. He was the young girl! As his daughter grew, he was doing the same, both with her and in his own right. I felt in some ways that I had an ally as a therapist in this little girl. I felt that what this man and I were working on would never have had the impact it did if it hadn't been for his engagement with her and her development."

At first glance, Noah Richardson has nothing in common with Archibald Craven. Noah is what is known as a people person— outgoing, enthusiastic, witty. Students at the small liberal arts college where he teaches mathematics have always looked to him for personal, not just academic, guidance.

But when Noah, who, incidentally, had never read *The Secret Garden*, began filling me in on his own personal life, I saw some similarities to Archibald Craven. After Noah's wife, Lorraine, died suddenly at the age of thirty-nine, Noah, also thirty-nine, was overwhelmed both by grief and the responsibility of raising their eleven-year-old son, Danny, by himself.

"Actually," Noah said, "for a long time I felt Danny was a burden—this sounds awful, I know, but it's true. I had sort of seen him as another problem, I guess, before Lorraine died, because she was sick for a while. Her death was sudden in that it shocked everyone. But she hadn't been well for some time, and during that time I had to take care of everything, including Danny, of course. So while I loved him a lot, it did seem, at times, that he was just something else I had to tend to. I wasn't a bad father, I don't think, but I was a very distracted one, preoccupied with just getting through, getting everything done —to the detriment of my relationship with Danny."

Then, after Lorraine's death, Noah "just fell apart. That's what it felt like—as if I were leaking out from my body." He began having panic attacks; in a meeting or in a class, he would "have to leave, get out." One time, having driven to Danny's school to pick him up, Noah was unable to sit in the car and kept driving around the block, "just to keep moving. I had to keep moving."

Soon the idea of moving took on larger dimensions. Noah, looking back now, seven years later, admits that "I probably didn't know what I was thinking then. Nothing made a lot of sense. But I know I had these plans to get out, to leave that house, to leave that town, to leave my job, to—go somewhere and be somebody else. It's as if you lose your moorings. There's nothing to hold on to.

"In the mornings, I remember, I guess either the alarm would go off or Danny would come in because it was time for school. And I would just pull the covers over my head and think I didn't want to get up that day. It was much too difficult."

But Noah did get up. Every day. "I didn't have a choice, because my son just by his being, not because of anything he may have done or said, forced me to face life, to get him breakfast, to make sure he was dressed, to pack his lunch, and to take him to school."

And eventually Noah found himself getting up because he wanted to get up. The responsibility of caring for Danny had gone from being "another thing to do" to "another thing to do that was really good. I was focusing on him. I wanted to focus on him."

That summer, Noah and Danny traveled—to visit a former colleague of Noah's, to visit relatives, to see the Grand Canyon. Noah was on the move but not, as he had envisioned, away from everything. As he told me about his and Danny's adventure—"I have this great picture of Danny in one of our albums; he's pointing to the Grand Canyon as if he discovered it"—I understood why Noah had this quotation from T. S. Eliot framed on his desk:

> We shall not cease from exploration
> And the end of all our exploring
> Will be to arrive where we started
> And know the place for the first time.

"It was Danny's presence—his very presence," Noah concluded, "that forced me to attend to life, to focus on life, on living, on being. I couldn't escape. I had a son. I had a child who needed a parent, so I had to be a parent. I had to be an adult. I had to be okay for him.

"I remember thinking how grateful I was to him for forcing me to get up and get dressed and get him ready and go to work and face what I didn't want to face. I was grateful to him because I felt he was saving my life. And I'll always be grateful."

V

Creativity

How Parenthood Can Enrich
Our Powers of Self-Expression

The linkage of childbirth with other forms of creativity goes back to the very roots of human expression. The Sumerian princess, priestess, prophetess, and poet Enheduanna was not only the world's first nonanonymous author but possibly the first to formalize this connection. In her poem to the goddess Inanna, she used the language of childbirth to describe her literary labors: "It is enough for me, it is too much for me! I have given birth, o exalted lady, [to this song] for you."[1]

WE ARE IN THE KITCHEN of the average American two-child home. A parent (mother or father; take your pick) is seated at the table, talking with a reporter who has just commented that she thinks parenthood can be a fountainhead of all kinds of creative expression.

The parent agrees wholeheartedly and directs the reporter's attention to the refrigerator, which is plastered with artwork: a construction-paper garden of glued-on paper bake-cup flowers; a cardboard square covered with paint splatters ("That was his Jackson Pollock period," the parent observes of the preschooler); drawings suggesting mermaids, hot pink dinosaurs, and genies (showing the children's keen awareness of their culture); a mishmosh of guns, tanks, and planes with the slogan DONT HAV WAR—which the proud parent is thinking of having printed on note cards.

No doubt about it. There is plenty of evidence on this refrigerator, as on millions of others, that creativity is of major importance to parents. Refrigerator magnet manufacturers know this, which is why they woo parents with products that say things like "My Kid Made This" and "Look What —— Made in School."

What the magnet manufacturers don't seem to acknowledge, however, is something else that's evident in this kitchen art gallery and millions of others: that children can foster their *parents'* creativity. Where are the magnets with "Mom Made This" and "Dad Made This" to hold up all the photos documenting children's lives and family life? Where are the magnets acknowledging parent-child collaborations ("Look What Dad and I Made"; "Look What Mom Helped Me Do")?

When we (and there must be some refrigerator magnet manufacturers among us) consider creativity from the point of view of ourselves as parents, it's almost always in terms of how we're helping our children to develop it—with the lessons, the arts and crafts projects we encourage and supervise and participate in, our respect for their play—which, unlike ours, does not involve stepping "sideward into another reality," as Erik Erikson described it, but "forward to new stages of [self-] mastery," with our conscientious gift to them of lots of time in which to dream so that their imaginations will open and expand.

But what about us? How do our children open and expand our imaginations?

The artfully arranged refrigerator display of the parent's prize snapshots and of masterpieces by parent and child are, the reporter suspects, only the surface ripples of the parent's creative output. Moving beyond the refrigerator, the parent begins to focus inward.

Parenting As a Creative Process

"I know that a lot of people wouldn't think this looks like fun," Frances Brent is saying. She is in the midst of trying to convince her two-year-old son, Jesse, that the floor would be a safer place to play than his little chair, which he has placed on a big chair, and on which he is now bouncing. "But to me it's fun."

For a long time, Frances and her husband thought their older son, Ben, now nineteen, would be their only child. But, to their amazement and joy, along came Jesse and, shortly afterward, a daughter, Jennie, now six months old.

A lot of people wouldn't call what Frances is doing now (in contrast to writing poetry, teaching, writing short stories, and editing) creative, but to her it is. Absorbing, exhausting, and indisputably creative. To spend an hour or so trying to have an adult conversation with Frances in her sunny family room is to see parental creativity in action.

Jennie, crooning and crawling on her blanket, isn't much in need of imaginative input—until Jesse, now down from the chair, grabs the toy she is chewing. Frances comes to her rescue, then to Jesse's rescue when he can't find the *right* wizard puppet. "Oh, but this one's the good wizard!" Frances tells him, and then delights him with an impromptu puppet show. This is a woman whose entire being these days is invested in doing things like making her children's stuffed toys come to life.

"I think that when you have a baby," she says, "you become merged with the baby creatively and that's where your creativity goes, at least for me. That's my experience. It's not going into anything else right now. And I don't resent that; I'm not worried about it. Because I also know that I'm going to re-emerge as an individual and the experience of having lost myself in my children will have enriched me. I don't think this is necessarily a better experience than had I not had children. I have friends who don't have children and are very imaginative and productive. Their travels or professional lives enrich them. But I'm getting enrichment through my children now."

Almost all of the mothers and fathers I talked with believe, as Frances does, that parenting is a creative process quite on a par with those which can win us accolades in the world at large. A father of four, shouting over the racket of Batmobiles circling his driveway, said that "becoming focused on trips, projects, activities that would please the kids, calls for creativity. And of course they don't all like the same things, so I guess I've become four times more inventive."

The father of two grown sons looks back on their—and his —youth as a period of "adaptation for survival—but you could call it creativity. With children, you're an individual, and each child has his own personality. What you can do with one to get a desired response may not work with the other—to develop an intellectual curiosity in the child, to encourage a hobby, to pursue a job till it's finished, to inculcate ideas you feel are important for success in the world later on. Our children are two different personalities, and I think we had to be very creative to find different pathways for each of them to get where we wanted them to go."

"Parenting is creative in how you relate to your children's world," Tanya Landau told me, "or how you think of ways to bring the world to them, on their level. Your impulse is just to present it to them as you know it, but they don't always understand it like that."

"Maybe it was two weeks ago," recalled Greg Weber, who clearly delights in his ability to bring the world to the level of his "bright and perceptive" seven-year-old son; "he was in the tub and he happened to have a Cool Whip container. He's into the reading thing, so he asked me what the C inside the circle was. And I had to think, how can I make him understand the concept of copyrights? It's a challenge, all the time, taking each complex thing he discovers and reducing it to its core element so that he can grasp it. I feel I've really accomplished something when I succeed. Now he goes around saying, 'Oh, they can't copyright this one; this one's copyrighted already!' He's in the know!"

Sally Tenzer has always channeled her need to make and do things into one artistic form or another—playing the violin and the piano, painting watercolors, gardening, making pottery—

and parenthood, which, when she thinks about it, seems to demand as much creativity as her other pursuits. This has become particularly apparent to her now that the older of her two daughters, Amy, has become a contrary adolescent. "What's happened with Amy is I say black and she says white. So trying to guide her toward the ends that I think are right—but in a way that doesn't incite revolution—takes a great deal of imagination on my part. It's very, very difficult."

As Sally talked, I remembered the father who said that meeting the needs of his four children has made him "four times more inventive." But Sally's situation suggested that we can also become more or differently inventive with each stage of a single child's development. Nothing in her experience of raising children, she says, has called for more creativity than coping with "this need a teenager has to be her own person."

We tend to think of self-fulfillment as something we must pursue by ourselves, going into a room and drawing or playing an instrument, taking a walk and consolidating our ideas. Feeling whole, complete, self-actualized; we think of this aspect of existence as attainable only when we get time to ourselves, when we are doing things for ourselves.

But as Sally, Frances, and so many other parents have discovered, often to their surprise, the time and energy put into raising our children can be just as self-expanding.

As Frances explained, by way of linking herself as a mother with her friends who are childless and therefore able to engage wholly with the world at large: "This is what I think. I think that when you love somebody—your child—it is an experience of traveling outside yourself to some other place. That experience, like going to another country or entering into what you're writing or painting or working on, enriches you. You come home with more than you had before. I think that's what happens."

The reason that our accomplishments in the big world, or in the worlds we inhabit when we are absolutely alone, are more easily labeled "creative" than our daily or even long-range achievements as homemakers and parents has to do, I think, with the notion that where there is creativity there is a palpable product.

I once attended a PTA meeting at which the major topic was the school play that had just ended its triumphant two-evening run. A young mother who had put considerable time and talent into this production was reminiscing about all that it had meant to her. "Being at home with the children all day, everything you do, there's no product!" she said. "It was so wonderful being involved with something that was a product!" And the other parents nodded to show they knew what she meant.

Lots of parents know what she meant. Ruth Sack, a gifted graphic artist and the mother of two boys, ages ten and six, was taken aback when I asked her about creativity in parenting. "It's funny to think of it that way," she said. "I'm so oriented in my work to thinking about a tangible goal. And a child is intangible; a developing personality is something so intangible."

Ruth, like many artists, channels her more readily perceived creativity in two directions—the work she does for money and the work she just does. "The art I do for my career is creative, but I don't consider it as creative as the art I do for myself."

Ruth hopes that someday the paintings and drawings that spring from her will prove as profitable as the catalogues, pamphlets, and posters she is now paid to produce. But after her first son was born she found that "since I only had so much time in my life, I had to eliminate projects that didn't have to happen right now, and I eliminated much of the creative, automatic, personal stuff.

"And now that I think about it, I can understand why I haven't done a lot of highly creative things since becoming a mother. Maybe I haven't needed to. Maybe parenting has fulfilled those needs. I think a lot of the best parenting is extremely creative. Finding the way to settle a conflict between two children seems creative to me because it's not something you can learn from a book. Each situation is unique. Each solution has to be unique. You have to jump out of yourself and try to know how the kids see the thing at that moment and decide how to handle it.

"There is a half-empty and half-full way of looking at things. You can say, I'm depleted by these children, so I cannot fulfill my creative side; I can't find time for it; the children are robbing me of it. Or you can say, I don't need to push these feelings out through my painting because they're coming through this other channel, my children. And I guess, depending where I am in my menstrual cycle, I could give you two completely different answers on that!"

But for the most part, Ruth seems to lean toward "the half-full way of looking at things." Raising children, she told me, gives her "the same kind of satisfaction that I get from my art, but when you're dealing with children, you have to get out of yourself and understand *them.*"

She also finds that the payback she gets from her children is, in a way, comparable to the paychecks she gets from her art. "Right now," she said, "I see my older son flowering into a very lovely person. And he was such a jerk last year! But the pieces are falling into place and he's becoming a kind older brother and a very nice child. And I am tickled. It's like when you catch yourself in a mirror or in a window when you're walking by and you almost don't recognize yourself. It's a curious feeling: look at that!"

It is in these moments of glimpsing ourselves in the mirror that parenthood can seem perceptibly creative. Sometimes, as Ruth suggested, we're successfully mediating a battle between siblings or otherwise helping our children learn to control their behavior or emotions. Sometimes we're figuring out ways to translate the world into language they understand. Sometimes we're doing for them, or with them, little projects that we do see, at the time, as "creative." "I'm a good storyteller," Ruth told me. "I can sit down and weave tales with the kids. And that takes a lot of energy and imagination. It's extremely creative, and it's a wonderful time when I sit down with them and do that."

Sometimes these projects yield actual products. When Ruth mentioned storytelling, I thought of all the homemade

Halloween costumes I'd heard about, the birthday cakes from scratch, the tree houses, the entire Lego cities.

I remembered the Saturday morning I helped Jonathan build a birdhouse, and all the time we put into constructing a big Indian doll from paper plates, snippets of felt, wire, beads, and cardboard tubes from paper towels, among other odds and ends. Then there was the parental masterpiece I had only read about, in Laurie Colwin's novel *Family Happiness:* a "barnyard lunch" for a child's birthday with "pigs made of eggs dipped in beetroot juice and a pig yard made of spinach and a little fence of fried potatoes." One character exclaimed that seeing it "made me feel my girlhood once more."

News of such parental ingenuity does not normally leak beyond the home or the neighborhood. It seldom earns us pats on the back from the general public. Nor, to be frank, does it usually deserve public acclaim. A pig yard made of spinach? A scrap-heap Indian? Clever, yes. Earthshaking? Well, no. But within the child's world to which we travel and in which we live much of the time, these achievements can seem monumental. We cherish them as talismans of our children's delight in making them, in having them, and of our own pleasure at having done something many of us never imagined ourselves doing. Would I have built a birdhouse (or, for that matter, expressed myself through any art or craft) if it weren't for Jonathan? Would Ruth, the graphic artist, ever have discovered her penchant for storytelling if she didn't have two little sons to inspire her?

These products, the things we make and do with and for our children, like the school play that the young mother at that PTA meeting remembered so fondly, like our daily, creative dealings with our children's moods, crises, and behavior, can make us more inventive in general. They can unearth talents and traits we didn't know we had, open areas of our imagination we've never used before, stimulate interest in things we never thought interested us.

And they can, viewed collectively and from the half-full perspective, make the intangible tangible. Stephanie Hickson has a clear vision of the way children can prod, feed, and reward their parents' creative impulses. Stephanie is thirty years old, divorced, and works as a chemical technician to support herself and her two-year-old son.

"You're molding this kid," Stephanie explained, "and it takes a very long time. You've got to think about it, sit back, look at it—just like an artist with a block of clay. You see an image in it, and other people see a block of clay. Then you go there with your hands and you try to make it do what you want it to do—except that the clay can't rebel. But sometimes I guess the wheel makes it lopsided. So you straighten it out; you correct it. I see rearing a child as being a creative artist. You have to pay close attention to your work if you want to have a masterpiece at the end. I think when I work with Earl, when I teach him, I feel the same way artists must feel when they create. When I teach him something, that's like another stroke of the brush. And eventually at the end I'll have my picture."

I heard many mothers and fathers second Stephanie's satisfaction at the thought of her child as a work in progress, albeit one over which we have less control, ultimately, than, say, a real potter working with a real block of clay. ("You're like a gardener with a tree," one father said. "You know the tree has a life of its own. But you can do a lot to help it come into its own.") And they feel—as Freud wrote in *The Interpretation of Dreams*—that this creative investment and expression ultimately can be more rewarding than any other.

"Children may perhaps achieve what their father has failed to," Freud wrote.[2] He believed not only that his children might fulfill some of his own aspirations but might finish projects he had started—for instance, this very "book upon dreams" that he was writing and that he occasionally feared he would not live to finish.

In his letters to Fliess, Freud intimated that he hoped the book would bring him a measure of the immortality (not to mention the royalties) he craved. But in the book itself he indicated that it was his children whom he regarded as his more significant and lasting legacy. "After all," he wrote, "[is] not having children our only path to immortality?"[3]

Both men and women told me that their perception of

parenting as highly creative does stem in part from this sense of participating in the process of molding people who will reflect and perhaps extend and improve upon them. Above and beyond that, they look upon their children as a contribution to the world that is as valuable as any political, professional, or social contribution they might make.

When Melinda Stern began studying for her bat mitzvah at the age of thirty-two, she had no knowledge of Hebrew. Like anyone struggling with a foreign language, she found certain phrases particularly charismatic, and two of them stuck in her mind like fragments of favorite songs even before she really understood what they meant. Later, after she had internalized the meaning and connotations of those phrases, they became even dearer to her. Both of them concerned parenthood, her reason for becoming bat mitzvah: *l'dor v'dor*—"from generation to generation"—and *Tikkun Olam*.

Tikkun Olam is a central concept of Judaism. It means "repairing the world," perhaps the ultimate creative process. For Melinda, at this point in her life, parenthood is the medium through which this creativity is expressed. Her work, as she sees it, is trying to make good on all the promise contained in the two human beings she and her husband created.

"There are so many ways to repair the world," she told me. "A lot of times I become self-disparaging. What am I doing that's repairing the world? My husband, a doctor, is trying to heal people, save lives, every single day. I'm not doing that. But then I think my contribution is to try to make two good human beings. Motherhood is shaping and guiding and instilling values and helping to create a complete, thinking, feeling human being who will go out in the world and try to make it better. And that is *Tikkun Olam*."

This feeling, which Melinda shares with many parents, that through making "good human beings" we are doing our bit to improve the world, cuts right to the heart of creativity, as Abraham Joshua Heschel did when he wrote: "The key to the source of creativity lies in the will to cling to spirituality, to be close to the inexpressible, and not merely in the ability of expression.

What is creative comes from responsive merging with the eternal in reality, not from an ambition to say something."[4]

Heschel was not referring to parenting when he wrote this, but he might well have been. The emotions too deep to communicate, the acts that seem commonplace, the daily achievements that don't win medals, all the ingenious and inventive efforts invested in the process of parenting, are no less creative because they remain at an experiential level and aren't given form in plaster, stone, paint, music, or words.

But sometimes being intimately involved in the continuing creation of another human being becomes rewarding both in itself and as a catalyst for other creative endeavors. Sometimes our children awaken in us the "ambition to say something." Sometimes giving so much of ourselves to our children contributes to—does not detract from—pursuits that we have no trouble labeling as creative.

"The advantage of motherhood for a woman artist," according to the poet Alicia Ostriker, "is that it puts her in immediate and inescapable contact with the sources of life, death, beauty, growth, corruption . . . If the woman artist has been trained to believe that the activities of motherhood are trivial, tangential to the great themes of literature, she should untrain herself."[5]

This is also true, according to some male artists, of fatherhood.

Parenthood as a Source of Creativity

"Middle age and fatherhood have done nothing to diminish Bruce Springsteen's exuberance for performing on stage," says the caption under the *New York Times* photo of the new Boss, looking, however, very much like his old—dare I say it?—macho self as he tears up the stage. But according to the accompanying review by Jon Pareles, this Bruce Springsteen is no longer the blue-collar Job of "Born to Run." Not with one-liners like "Have we got any moms and pops out there?" Not with philosophical asides on "the legacy we leave to our children." And not, heaven knows, when reciting nursery rhymes!

This Bruce Springsteen is, in his offstage life, a father, a
fact that has significantly colored his onstage personality and
the music he composes and performs. The metamorphosis of
Springsteen from working-class hero to family man began nine
months after his son was born, as he told the *New York Times*
reporter Stephen Holden.[6]

"I was a father," he said, "and I had a real relationship with
Patti, which was something that had evaded me for a long time.
I'd just finished the album 'Human Touch,' but it felt unfin-
ished." Seized with "an intense creative fever," as Holden described it, Springsteen composed "Living Proof," a moving
rock ballad that "portrays fatherhood as a transcendent deliver-
ance from a prolonged period of self-doubt and unhappiness."

"Living Proof," as Springsteen explained, was only the beginning. "[It] was the key unlocking the door into the next
room, where a lot of songs were waiting. I wrote one a night
over the next three weeks, and they became [the album] 'Lucky
Town.' "

Springsteen's discovery of family life as fertile soil for his
art (the headline of Holden's article put it nicely: "When the
Boss Fell to Earth, He Hit Paradise") affirms something Gertrude Stein once said to a younger writer: "Don't think so much
about your wife and children being dependent upon your work.
Try to think of your work being dependent upon your wife and
child, for it will be if it really comes from you, and if it doesn't
come from you—the *you* that has the wife and child . . . then
it is no use anyway."[7]

Be yourself, Stein was saying, your real self. It is within that
self that you'll find the wherewithal to write, to create any form
of art. Even though the inspiration may come from outside, it is
what happens when the artist internalizes, synthesizes, and finally interprets the idea or experience that turns the raw material into art.

Usually, when artists write or talk about themselves, they
don't mention bringing up the kids, or, if they do, we get the
impression that they function as artists *despite* the kids—which is
why Gertrude Stein's remarks seem so refreshing and the new

Bruce Springsteen seems enchanting enough to warrant exploration in not one but two *Times* articles.

We often find—and have come to expect—men who are successful artists attributing a good part of their success to the women who kept the children out of their studios, offices, basements, garrets, hair, sight, and minds as they struggled to create their great whatevers. Joseph Conrad was profuse in his gratitude, calling his wife "a silent, watchful, tireless affection" who made "the . . . flow of daily life . . . easy and noiseless for me" so that he could "wrestle with the Lord for [his] creation."[8]

As for female artists—we've grown accustomed to hearing them regret that *they* don't have wives who would allow them to spend more time with their muses, undisturbed by their offspring. We don't often hear about their offspring being muses.

Tillie Olsen, for instance, who didn't publish a book until she was fifty, explained that "children need one *now*," and that as we tend to their needs out of "love, not duty . . . one feels them as one's self," our own work is "interrupted, deferred, postponed" and that "makes blockage—at best, lesser accomplishment. Unused capacities atrophy, cease to be."[9]

Even after Olsen was "free of these domestic labors of love," her creative efforts were, she wrote, hampered by "the habits of a lifetime when everything else had to come before writing . . . What should take weeks takes me sometimes months to write, what should take months takes years."[10]

But the assumption, however well documented, that our muses cannot be heard above the tumult of children does not remotely approach a general rule. Bruce Springsteen, Gertrude Stein, and Alicia Ostriker are far from the only artists who have taken a holistic approach to creativity, who have noticed that letting in the tumult and, concomitantly, glimpsing the eternal truths and mysteries that are so bound up in it, can actually release ideas and energy that otherwise might have remained untapped.

Cecil Day Lewis would have been very much in tune with the new Bruce Springsteen, since he too found his sensibility revived by fatherhood, by the wonder of it all. Cecil Day Lewis was a poet laureate of England, a detective story writer (under the pseudonym of Nicholas Blake), translator, professor, Commander of the Order of the British Empire, and the father of the actor Daniel Day-Lewis, whose birth inspired him to write a little poem that ended with these lines:

We time-worn folk renew ourselves at your enchanted spring.
As though manhood's begun
Again in you.
This is your birthday and our thanksgiving.[11]

In the essay called "Fires," Raymond Carver tells us—and it does sound as if he's just telling it, chatting with us, his readers: "I have to say that the greatest single influence on my life, and on my writing, directly and indirectly, has been my two children."[12]

But their presence, Carver goes on to explain, was not entirely uplifting. From the moment they were born, both of them before he was twenty, "their heavy and often baleful influence" determined the way he would write and the way he and his wife would live. They were "in the driver's seat."

One day, trapped in a crowded Laundromat in Iowa City, desperate to finish five or six loads of mostly kids' clothes and get on with his other chores, frustrated almost to the point of weeping, Carver had this epiphany: "Nothing—and, brother, I mean nothing—that ever happened to me on this earth could come anywhere close, could possibly be as important to me, could make as much difference, as the fact that I had two children. And that I would always have them and always find myself in this position of unrelieved responsibility and permanent distraction."

This was "real *influence*," he emphasizes. Not like reading Ernest Hemingway and Lawrence Durrell. Not like a chance phone call that somehow wove its way into a story he was writing. Not like the cheers from the Saratoga racetrack that put him in mind of events from his past in El Paso that then found their way into his narrative. This was "the moon and the tide."

During his nineteen "ferocious years of parenting," Carver

wrote, he seldom had "the time, or the heart" for sustained creative work. Between the kids and the menial jobs he and his wife both undertook to make ends meet (at one point, he was employed as a tulip picker), he was left with an hour or two a day in which to write, and some days not even an hour. This was the reason that he never became a novelist. "I had to . . . write something I could finish now, tonight, or at least tomorrow night, no later, after I got in from work and before I lost interest." And so, instead of becoming a novelist, he became a writer of short stories and poems.

Although Carver looked back on all those years of "hit-or-miss" writing with sardonic candor—"I'd take poison before I'd go through that time again"—he saw that the limits placed on him by his children were not entirely a bad thing. Like Tillie Olsen, he found that his writing habits from those days persisted beyond the years that were formative both for the kids and for him. Even after he had "a great swatch of time in which to work on . . . anything I want," even after he was successful enough to write rather than pick tulips for a living, he continued to write short stories and poems, not novels, although now it was his choice, not his fate.

To an extent, his choice may have been dictated by his coming to feel comfortable in these forms as well as by winning recognition as a master of them. Perhaps Carver knew that the constraints parenthood placed on his creativity, however onerous they seemed at the time, worked, in the long run, to his advantage. Perhaps that was why he was able to say, "God forbid, I'm not complaining now, just giving facts from a heavy and still bewildered heart."

Perhaps he also realized, more fully than he let on in "Fires," the extent to which his children influenced not only the form of his work but its content. In "Fires," he touched on parenthood as a source of the material that led to some of his best, most universally appealing, stories. He noted that Flannery O'Conner's observation—that enough of "the stuff that makes fiction" has happened to writers before they are twenty to last a lifetime—proved untrue for him. "I really don't feel," he wrote, "that anything happened in my life until I was twenty and married and had the kids. Then things started to happen."

These "things"—the financial struggles, the dashed dreams, the interruptions, the commotion, the demands, the feelings of being oppressed, suffocated, as well as the overwhelming love and worry and fear and responsibility—all the things that make up the drama of so many people's daily lives, informed and colored Carver's writing as powerfully as life in exotic settings, unhampered by children, influenced Hemingway and Durrell.

Carver's children, even as they sapped his creativity, also fed it. "Distance" explores a young father's conflict between going on the hunting trip he longs for and staying home to help his wife with their sick infant. "A Small, Good Thing" lays out the anatomy of the parents' anguish as they sit helplessly by their comatose eight-year-old son. "Fever" tells of a father's struggle to come to terms with his wife's desertion of him and their two children, and, not incidentally, to find someone reliable to care for the children while he is at work.

These stories could have been written only by someone who had lived through, not just observed, parenthood. It is impossible to separate Carver the writer from Carver the father. His children made him who he was. Their proximity, their "heavy and often baleful influence," gave him ideas and, even more, insights, sensitivity, a depth of understanding about family life and about what really goes on within children and within parents and between children and parents that he could not have acquired in any other way.

Recently, I glanced through a book about Carver, looking for further evidence of his children's influence, anything that might not have come up in "Fires," any secrets only hinted at in the stories and poems. There was no mention of Carver's children in the book. "Fires" was discussed, but just about all that the biographer seemed to glean from it was that Carver's early marriage, early fatherhood, and utter poverty had indeed placed a great burden on him. That was it. The influence of his children, their importance, had, incredibly, eluded the author. Or maybe not so incredibly.

In books about artists, connections are often made between their lives and their work, but not between their parenthood and their art, even though parenthood is such a significant part of the lives of so many people and, if these people are artists, of their art. Maybe if parenthood weren't so commonplace, its impact on art would be more noticeable and intriguing—like bullfighting, for instance, or war, or expatriatism.

In the vast silence on the subject of how having children can make an artist, "Fires" was a real ice-breaker. So is "The Making of a Poem" by Stephen Spender. Carver did not go into the creative process itself—that is, how he actually processed truth in writing fiction. Spender did.

There are any number of ways in which children can kick-start creativity. One is by inspiring—by doing something, saying something, taking on a certain look—a specific work or part of that work. In the case of Stephen Spender, as with his friend and contemporary Cecil Day Lewis, it was his child's coming into existence that did the trick.

In "The Making of a Poem," he details the way the birth of his son generated a progression of thoughts that grew into a full-fledged poem. Like most fathers in those days, he apparently missed the delivery itself but was nonetheless profoundly moved by it. As he rode to the hospital on the bus to visit his wife and his baby, he was struck by the cleanliness and orderliness of the city. He thought that "everything was prepared for our child . . . any child born today inherits, with his generation, cities, streets . . . the most elaborate machinery for living" from people of previous generations.

But then "sadder thoughts" crowded in, "naturally enough." Spender thought how his son was also heir to "vast maladjustments, vast human wrongs." And it occurred to him that this baby was "like a pinpoint of present existence, the moment incarnate, in whom the whole of the past, and all possible futures, *cross*." His mind snagged on the word "cross," which seemed to him to contain not only the "situation . . . of a child born into the world" but "the form of a poem about his situation," a poem where "the *cross* in which present and future meet is the secret of an individual human existence."[13]

Terry Eicher once came up with an idea for a poem in a manner much like the one Spender described. The poem was about the uses of the baobab tree, a source of paper, cloth, rope, and food for generations of Africans. But Terry's inspiration was not the tree itself, how it looked, what it meant to him. Nor did the poem evolve directly from the years he and his wife had spent in Africa as Peace Corps volunteers. The poem came from another direction entirely, through his older daughter, who was born soon after their return from Africa. "Her first word sounded like 'baobab,' " he explained, "and it was hearing this sound from her that brought to mind the tree. In the poem is the idea of this baobab tree, which is supposed to be the oldest tree on earth—and how its name is the first word of not just my child but any child. That word, baobab, sounds like every child's first word—babble, the beginning of language, the oldest tree, the child beginning to talk."

Ruth Sack has, on occasion, sketched or painted her two boys. But their creativity has also proved inspiring. "One time," she told me, "Matthew [her six-year-old] was upstairs on the landing, a space about eight by twenty feet, and he traced a magnificent pattern in the carpet with his finger. He just pulled his finger across the carpet and created lines on it. It was a landscape covering that very long space on the floor, and I thought, My God, this is phenomenal. This is really beautiful. I wish I could buy a carpet that looked like this. Imagine!

"And I got all these ideas about how to create a tapestry that has that look. Children are so liberated in their use of space, in their drawing; it's been very stimulating for me to have kids."

Many of Pamela R. Lopes's poems were inspired by her only child, a son, who was born when she was fifteen. From the time he was three and a half, she has raised him as a single mother—"but not entirely alone," she says. "I insisted that his father be an integral part of his upbringing, and I had caring friends who were there for me—and him." And she put herself through college in the process.

Her son is now in college himself, on his way toward becoming a psychologist. Pamela does some writing to supplement her income from "networking" for a municipal substance
abuse prevention program. Her romance advice columns appear
regularly in "two magazines I'm sure you've never heard of."
She has not yet tried to market her poems, but they are her
"real writing," and she wants them in print. Her agenda is more
than self-expression.

In a poem that means much to her she speaks to other
parents out of her own hard history, telling "how the world
tries to rip your children away from you and all the negative
influences that are out there and how you have to fight to maintain and keep your child against all these odds. And I think
that's real true, because I see so many people who just gave their
children away. There are a lot of children who are lost, who
didn't have parents who rallied for them and championed for
them."

Ever since Pamela's son was two and she was a freshman in
college, she has been writing letters to him. Over the years they
have become a book. "There are also some poems in it that I
wrote, stories about how I was feeling, and things I was experiencing at the time. And there are some poems I liked from
other poets. That's basically it.

"I'm going to give it to him in a few months for his
twenty-first birthday. I hope he'll read it, get some insights into
who I was, who I've been. I want him to look at some of the
poetry I've written, some of the poetry I've collected from others, and I hope he can use it. I hope it'll help him get through
life successfully. You know, I never before looked at it as a creative endeavor, but I guess it is. It's a 'life book.' No chance it'll
ever be published. It's just for him. But maybe, except for raising him, it's the most creative thing I've ever done."

Sometimes, the line between art and parenthood is not neatly
traceable from point of origin to destination. Sometimes, art
and parenthood are inextricably bound together.

"When there is an organic relationship between childrearing and art," Emery Bernhard wrote in an essay that affirma-

tively answers its title "Can Art Survive Parenthood?," "the domains interweave and cross-fertilize. Children show us how work can be play and play can be work . . . We must have faith that an artistic impulse denied—due to a child with colic or a job we cannot turn down or a burned-out coparent who needs relief—will not die, but will melt back into the subconscious and re-emerge when the time is right."[14]

For some creative people, that time does not necessarily have to be when the children aren't around. Ursula K. LeGuin, mother of three and author of over twenty fiction and nonfiction books, believes that "the supreme value of art depends on other equally supreme values."[15] (And also that "it's a lot easier to write books while bringing up kids than to bring up kids while working nine to five plus housekeeping. But that is what our society, while sentimentalizing over Mom and the Family, demands of most women.")

According to LeGuin, the autobiography of the prolific nineteenth-century Scottish novelist, historian, and biographer Margaret Oliphant "gives us a glimpse of why a novelist might not merely endure writing in the kitchen or the parlor amid the children and the housework, but might endure it willingly. She seems to feel that she profited, that her writing profited, from the difficult, obscure, chancy connection between the art work and the emotional/manual/managerial complex of skills and tasks called housework, and that to sever that connection would put the writing itself at risk, would make it, in her word, unnatural."

Oliphant's byline—frequently, it was *Mrs.* Oliphant—reflects that "connection," the years and years of writing in tandem with raising her own three children and her brother's three children. She wrote this explanation of how she did it: "The writing ran through everything. But then it was also subordinate to everything, to be pushed aside for any little necessity. I had no table even to myself, much less a room to work in, but sat at the corner of the family table with my writing-book, with everything going on as if I had been making a shirt instead of writing a book . . . My mother sat always at needlework of some kind, and talked to whoever might be present, and I took my share in the conversation, going on all the same with my story, the little groups of imaginary persons, these other talks evolving themselves quite undisturbed."

Dorothy Canfield, in the first half of this century, also wrote a great number of fiction and nonfiction books while keeping her home fires burning. It is no accident that throughout her career, her maternal and professional identities merged from time to time to produce works such as *Mothers and Children* (1914) and *Our Children, A Handbook for Parents* (1932).

Canfield once described a story's unfolding as a leitmotif of her daily occupations. After having taken a long walk, during which the kernel of the story popped into her mind, "I had come again to our own house and was swallowed in the usual thousand home-activities. But underneath all that, quite steadily my mind continued to work on the story as a wasp in a barn keeps on silently plastering up the cells of his nest in the midst of the noisy activities of farm life. I said to one of the children, 'Yes, dear, wasn't it fun!' and to myself, 'To be typical of our tradition-ridden valley-people the opposition ought to come from the dead hand of the past.' "[16]

In her diary, the German artist Käthe Kollwitz wrote: "I am gradually approaching the period in my life when work comes first. [Her sons were then eighteen and fourteen years old.] When both the boys went away for Easter, I hardly did anything but work . . . And yet I wonder whether the 'blessing' is not missing from such work. No longer diverted by other emotions, I work the way a cow grazes . . . The hands work and work, and the head imagines it is producing God knows what; and yet formerly, in my wretchedly limited working time, I was more productive because I was more sensual; I lived as a human being must live, passionately interested in everything."[17]

These illuminating excursions into the two-track minds of women leading dual-track lives make me think of the domestic scene Anna Quindlen described to Judd Rose during a "Prime Time Live" interview. Quindlen was sitting on her porch with her daughter the day the Supreme Court handed down its 1992 decision upholding the states' right to place certain restrictions on abortion but at the same time upholding women's right to abortion. She was spending time with her daughter and reading the decision at the same time—much as Dorothy Canfield talked to her child while spinning a tale in her head.

Quindlen, however, did not bring up the scene to illustrate how she can parent and process information for her writing simultaneously. What she was processing at that moment, the abortion decision, was more than grist for a column. What the Supreme Court decides on abortion affects her daughter's future. A lot of the subjects she writes about affect her children's future. So her children have fed her creativity not only because they have directly provided her with some of her richest and most amusing material, but because she writes in part to improve the world for them.

I also thought of Ruth Sack projecting into the future about how she'll someday remember this period of being the mother of two young children and at the same time a hardworking professional artist. "I'll look back on this pretty house surrounded by trees with lots of things happening, all this work coming out of it, and children running in and out. You know, it's really kind of neat in the afternoons when the kids get home from school. The dog comes alive. I guess she's been conserving her energy for when the kids come in. And I'm getting my work done."

Her words sped up, rapid-fire, as she went on: "I have a few phone calls to make, a few little things to do. But I have kids running in and out and asking me for things and I'm talking with them and then I go back to what I'm doing and then they run outside. And then they come back with their friends. And then I take them to pick up the pizza and then we all eat pizza, and there's a lot of, you know, just noise.

"And that's what I'll remember, this little orchestra here, things that go on. And clients come in while all this is going on. The children run past them and I'm handing them envelopes at the door and the Federal Express person comes in. You know, I'll be remembering it in stop-action photography, really fast. That's how I'll remember it because that's how it is.

"And you know what? It's too empty when the kids aren't here. I love it when they're here and I'm working. It's—it's really all the same stuff."

VI

How Our Children Can Improve Our Work and the Way We Work

It was on November 12, a day dominated by a left-sided migraine, on the afternoon of which Martin sat down to write a new poem, on the evening of which Oli lost his second tooth, that, after the frightful labor pains of the last few weeks, I gave birth to a new piece of knowledge.
—SIGMUND FREUD, *The Complete Letters of Sigmund Freud to Wilhelm Fliess*

RUTH SACK'S CAREER as a graphic artist was born with her oldest son, Daniel. "I was always uptight and maybe insecure as a young person," she told me. "And my art career never got a tremendous start. But I sort of put the pieces together around the time I had my first child. Before Daniel was born, I was a fine artist and I had a job working at an art school. But I knew this wasn't it. Then I became pregnant. And for me the pregnancy was a wonderful time to change careers. It was a new stage in life, giving birth, and a great time to start something new.

"I began going to design school," Ruth continued, "and after the baby was born I took him to class with me. I was attending classes and working part time and I had a little baby and it all made perfect sense. I have a friend who's also an artist —she taught me print-making—and she said she'd had the same experience. The feeling that I could do it, channel my creativity into a real career, came from the confidence that I got from accomplishing this incredible thing, having a child, being a mother. It gave me a tremendous feeling of confidence that I hadn't had before."

I remember thinking, as Ruth talked, that what she described did indeed make "perfect sense." But, let's face it, the idea of parenthood as career-enhancing is not part of the national mindset. Depictions of the working parent in magazine and newspaper articles, in books and movies, on television, and in advertising focus unremittingly on all that work plus parenting takes out of us, not on all that we can get out of it. In the commercial for Mitchum's Antiperspirant, for example, the camera lingers on a black-and-white close-up of a worried-looking woman, who confesses, "Between work, kids, the house, I'm so stressed . . ." Then the camera turns to a worried-looking man, who confides, "I'm a good father. I work hard. But all I get is stress, stress, stress . . ."

When we hear about how having children affects our working selves, it is almost always of the conflicts in balancing both responsibilities. And there is no doubt that our struggles with these conflicts represent a substantial chunk of our collective consciousness.

I noticed soon after Jonathan was born that, although my horizons were expanding in a number of areas, work was not one of them. During his first year I managed to get one little essay together. It was called "Why Mommy Can't Read." (Let alone write!)

And now, reporting from my home office, I have to say that working while mothering is still an uphill struggle. This book was indeed inspired by Jonathan, but on a day-to-day basis

I've been much more aware of how it's been inhibited, inter-rupted, and stalled by Jonathan—and by the children of many of my subjects.

It is often harder to get an interview with the average par-ent, I found, than with the average head of state. And once dates have been made, they're often canceled due to things like chickenpox. And once we sit down to talk, the flow of conversa-tion, often enough, is directed by the comings and goings of the children.

Because of the hurdles that parenting has thrown in the way of my work and that work has thrown in the way of my parenting—not to mention my having amassed a small library of evidence that mine was a far from unique experience—I sus-pected that "work" would be one area in which the influence of parenthood would be largely negative or, at least, inhibiting. I thought I would hear from stay-at-home parents about the frus-tration of careers postponed and the fear of never being able to make up for time lost from the job. I expected to hear from those parents who cannot afford to stay home with their kids about the unrelenting "stress, stress, stress" of having to make ends meet at both ends. I anticipated stories about important meetings and deadlines missed because of child-related emer-gencies, inability to perform on the job because of child-related worries, being passed over for a promotion because of the child-related inability to work overtime, getting a promotion and finding that what is good for one's work life can wreck one's home life.

And all of the above did come up in my conversations with parents. But even as they discussed these conflicts and their con-comitant frustrations, some parents brought up ways that their children had affected their work for the better, not for the worse.

Talking with these parents and reading about others, I found that our children can influence our work lives in many more ways than by giving us additional people whose survival depends on our work. I found out, and not only from Ruth Sack, that having children can lead to a new career, a new direc-tion, that can be more rewarding than whatever the parent was doing before. I learned that children can inspire insights and approaches that improve the way a parent works or the nature of the work itself, and that, through raising children, parents can develop personality traits and personal qualities that may help them do their work or get along at work—even get ahead at work—more effectively.

The Careers-Inspired-by-Babies Boom

Remember *Baby Boom*, the 1987 comedy with Diane Keaton as a hard-as-nails female executive who "works five to nine," earns six figures, and has a fabulous Manhattan apartment, a fabulous wardrobe, and a significant other who is equally work-obsessed? For "the Tiger Lady," as they call her in the business, every day is a good hair day. Until she inherits—from a British cousin whom she hasn't seen since 1956 and who has died in a car accident—a baby named Elizabeth.

"But I can't be a mother!" she says to the social worker who delivers the child to her at Kennedy Airport. "I have a twelve-thirty lunch meeting!"

Then comes a series of scenes in which the summa cum laude Tiger Lady flunks Child Care 101 (ushering in a whole new era in sitcom-style humor—the Murphy Brown era—in which babies make fools out of moms, not dads, in which moms, not dads, are the ones fumbling with diapers and finally resorting to electrical tape to make them stay on the squirmy kid).

Tiger Lady puts Elizabeth up for adoption. Fails. She can't bring herself to go through with it. Something has happened to her. Motherhood has happened to her. Her significant other, returning from a business trip and finding her still with the child, decamps.

Things aren't going too well on the job, either. Her boss, who boasts about not knowing how many grandchildren he has but knowing exactly how many millions of dollars he brings into the firm each year, arrives in her office with a Very Important Suit. Tiger Lady tries to talk shop while wrestling with Elizabeth. Fails. The boss explains to the other guy that it's not really her baby; she's just keeping it for a while.

"I'm keeping her a little longer than that," Tiger Lady says.

"Oh? How long?"

"Forever."

Tiger Lady loses her partnership prospects, then the job. But, trouper that she is, she adds a new dimension to the term "home shopping" by calling a number in Vermont and buying a farm, complete with apple orchards. She arrives there as determined to enjoy as she ever was to succeed.

It all looks too good to be true. And it is. First the heating system goes. It's a bitter winter. The roof caves in. The well dries up. So does her savings account. Every day is a bad hair day. She's desperate. How can this be happening to her? She graduated from Harvard *and* Yale! Yet here she is, filling the cupboards of this disaster-prone house with jar after jar of the baby applesauce she has invented—using her own apples—for Elizabeth. This gives her something to do when it snows.

But wait a minute. (And here comes the reason I got into this story in the first place.) When she consigns some of the applesauce to the local grocery it's instantly snapped up by visiting New Yorkers. She decides to market it. And succeeds.

Soon Country Baby becomes an entire baby food line that goes way beyond applesauce and way beyond Vermont. Naturally, Tiger Lady's former employer back in New York, the Food Chain, reads about her entrepreneurial triumph and offers to acquire Country Baby. It makes her an offer she can't refuse.

But she does refuse. Because she has discovered that she already "has it all." The baby. The business inspired by the baby that the baby's presence does not interfere with and that does not interfere with her spending time with the baby. And, not incidentally, romance (in the form of the local veterinarian who, lest we fear he's not quite on her intellectual level, also teaches at Bennington).

What a satisfying movie! Our heroine escapes from the rat race, succeeds spectacularly on her own terms, and then gets to tell the rat race to go jump! This is truly the stuff of which many harried working parents' dreams are made. Truly a triumph of parental ingenuity over the working parent's trap. And truly a triumph of the art of filmmaking over real life. Or is it?

The ongoing emergency often caused by childrearing while holding down a full-time job is not usually resolved as glamorously as in this movie. That's for sure. But the idea of a child providing a parent with the impetus to persevere in creating or finding work that will satisfy both financial and personal needs is not so far-fetched. It has happened.

There is, for example, Earth's Best, a real-life manufacturer of none other than baby food that was just getting under way in Vermont around the time that *Baby Boom* was in production. Ron Koss, who founded the company with his brother, Arnie, says that the movie was not inspired by his business and his business was not inspired by the movie. Nor, he is quick to point out, is his story really analogous to the Diane Keaton character's.

"I can't say," he told me, "that I had a baby and therefore came up with the idea of manufacturing baby food. The way it happened was very different from the movie." But Ron did have a baby, and the baby did play a strong supporting role in the development of his business.

Ron's interest in doing some good for children and for the environment began before he had children. He had had several "human services" jobs, working with children. He had also worked in a natural food store where—this was in the late seventies—he noticed that there were no organically grown "convenience products" for children. So he thought of producing organic baby foods, "but it was more about how to do something on a wood stove than how to do it in a real food-manufacturing facility."

Ron knew that the wood stove approach was impossible in real life, where there are such things as health regulations. "Making the food in your kitchen and selling it in stores is the romantic picture of what it would be like to start your own little baby food company. And maybe you could do it if you're just going to do applesauce. But when you start putting carrots in a jar or sweet potatoes or peas, it's a whole different processing reality, and there's more potential hazard, even deadly hazard, if you're not doing it properly."

And, back in the seventies, the thought of going into big-time manufacturing was overwhelming to Ron. "So the idea just rested, although my brother and I discussed it from time to time." But by 1984, when his son, Gabriel, was a year old, Ron and Arnie felt ready to do more than dream and talk. And little Gabriel had a lot to do with motivating them.

Their ambition was not only to produce high-quality organically grown convenience foods for babies but, in doing so, to stimulate the market for organic foods. "This is especially important for children, who are the most vulnerable to pesticides and chemicals because their immune systems are just getting going."

Having his own child constantly encouraged Ron. "In seeing how vulnerable he was and how vulnerable I felt in just having the responsibility of caring for him, I was able to keep going and survive the start-up process. Because starting Earth's Best was very trying. I think without that connection to Gabriel it would have been impossible to survive."

Gabriel contributed to the company in a more pragmatic way, too. "He was a major experimental model for product development," Ron said. "We were always feeding him the products we worked on. If he didn't like something, we'd have to look at why."

And what did Ron think of *Baby Boom?* "I haven't seen the movie. I read the script; it was sent to me. But when the movie opened in Vermont and my brother and I went to see it, about ten minutes into the film, the film started playing backward from the end of the movie to the beginning. The theater had to give us our money back. And I never went back to see it. But I'm content to have read the script. I thought it was really cute."

Even the briefest glance through the Right Start catalogue (which offers over sixty pages of mostly ingenious paraphernalia "for infants, young children, and the families who love them") suggests that the markets stimulated by people who were stimulated by parenthood extend way beyond organic baby food.

Although the product descriptions in this catalogue and others like it do not say "made by a parent," it is hard to imagine anyone else having so clear an inside track on how small children operate. There are devices for preventing spills, chills, leaks, teething pain, and so forth, not to mention enough baby furnishings to constitute, as the writer Dorothy Kalins found when she became a mother, a major influence in interior design. "Bunny Modern," she called her home's new look in a *New York Times* article, full of "objects . . . invented by some harried parent at the end of her rope . . . from the 'if only I had . . .' school, as in, 'If only I had a safe little chair on wheels to put the baby in.' "

It's no coincidence, either, that a number of parents have wound up writing children's books. Although some of the legendary children's book authors, including Maurice Sendak, Dr. Seuss, and Margaret Wise Brown, have been childless, the experience of A. A. Milne, whose son and his stuffed animal collection launched Winnie the Pooh, is probably more the rule than the exception. For instance, Marguerite de Angeli's first three books evolved from the experiences of two of her five children. And Julius Lester's books for children and young adults about African-American history and culture resulted from his inability to find such books for his own children to read.

Art seems to emanate as naturally from the writer Emery Bernhard and his wife, the artist Durga T. Bernhard, as love does from children. But by the time their second child was born, it was apparent to them that supporting both their "biological and creative offspring" by taking turns at "grunt jobs" was not working out. They decided to work together on children's books as "a way to cultivate art, career, and kids in the same garden." In less than two years, they managed to sell six books, including *What's Maggie Up To?*, *Ladybug*, *Spotted Eagle & Black Crow: A Lakota Legend*, *Alphabeasts: A Hide & Seek Alphabet Book*, and *Dragonfly*.

"We were finally collaborating in both art and life," Emery Bernhard wrote, "and 'we' included [the children]. Who better could tell us when a story was good or 'poopy'? Who better could test the child appeal of an illustration?"[1]

"Nobody," would be Ann Ruethling's reply to those questions. Ann's daughter, Elizabeth, who is now thirteen, and her son, Evan, now ten, have helped her "test market" books for her famous children's book catalogue, the Chinaberry Book Service. Ann also has received a lot of input over the years from her customers and their children. In fact, a considerable part of the catalogue's charm (and, therefore, its success) lies in Ann's melding this parent-and-child private reading experience with her own observations to produce chatty, detailed "annotations" on each and every book in her catalogue.

Today, that's a lot of books. The catalogue is now 122 pages long; it grosses $5 million a year. Its customers live as far away from its California home as Japan. Yet it still has the aura of Ann sitting with you, the reader, at her kitchen table, talking books. Which is exactly how Chinaberry began.

In 1981, Ann and her husband, Ed, were living in a rainy, depressed, and depressing Oregon town. Ann had quit her airline-marketing job to stay home with her baby daughter. Ed was working as a carpenter. "For Elizabeth's first birthday," Ann recalled, "she got a Mother Goose nursery rhyme book, full of all the rhymes you and I grew up with. But as I read it to my twelve-month-old, who still had a song in her heart and was very innocent, I was taken aback by the violence and sexual stereotyping in those rhymes, and I didn't want to do that to her. So instead of the little old woman who lived in a shoe spanking them all soundly, I had her kissing them all soundly. I just changed negative words to positive words and went along, but when the Peter Peter Pumpkin Eater page came up, I couldn't think of how to ad-lib that one."

Ann, shaken by the messages in this book and others that she remembered by rote but then, when repeating them to her own child, suddenly realized were not good for children, became "sensitive" to the point where she even had trouble singing Elizabeth "The Mockingbird Song." " 'Papa's gonna *buy* you . . . Papa's gonna *buy*'—I didn't change 'buy,' " she said, "but I didn't feel comfortable with it."

Ann's awareness of her daughter's vulnerability and her sense of her own power as a parent led her to "go through" books she took out from "our little-bitty library" for Elizabeth at that moment and "down the road," so that she wouldn't have to "rearrange them" in mid-read. She wrote her impressions of them on index cards.

"I had to screen them," she says, "not censor them, because I wasn't just looking for bad stuff I didn't want to read but for good stuff I did want to read to her. Good role models and people being brave and kind and respectful to each other, and humorous stuff. I think humor is really important."

When the stack of index cards was four or five inches high, Ann began thinking that other parents, as concerned as she was, might welcome her research. And if they lived, as she did, where they could not easily get good children's books—more the rule than the exception in the days before publishers discovered the huge children's market—then they needed a source.

The name Chinaberry came from a friend's recollection of a favorite and apparently long-lost childhood story, "Under the Chinaberry Tree." ("It was such a pretty word," Ann said.) The first catalogue, thirty-two pages long, was hand-lettered by Ed, "who at this point was sort of humoring me because he knew I needed to do something to keep my sanity but he also knew there was a good chance this was going to eat into the grocery money. Which it did."

Ann took out an ad in *Mothering* magazine, offering "positive and uplifting books for children." Elizabeth, who was around two and a half by this time, pitched in at the kitchen table as Ann filled orders. "She'd hold down the flap while I closed the package, and she kept me company." Ann always included postcards when she responded to the letters that always accompanied the orders, letters telling her that "after reading the catalogue, I feel as if I know you." And sometimes, thanks to Elizabeth, pieces of the family silverware also went into the packages—"which we could ill afford."

Soon after Evan was born, in 1983, the family moved to San Diego. Although Chinaberry was attracting more customers, it was hardly profitable. Ann, whose marketing skills had never included budgeting, remembers the business back then as "like having a sick child." She credits Ed, who, moved by the "real relationships between me and the customers and how much this service must be needed," made the catalogue "into something that could survive more than another three months." Through trying to find the best books to help mold her own children, Ann founded a service that helps innumerable other parents do the same thing.

Professional Loss, Personal Gain

There is nothing wrong with this picture. Sally Tenzer's home, a "modified Cape," is filled with fine American antiques that she and her husband, Peter, have collected since the early days of their marriage. There is a screened-in porch. The back yard is large and bordered with garden plots alive with last year's flowers and spinach.

On this bright spring day, I find Sally hauling soil from the plots to her patio so that she can plant dozens of pots of snapdragons, marigolds, zinnias, and other annuals that she bought at the Mother's Day sale at her younger daughter's school. She talks to me as she transfers the young flowering plants to their hanging baskets.

This is not a woman who enjoys sitting still. She describes herself as "obsessive." Right now her focus is on gardening and pottery and volunteer work. Not long ago, it was on her career. She had a sixty-hour work week, including a two-hour-a-day commute. For a while, on top of that, she was going to business school. Her husband pitched in whenever and wherever he could, but his work often took him away from home. At that time there was plenty wrong with the Tenzer family picture.

Every moment Sally was not on the job or commuting, she seemed to spend coping, like so many other parents, with what to do with the kids during the hours they were not in school and she had to be at work. "What I found terribly frustrating was that schools do not cooperate," she recalled. "We don't as a society have a system set up for working parents of school-age children.

"It's not just afterschool that's the issue. It's before school. Not everyone's job begins conveniently after the schoolday begins. And what about those days when the schools are closed? People can't just leave their job because it snowed and the schools are closed! What about when your child suddenly gets sick? It would make great sense, with so many people having to work today, if we had quality before- and afterschool care in all the schools. That's what we need. You can't leave these children alone.

"So how did we cope? I don't know. We scrambled. We had been living here for only two years, so we didn't have a great network of friends. We have no family here to help out. I'd hire baby sitters; they'd quit. I was always looking for help. But the worst thing wasn't all this stress; it was not being here for the kids and the toll this was taking on them. I should have recognized much sooner what was happening and the reason it was happening. Samantha had a temper tantrum every night. Seven-year-olds don't do that. Preschoolers do that, but not seven-year-olds! And Amy, who was thirteen, was also being very difficult. Miserable. Nasty."

Often when we talk about life-altering events, occurrences important enough to steer us decisively in one direction rather than another, we liken them to overwhelming forces in nature. But when Sally started talking about the tornado that turned everything around for her, she was referring to the real thing, a tornado that reared up out of nowhere on a summer evening in 1989, ripping through her town.

"Lightning struck a huge tree in our front yard, and it fell across the power line that connected our house to the power pole across the street. There was this live wire hanging down in the middle of the street. I don't remember what the reason was, but I had stayed home that day and my children were out in the street within two minutes after the tornado was over, dancing around that live wire. That was the last straw. I said to Pete, 'That's it. I've had it.' My children might've been dead if I weren't home. I mean, even with me home, they were almost killed.

"I felt I'm too far away; if there's an emergency, I can't be here. And I decided I wasn't even going to start looking for another job; I'm just going to come home."

Now, two years later, Samantha, who has long since stopped her nightly tantrums, is doing well in school and at all her other activities and "has a real joie de vivre." Sally says, "She was still very clingy for a while; she needed me in her sight. She still doesn't like me to go away from home. I'd been working since she was two. But now she's doing much better. She's having the kind of childhood I want her to have."

Amy, though still in the throes of a "rocky adolescence," is "blossoming, feeling more confident, looking beautiful. And as a result she's getting nicer. She feels better about herself, so she's relaxing and able to give a little more."

"And you feel this is all because of your full-time presence at home?" I ask.

"Who knows what would've happened if I hadn't stayed home? But things probably would have been different. All I know is that it's been worth every minute of it, staying home. I loved working. I'll work again. But I love mothering, too. That's always something I wanted, and I want to do it well, so that . . ."

Suddenly Sally's voice rises, the words come fast, the tone is indignant, almost defensive. "That's really important. Maybe it's more important than my going out and working for somebody. Because let's face it: who cares whether you open a bank branch or you don't? In the whole span of things, what contribution do I make opening and closing bank branches? But I'm making a contribution with these two children. I see that as my work, too. And I need to put it first now."

I doubt that it is possible to find any two psychiatrists who would come up with the same list of attributes that constitute a mature personality—or who would agree on what maturity is. But it doesn't take a psychiatrist to figure out that one of the qualities that separate the mature from the immature is the ability to put things—particularly one's own life—in perspective, to see the course of one's life as a continuum, and to know that wherever one is at any given moment is not one's whole story.

It is only through this view that one can avoid the mistake of applying the magical thinking that so easily can determine our consumer choices—"If I buy this Lancôme makeup, I'll be as beautiful as Isabella Rossellini"—to our life choices, to, say, the belief that working or staying at home with the kids, whichever we are not doing at the moment, will bring fulfillment or perfect happiness.

The parents I talked with who have compromised their careers for the sake of their kids do not spend a lot of time thinking about how much happier or more fulfilled they might be had they made another choice. Parenthood has lowered their career expectations temporarily, sometimes permanently. But they regard this as a positive factor in their lives. They feel, as Sally does, that the time they took away from their work to spend with their children is a better investment in the long run, not only for the children but for them. And they regard their decision as a sign of maturity.

Tanya Landau, who was twenty-five and left graduate school when her daughter was born, sometimes felt at first that she was "missing out on something—what with my husband still in school and always hard at work, and the pressure in our society for women to work." But now, two years later, she has "grown out" of the conflict.

"I don't feel I'm missing out at all now," she says. "What I do feel, more and more, is that this is a short phase in my life. Before this phase, I did a lot—I traveled, was in school, read—I did a lot of things. Recognizing that helps me feel I can be doing this without losing out on—what? I don't feel I'm missing out on life. The time will come again when I'll be doing those things, things that I like to do. But I love to do this also, and I'd hate not recognizing that this is such an important time and then twenty years later realize that I've sacrificed it. I have the sense of having chosen one thing I love over another thing I love, not of having given up anything."

"I've given up a little salary, but that's it," says Stephanie Hickson, the young mother who likened her two-year-old son to a masterpiece in progress. Stephanie is a chemist, but after Earl was born she took the lower-paying position of "chemical technician" because "the responsibility of being a chemist is too much. All those hours would interfere with my being a good mom."

Greg Weber's identification with fatherhood, the unexpected "fatherly feelings" he experienced "about an hour" after being introduced to the infant he and his wife were about to adopt, enabled him eventually to break the absentee tradition of his own father that he had feared he was doomed to repeat.

Greg compares himself, around the time that he became a father, to "a plough horse," like his own father. "I had a boss at one job," he told me, "who said anyone who leaves before six, he doesn't consider a professional. That was pretty typical. A lot of men, I think, have to put on the harness and pull the plough. And the plough horse doesn't think too much about whether or not he's having a good time or being fulfilled. He's measured by how well he does his assigned task in life, which is to plough the field."

But Greg's plough horse analogy falls short because it doesn't take into account the pleasure he's felt in successfully shouldering his burden. He has always liked work; so did his father. On some level, even the long hours and the commute were enjoyable. They went with the job.

So, however, did missing his sons, missing out on time with them. Greg definitely did not enjoy that. His present job has shorter hours. "I chose it because I knew they were working basically eight to four-thirty, and people were actually sticking to those hours. It's not the greatest job in the world, but it was definitely a life style choice. By being home at five o'clock I can do things like go to the baseball games and have dinner with the kids and be out there when they're playing. And it's made things easier for Sheila, too, because now I can give her support during the hours the kids are still awake."

Like Greg, Kevin Marks works with computers. And, like Greg, his decision to modify his career goals in order to expand his fatherhood potential had to do with his own father. Kevin's father died young, "before he had a chance to watch his kids grow up. I still have that chance and I'm taking advantage of it."

Kevin remembers being "more ambitious in my younger days." But now "my goals are not to head the office. The manager and the two assistant managers are all people without children. They can put in longer hours. They don't have to take time off when the kids are sick. Whereas I have to, and I do.

"I hear people say, 'I want the best for my children. I want to provide the best so I'll work harder and earn more money.' But then you look at someone like my father, who died when he was almost my age. To me, spending time with my kids is more important than having more money. Definitely. As long as I have some kind of job."

For John Petaway, who is divorced and is raising his son and daughter singlehandedly, the fact that he hasn't gone as far professionally as he might have has proved "more than worth it." The latest of John's many and varied jobs at the time I talked with him was as an administrative social worker in a family support program that was about to lose its state funding. But John seemed more worried about how to deal with his daughter's thumb-sucking habit. He's always managed to find work; he'll manage this time, too. He hopes that his next job will involve working with children.

"I've actually enjoyed raising my children so much I've often wished it could be my job so that I could spend all my time doing it. I have kids around me all the time—my kids, my nieces, nephews. They do need more men in day care. I go sometimes to the day care and just visit. And when the children hear a male voice, they come and they sit. It's as if they can feel my love for them. So, no. I don't feel bad about having given up part of my career to raise the kids. I wish more men were able to do it."

"There's no doubt that my personal aspirations have been scaled down by motherhood," says Becka Moldover, whose four children have, for the most part, kept her from her nursing career. "I'd love to have advanced degrees and be doing all sorts of intellectual and esoteric work. I like to fantasize about walking down the street and have people go, 'Oh, look! Isn't that BECKA MOLDOVER?!' instead of 'Oh, there's Joe's—or Anna's or Abby's or David's—mom.' It is easy to fantasize, 'If I didn't have kids, I'd have glory!' Dreams of glory are among the first things punctured by motherhood. I'm currently pleased if I can have a coherent conversation.

"But despite the occasional fantasies, I get more pleasure from being with my family than from any work I've done. I've become much less interested in the 'career world.' The kids have been of primary interest and importance to me, and my enjoyment, which seemed tenuous with my first child, has increased as I've worked my way up to four. I like being home because I think that 'being there' creates a center for them to explore from and relate to. Some people have the energy to provide this while they're pursuing other work, but I don't have that energy—or that sort of ambition."

How Parenthood Can Spark New Approaches to Our Work

Obviously, the additional time that parents get to spend with their kids by cutting back on work hours or giving up big career plans can be rewarding in itself. But some parents find an added bonus, a perk, in raising their children, in absorbing so much from their children during all this time. In one way or another through their children they hit on ideas or attitudes that they can use in their work, that improve the work they do or the way in which they do it.

Some of the more famous examples of children enriching a parent's outlook and thus his output can be found in the work of Sigmund Freud. In *The Interpretation of Dreams*, Freud used some of his young sons' and daughters' dreams to show that children's dreams, unlike those of adults, are "frequently pure wish fulfillments." "In one charming instance," Peter Gay reported, "Anna, the future psychoanalyst, makes her appearance by name," having cried out in her sleep " 'Anna F'eud, stawberry, wild stawberry, om'let, puddin,' " all of which, according to Freud, "comprised about everything that must have appeared to her as a desirable meal."[2]

Some of Freud's own dreams about his children not only provided further nourishment for *The Interpretation of Dreams* but contained, according to the distinguished psychoanalyst

George F. Mahl, "seeds of his later ideas of the importance of the father-son relationship in the development of religion, other social institutions, and morality."[3]

One well-known instance of the influence of Freud's personal experience on his ideas was his close observation of a "puzzling and continually repeated performance" by one of his grandchildren (his daughter Sophie's eighteen-month-old baby, Ernst). It led to his thinking and writing about the "repetition compulsion," the need to re-enact or to talk repeatedly about distressing, painful, even traumatic experiences.[4]

The work of Jean Piaget also profited enormously from his sensitivity to his children. Piaget, the Swiss psychologist whose discoveries about the way children develop and learn have dominated the fields of child psychology and education for the last forty years or so, had three children—Jacqueline, Lucienne, and Laurent. He and his wife kept meticulous notes on their behavior, both spontaneous and in response to certain "tasks" he created for them. He presented the theories that evolved from this "work" with his children in three books, which became classics: *The Origins of Intelligence in Children, Play, Dreams, and Imitation in Children,* and *The Construction of Reality in the Child.*[5]

Dorothy G. Singer and Tracey A. Revenson have likened Piaget's recording of his children's behavior to the diaries kept by Charles Darwin, Bronson Alcott (Louisa May Alcott's father), and other " 'baby biographers' of the nineteenth century" who painstakingly documented "what their children wore, ate, said, and learned each day."

"For most parents," Singer and Revenson wrote, "when a toddler knocks down a set of blocks it means another mess to clean up; for Piaget it was a valuable clue as to how the human mind reasons. He would ask: Did the child knock the blocks down in any particular order? According to size? shape? color? Did he laugh while he was doing it? From such observations, Piaget traced the origins of mental growth through early childhood."[6]

Most parents, fascinated though they may be with their children's behavior, never approach this level of absorption in it. Nor does word of the way children can enrich the work of the average parent usually reach the public at large. But the parents I spoke with echoed, in one way or another, Joseph Brodsky's quip on winning the Nobel Prize—it's "a giant step for me" if not for mankind.

For example, Stanley Friedman, an otolaryngologist who has two grown sons and whose practice is partly pediatric, does not recall any specific innovations that resulted from his involvement with his children—except for the little trick of putting their cough medicine, which had a "vaguely grapey" taste, into grape juice in order to get a finicky child to swallow it.

His children's influence on him as a physician was more subtle, but he's continually aware of it. "I think what I've gained from parenthood," he told me, "is an unconscious ability to relate to my patients and therefore to be more helpful to them." On many occasions, his having been the parent of an ailing child has made him "more empathetic" with his young patients and their parents. "When you've gone through it, you understand what the mother is going through when she calls you up and says the child is screaming because of an earache. You know the feeling of helplessness the parents have when either it's an infant who can't articulate and they know something's wrong or a child who can articulate what's wrong and the parents can't do anything about it."

Sheila Weber, Greg's wife, told me that she has become more effective in her job as an adoption counselor through being a mother herself. "I have a different understanding of parenting now. There are some things that, no matter how much you read about them, are hard to understand in the same way as someone who's living them. The way children develop and grow is one of those things.

"Even though I was a child development major in college and certainly learned a lot about children and their stages of growth, it didn't sink in until I had children and observed them and really learned how kids change at different stages and how they're always changing.

"I do mostly adoptions of older kids, so the ability to determine what this child is really like, whether this is a stage he's going through, has been very helpful to me in helping adoptive parents. When people adopt older children who have a history they weren't part of, this issue—figuring out who this kid is—is really, really important.

"I see it all the time with families who adopt older children; they see bad behavior and they get scared by it. You know, they attach a meaning to it that sometimes isn't the right meaning. Sometimes the behavior is a reaction to the stress the kid feels because he's just had his world thrown upside down and he's moved into a completely new environment. The stress comes out in that way. But it's hard sometimes for the adoptive parents to see that.

"And I think I've become a lot more insightful and am more able to help those parents because of being around my own kids."

Joanne Marks has found that being the mother of an infant and a toddler has given her a greater rapport with her students. "Now I have a new appreciation of how young my students really are," she told me. "Sometimes we assume kids know or should know much more than they're capable of at a certain age; or we think they should behave better than they can realistically be expected to. Well, my expectations now, I think, are more realistic. Also, I'm much more in tune with parents' feelings, so I'm more empathetic and responsive in my dealings with the parents."

Like Joanne, Helene Sapadin works with students from all elementary school grades; her subject is "social skills." And she's found that being a mother, a single mother, has given her a distinct edge in getting her students to relate to her, which is a prerequisite to her reaching them. She has become more of "a role model" for her students, most of whom are disadvantaged and live in neighborhoods where single motherhood is usually an accident, not a choice; where babies are often unwanted. "I remember one boy asking me, 'Well, do you have a husband?' And I said, 'No.' I talked about adoption, that Molly and I had adopted each other. And the boy looked at me and said, 'You *wanted* a baby?'

"My experience in adopting Molly and being her mom is an amazing thing to them," Helene says. "I share this with them to show that you can be a professional person and a mother, that you can choose to be married or not or to be a mother or not. You can make choices within your situation. And that's been very exciting.

"Even though Molly and I are not your typical American family, I feel more normal than I've ever felt. So it's natural to bring this up in teaching, and the kids respond to it because they come from all kinds of situations that are not typical and that have made them feel not normal. To be able to help them feel that they can be okay and normal and accepted and empowered to make choices, no matter what their situation, is a very important thing."

Before Molly, Helene could talk about this. Now, she's living it. That makes a big difference in getting her message across. On one occasion, the way Helene and Molly live and interact became a teaching tool. As Helene put it, "Molly came to school with me one day and she became the greatest teacher for one of the kids." Molly was just over a year old, and Helene was teaching at a special school for delinquent children. A boy of eight or nine, whose eruptions of anger reflected, Helene was sure, what went on in his home, was sent to "cool off" in a room that was used for "time out" and that was also where Helene was feeding Molly her lunch.

"Molly finished eating," Helene explained, "and that was fine. But then she proceeded to finger-paint with her baby carrots. My rule is that I don't care if she gets messed up while eating, but I don't want her to play with the food, so I took the jar away from her and she started carrying on.

"I was conscious of this kid in the 'time out' chair who was cooling his jets—and watching my every move. I said to Molly, 'Even babies have rules. You cannot play with your food.' She decided to have a tantrum, so I put her down on the floor and said, 'I'm here and I love you.' And the tantrum took about thirty seconds and then she was fine.

"Meanwhile, this boy was looking; his eyes were like saucers. And his ears—if you could see ears flapping out to catch all the sound—he was right there. After a while, not to be totally obvious, I walked over to him and said, 'See what happens?

Even babies get into problems.' And he sort of smiled. And I said, 'Well, what did I do?' He couldn't answer. I said, 'Did I hit her? Did I yell at her?' He said, 'No.' So I asked him again what I had done and he repeated it exactly, with a major smile—and this is a kid who hardly ever smiles. 'You said that even babies have rules . . .' But when he got to the part where I'd said, 'I love you,' he couldn't bring himself to say it. I think he'd probably never heard that. So I said it for him and he smiled and nodded; he'd remembered.

"I thought of a million follow-ups to reinforce that lesson, that you can get your point across and communicate without hitting, without yelling. Unfortunately, this was on the last day of school. It makes me sad that I never got to reinforce that message with that kid. But I think the experience with him has enriched my ability to get it across ever since with lots of other kids."

I spoke with Jeffrey Lustman in his office on the seventh floor of the Veterans Hospital in West Haven, Connecticut, where he is the director of the psychiatric emergency room, the clinical director of the psychiatry service, and the associate chief of staff of education. He is also the father of fourteen-year-old Emily and ten-year-old Andrew, whose influence on the way he functions in his other roles has been profound, far-reaching, ameliorative, and permanent—starting with their births and his experiences of them as distinct personalities right from the start.

"Emily, within the first seconds of life, looks around briefly and collapses into this shapeless catastrophic reaction, which is what kids do, totally normal, engrossing, absorbing, immediately wiring us into her experience. Here we were, all of a sudden, with work to do. What's wrong? How do you comfort her? My son Andrew, on the other hand, is born, he looks around, and he bubbles, almost like a teapot boiling over; tension is welling up but it's not getting out, a very primitive kind of regulation. And then he falls apart and he has a shapeless catastrophic reaction.

"And that's the way each of them still is. If I ask Emily, 'How was your day?' I'll get an hour, two hours. She likes to involve us in all the details. Whereas my son, you ask him, 'How was your day?' he'll say, 'It was fun.' 'What'd you do?' 'Stuff.' Prying things out of him is an achievement."

So, through his children, Jeffrey became convinced of something that he may have grasped from his years of medical and psychiatric and psychoanalytic training and practice, but perhaps not so conclusively—that "so much of what we are is biological, genetic." This has helped him in treating patients and in teaching others how to treat patients.

"Now I remember, and I teach my students to remember, that when we work with patients, we are not dealing solely with motivated phenomena. We're dealing with biological organizations that have had rich histories in their own right, so our expectation of what we can and cannot change, or should and shouldn't change, has to be a little less simple-minded."

Then Jeffrey told me an unforgettable story. It was about something that happened a few years ago with Andrew which taught him, in a way that all his education and experience never had, how to be a better doctor. He began by describing "the classic doctor's dilemma": how to "cope with the terror of being near someone's pain . . . and, sometimes, through your procedures, having to hurt them even more. Pain is right at the heart of it all, emotional as well as physical. You're exposed to it all the time, and you have to figure out how to cope with it. You have to be near it and function, not get lost in it, not collapse in tears—but not to be distant and cold and objective and all those awful things."

Jeffrey thought he had resolved this dilemma rather well, until the incident with Andrew helped him to resolve it better. "My wife and I were out of town at a wedding. The ceremony's over. We're looking forward to a lovely evening. And all of a sudden we get this panicked call. Our son has cracked his chin open and has been rushed to the hospital. We rush home, close to a hundred miles an hour, to the ER, and my son's chin is wide open. The chin had to be sutured, but he wouldn't let anyone do it but me. I have sutured kids up, but this is my son. This is not just a kid. This is my son with his chin wide open. And I have to be a doctor. I have to perform. And it was a whole new combination of all the same elements, all the same stirrings and feelings, but at a pitch that was ten times more intense."

After suturing his son and not collapsing under the emotional strain, Jeffrey realized that "I could get closer to patients. I can be more human and humane—and still function. I don't have to ward it off to the extent that I have. I can tolerate a lot more of other people's pain than I thought. Andrew's accident totally changed my experience of being a doctor."

How Personality Traits Developed Through Parenthood Can Enhance the Way We Work

The historian John Demos, in explaining how the separation of home and workplace brought about by the Industrial Revolution changed the role of the American father, wrote: "Sustained contact with the world touched men's innermost experience, indeed their very *character*. Many of the qualities most readily associated with success in work—ambition, cleverness, aggressive pursuit of the main chance—had no place in domestic life. At best, a man would have to perform an elaborate switch of role and behavior on crossing the threshold of his home . . . At worst, he would have to choose between effectiveness in one 'sphere' or the other."[7]

Needless to say, the more recent revolution, which sent so many American mothers into the workplace, accomplished the same split in the working woman's "character." It is now commonly assumed that the personality traits required by women as well as men to succeed on the job are entirely different from the ones needed to be a good parent. The economist Sylvia Ann Hewlett presented, in *When the Bough Breaks*, a Column A–Column B demonstration of the way some "hard-edged . . . traits cultivated by many successful professionals—control, decisiveness, aggression, efficiency"—may collide with the "passive, patient, selfless elements of good nurturing."

I have no quarrel with the validity of Hewlett's and Demos's observations along these lines, among them that the take-charge attitude which works on the job can prove disastrous in the home. It is also true—and this can be inferred from both Demos's and Hewlett's arguments and has become a common assumption—that the qualities which make for great parenting do not contribute toward making a great career, that the laid-back *modus operandi* which works so well at home could, transferred to the workplace, get the parent laid off.

But there is something missing from this equation. Is it not possible that through parenting some people cultivate characteristics that enhance the way they perform at work? That many qualities developed through parenting may, in some instances and in certain ways, contribute to career development?

A remark from a new congresswoman, Karen Shepherd of Utah, concerning her disapproval of the way men in Congress have scheduled hearings and meetings (all at once), suggests that parenting can indeed provide training that is valuable in our other jobs. "When you've done birthday parties for twenty two-year-olds all by yourself," she said, "that's actually harder than organizing Congress so that the hearings are scheduled coherently."[8] The ability and self-discipline to organize, schedule, set priorities, get things done efficiently and effectively may come from parenting as easily as from the courses required for an MBA. (Birthday parties are just the tip of the iceberg. Consider, also, the arranging and rearranging of each child's routines so that they don't conflict with the other children's or the parent's routines, and simply—simply?—running a household.)

The challenge intensifies, of course, for the working parent, who has to accomplish all of the above in a limited amount of time. "I remember when I was in graduate school getting my master's degree," the graphic artist Ruth Sack told me, "and I'd sit in my studio and look at what I was working on and I'd smoke a cigarette and I'd walk next door and talk. You know, I was pretty good at my work and I knew how to do what I needed to do to get my fellowship and get everything together. But having a child has given everything more meaning for me, including efficiency; it was just night and day. Now I can do in a day what would have taken me two days in the past. It's amazing how much I get done in so little time."

Kate Robicheau sometimes finds herself wondering, "What was I doing with all that time I had before I had kids? Why were things so hard? I'm amazed now at how much one can do with very little time. I've gotten to where I know this is my opportunity to do what I need to do. Whereas before, when I didn't have kids, when I didn't have to make sure it was a time when there was child care, et cetera, et cetera, I might have been different. I wasn't able to fit a certain task in a certain time. Now I can do that. I just accomplish a lot more in general."

Roberta Friedman's career interests were on hold during her two sons' early years, even as her husband, Stan, was finding that his ability to empathize with his patients and their families (he's the otolaryngologist we heard from earlier) was enhanced by fatherhood. Roberta entered law school when her sons were ten and twelve, and when she began practicing family law, she found that her experience as a mother had not gone to waste. In fact, it had given her valuable preparation for her work.

"Just the experience of juggling school with the kids' lives with my mother's illness, all of that gave me a kind of basic training in planning, projecting, all of those things I would really need when I went to work. And that was back in the days when we didn't have phones in our cars!"

Roberta described how, through parenting, "I developed a certain confidence about making decisions; I developed good judgment. There are these children who need you to make good decisions for yourself and for them and for the whole family. That may be three different kinds of decisions. I feel I've developed that skill by virtue of being a parent. I don't know if I would have been able to develop it any other way. And I can't think of anything else that helps me do the kind of law I do more than the experiences I've had of being a parent, being a wife, being in what I think is a very successful family unit that is strong and healthy."

Roberta was one of several mothers who told me she attributes her hard-won assertiveness—so useful, everyone agrees, in career building—to parenthood, especially to that aspect of parenthood we may call, borrowing from zoology, "defending our young."

"One of the things that was a huge step for me in learning

to be more assertive in the outside world, and not so complacent and accommodating, absolutely had to do with my children," Roberta said. "When the kids were in elementary school and were going on to the next grade, it was a no-no to ask for a specific teacher, but there were certain teachers who were abominable and some who were very good. I remember getting my nerve together and going to the principal and asking whether my kid could have this teacher or that teacher.

"I volunteered to do art projects in the school, and one reason was to make myself known, to participate, so I'd have less compunction about asking for things. These were acts of assertiveness that I wouldn't have been capable of if it weren't something as important as who would teach my kids. This has helped me in my work incredibly. I'm far more assertive than I would have been, better at asking for what I want, better at getting it. All because I had to look out for my kids in public school. Nobody else was going to."

Several other mothers mentioned "assertiveness" or "aggressiveness" as a trait developed in their private lives that has helped them in their professional lives. But none of the fathers I spoke with said so. Quite the opposite. They described ways in which parenthood had softened their personalities—"humanized me," as one man put it—and said that the development of these traits had helped them become better employers, employees, and co-workers.

Rich Garner, a thirty-five-year-old father of four, told me, "I entered into parenthood thinking you could line kids up like toy soldiers. I was very authoritarian, at work and at home. But over the years I've become far less rigid around the house, more relaxed. I learned that children don't operate like machines. And this has carried over to my job. Parenthood has really taught me to look at my standards for judging people, my standards off the job and on the job. People aren't machines."

Jeffrey Lustman had this to say: "Before I had kids I tended to function in a much more 'doing things to' and 'doing things for' mode. I was very directive, very authoritarian, do this, do that, let me do this for you. Not necessarily tyrannical; I'd like to think I wasn't that, although I knew I could be at times, and I occasionally felt that I needed to be.

"But I tended not to make space for facilitating, and it was from my experiences with my kids that I learned that the shortest distance between two points isn't really ever a straight line. If I want to get Andy to do math, I sure as hell better not approach it the way my dad did, namely [rapping on the desk], 'Do it!' He will hate numbers for a decade—as I did."

Now, Jeffrey says, he asks, "How do I instill an appetite for something or elicit a curiosity for something?" And he has found this approach much more effective than the old "do this, do that."

It is mighty tempting, at this point, to jump to conclusions about the wonderful way in which parenthood can help women (who are, after all, famous for their nonassertiveness) become more forceful and demanding, and how it can help men (who are, after all, famous for their aggressiveness) lighten up a bit— or a lot. But even if this were true, my sampling of the parent population is far too small to prove it. And I don't think it is true. There are probably some pretty unaggressive men out there who, through defending their young in various ways, have found themselves becoming more assertive, in general and on the job. I know that there are women who, after years of asserting themselves all over the place in their professional roles, find, through parenting, a gentler self that proves even more effective in the work world.

Remember Tiger Lady? These were her parting words to her former employers, by way of turning down their offer to buy her out: "I'm not Tiger Lady anymore. I mean I have a crib in my office and there's a mobile over my desk. And I really like that . . . And I'll be honest with you, I think I'm doing pretty good on my own. To be quite frank, if [you] can put Country Baby on every supermarket shelf in America, so can I. I'm sorry, I just think the rat race is gonna have to survive with one less rat."

The point is that, through parenting, both men and women can find their work enhanced not simply because they become the opposite of what they were before, but because they become, as Jeffrey Lustman put it, "just more human and more truly who I am. I'm angrier; I'm more loving. I'm more facilitating. I'm out to my margins more completely than I would be if I didn't have kids."

We'll hear in more detail and from beyond the world of work the meaning of being "more truly who I am" and "out to my margins more completely."

VII

"I Can't Fix the Cat!"

The Impact of Parenthood
on Our Self View and World View

A child's mind is a window not only to a family's psychology
and psychopathology, but to our world at large.
—ROBERT COLES, *The Moral Life of Children*

ONE OF THE FIRST noticeable effects that parenthood
had on me was that, after years of jumping on planes, suddenly I was afraid to fly. All at once, in place of my passion for
flying, there was the preoccupation with the big "what if" that
I'd scarcely considered: What if this plane crashes? If we don't
take Jonathan with us and the plane crashes, who will take care
of him? If we do take him with us and the plane crashes, that
would be even worse. What I had once thought of as the ideal
life equation—spending more time away from home than at
home—was reversed. Now home seemed more desirable than
any destination.

And in time home turned out to be a destination as valid as
any other—not a place to escape from, but a place in which to

explore myriad aspects of life that previously had escaped me. Now that I was no longer all over the map, I could focus more clearly on my place on it. I saw my life's direction as having gone from horizontal to vertical, from skimming over a great deal of terrain to digging deeply in an area that was truly my own.

I was discussing this with Greg Weber in his family room late one afternoon. Jonathan had come along with me and was playing with Greg's two sons in the back yard. Periodically, he'd crash our conversation with a sudden need to touch home base —me—before dashing into the fray again, underlining the very point I was making: how I have gone from being at large in the world to being primarily the place from which someone else is starting out.

Greg knew exactly what I was talking about, having experienced a similar shift in direction himself. He too felt that parenthood had broadened his horizons, though not in the same way I did. I felt that being a parent brought with it limitations that turned out to be liberating in certain ways. Greg felt his borders had widened; his emphasis was on self-expansion.

"There are dimensions of the self that—if you haven't had kids or have never had to care for anybody—would otherwise be unexplored or undeveloped. Before we had kids, our life was full, in a vertical direction. And having kids has turned it in a horizontal direction. I mean, our personal development was somewhat narrow before. With kids, you have to spend time with other things and other people, not just yourself, not just your spouse.

"Having kids exposes you to a whole new world. And it's not just the time you spend changing diapers and being with the kids; it's all the things that come with the kids: the day care involvement, involvement with the other parents, and then school and so forth."

Greg and I, then, coming from entirely different starting points, endowed with entirely different histories and personalities, have ended up in the same psychological place, a place where there's more room to move, each of us in a different direction, than either of us would have imagined.

The varieties of parental experience described below do not add up, by any means, to a comprehensive summary of every way in which parenthood can change the way we see ourselves and the world. What they indicate is how varied the parental experience is. These particular categories of experience were delineated mostly through parents' answers to an open-ended question: "Can you think of any specific areas in which parenthood has changed the way you see yourself and the way you see the world?"

It's a given that we've all lost something in the transition to parenthood. I can't go gallivanting around the way I used to; Greg's wife, Sheila, who used to be a world-class reader, now considers a hundred-page book heavy reading. And there are plenty of et ceteras for all of us. But what, I asked these parents, have you gained in terms of your relationship with yourself and your surroundings?

In their answers, I think, most parents will find bridges to their own experience—and hints of the possibilities available to any parent who is more open to the idea of adapting to parenthood than to the idea of prodding and pushing and whittling away at parenthood in order to make it squeeze into whatever his or her self-concept was before having children.

Changes in How We See Ourselves (Our Attitudes and Behavior)

SELF-CONSERVATION

The allergy to air travel that accompanied my own entry into parenthood was the first sign of a general "sobering-up" experienced by many parents, enough to make parenthood look, from a certain angle, like the world's largest conservation effort.

Parenthood can slow down even the biggest risk takers among us. It can make even the bravest of us risk-resistant. The daredevil airline-and-recording mogul Richard Branson attributed his uncharacteristic reluctance to take off on a transglobal balloon adventure to the existence of a son and a daughter. "If I didn't have young children," he told a *Vanity Fair* writer, "it wouldn't worry me." (He added, however, that "the idea of the balloon taking off without me is very, very painful.")

This new moderation, this caution, this preoccupation with staying alive and well—"I exercise now," Ruth Sack told me, "not to be lean and mean but just to be healthy; I've got to stick around for my kids"—comes not so much from our basic instinct to survive as from that other basic instinct—to protect our offspring.

Diane Foster (the same Diane Foster who told us earlier of losing her terror of flying when her daughter was born because she felt that she had accomplished her life's purpose) says that her daughter's safety is always the first thing on her mind. "Now, when we're driving in the car and a deranged person approaches, I instantly lock all the doors. Before, I probably would have engaged the deranged person in conversation."

"I'm constantly vigilant," says Kevin Marks, "always trying to think what might happen. If I don't see Amy for a minute, I run. You always have to be watching. It just takes one time, one second."

Even after I had recovered partially from my air travel phobia, I was plagued by other Jonathan-related phobias. I remember one incident—following a flight, in fact—when a bag containing Jonathan's formula went through an airport x-ray machine. I ran to the nearest phone and called Jane Brody, the health columnist for the *New York Times,* who assured me that the formula had not become hazardous to his health.

This extreme anxiety usually dissipates with time. But sometimes it can lead to pathological behavior in the interest of protecting either ourselves, as in the case of a woman who, unlike me, has not set foot on a plane since becoming a mother, or our children. (I'm thinking of the mother who, having read that hot dogs are a choking hazard for children, continued to cut her kids' hot dogs into thin vertical strips until long after they were old enough to protest. And of the parents who were so nervous about their son riding a bicycle that instead of giving him a helmet and safety instructions, they took away the bicycle. Forever.)

More frequently, however, parents end up welcoming their

newfound conservativeness as a sign of maturation and a means of expressing it. Reality has set in. It turns out to be not entirely a bad thing. Fearing for our children goes hand in hand with caring for them. Some of us discover that even as our children give us cause for fear, they help us temper those fears and sometimes give us the impetus to control other fears that predate parenthood. I had always been nervous about swimming, for instance, but because I didn't want Jonathan to inherit this attitude, I hid it and, in the process, overcame it.

A man who was an avid motorcyclist before he became a father—he is now a former motorcyclist—found that in learning to live with his own anxieties without making his children anxious, he "became brave in a new sense, learning to measure risks, to only take risks that are worth taking, not just to stick your neck out for the hell of it or for the fun of it."

A mother of four told me that she thinks her "new responsible-to-the-point-of-boring self" is an improvement over her "old, exciting, but irresponsible-to-the-point-of-self-destructive self." She expects that this new self will live a lot longer. "And if that isn't a positive effect of parenthood," she says with a laugh, "I don't know what is!"

BEING GOOD, BECOMING BETTER

It seems that the motivation to "clean up my act," as several parents put it, does not come only from the wish to protect ourselves in order to protect our children. Right up there as a catalyst is their impressionability. Recognizing the extent of our power to influence our children's behavior and attitudes can powerfully influence our own behavior and attitudes.

"I have to look at myself closer now," says Stephanie Hickson, the single mother of two-year-old Earl, "because I know that this little guy is looking at me, too. I can't say one thing and do another, because he'll see that.

"Now I think much more about the consequences of what I'm doing—not just for me but for him. I stick to what I think is right, even if it's not the popular choice. If I think a thing is right, I have to do it, because that's how I want my child to be.

When he comes to me later and wants to do something, and it's not what all his friends are doing but he knows it's right, I want to be able to tell him to go ahead—and he'll trust me because I set the example.

"As far as my dating—I prefer not to date. The women that I'm around who are single and have kids, they think you should always have a mate. But I want my kid to come first; I want to make sure he's secure before I try to fulfill some need of my own for companionship. And this is not a popular thing among the women I'm around. It's not popular, but I'm doing what I think is right."

Diane Foster described a scene that took place when Sophia was two and a half years old as an example of how her "awareness that before expecting Sophia to be something, I have to be that myself" has led to positive changes in her personality.

"There's a restaurant downtown that I go to a lot because it's near the library. But it has this one drawback. There's a really creepy guy who buses the tables and he's always annoyingly oversolicitous of me. I've wanted to tell him to get lost, but I've never been able to bring myself to do it. Well, one time when I went in there, I had Sophia with me. So of course this guy came running over and tried to do everything for her, put a napkin on her. And, as usual, part of me wanted to say, Go away, and part of me wanted to not be mean. So I did nothing.

"And after the guy left, I said to Sophia, 'Sophia, if somebody's doing something you don't like, you don't have to let them do it. You can say, Go away.' And then I thought—wait a minute; you're not talking to Sophia, you're talking to yourself. You should have been the model. You should have said to this guy, 'Let me ask my daughter if she wants that,' or 'We don't need that, thank you.'

"It was almost as if I want her to be what I'm not sometimes—and being with her teaches me what I've got to be. If I want her to learn to stand up for herself, I've got to stand up for myself—and for her. Instead of just saying, 'Come on, Sophia, you do it.' "

Therese Benedek pointed out that from the time children

are born, they offer to their parents "hope and promise for self-realization" and the warning that they themselves "may expose not one's virtues but one's faults." Benedek quoted Anton Wildgans, an Austrian poet, who wrote of his infant son, "Our judge you may become—you are he already." (She observed that this feeling may seem particularly familiar and even unsettling or threatening to "modern parents," who cannot look for support to time-honored rules, standards, and values that were in place to guide parents in cultures "less individualistic [and] more authoritarian" than ours.)[1]

As children get older, parents may want to shape up in part because the kids demand that they do. Children do become rather judgmental—particularly of their parents! At around the age of six or seven, as the psychiatrist Judith Kestenberg pointed out, children, imbued with "principles of fair play, impartiality, justice, and consistency of standards, learned in school," can be uncannily accurate in detecting little flaws in our character (not to mention our table manners), and are quick to crack down on us. "At no point in the parents' development," Kestenberg wrote, "are they more forcefully confronted with their double standard of morality."[2] Or behavior.

"Listen to me!" Jonathan shouts when I interrupt what he is saying with what I want to say. "You don't listen to me!" He's right. I'm wrong. My child makes me aware of something I've often been guilty of—and not only in my dealings with him.

Kate Robicheau said that she frequently feels as if both her sons, who are fourteen and six, are giving her the message, "Boy, in case you're about to slip up, we're going to really be watching you." She has noticed her kids expressing shock at things other people have said or done—"which made me feel, wow, I'm glad I didn't do that. My kids have made me raise my standards in general. It's true. They make you want to be good or at least better. You know, you can get pretty cynical about the way the world operates. And you can start feeling foolish for following the rules. You may want to bend the rules a little. But you've got these kids. It's not worth it."

BECOMING LESS OF A PERFECTIONIST

At the same time that parenthood can raise our expectations for ourselves, it can make us relax. Several parents reported that they have become far less demanding of themselves (and, consequently, of other people, including their children and their spouses).

"I think I have learned to be a little more laid back," Greg Weber told me; "a little more tolerant. I used to be such a perfectionist. I sometimes expected unreasonable things from myself. And I could be unreasonable with other people, too. I was trying to be perfect, so I expected them to try to be perfect. And, of course, with kids that goes right to hell; you have to adjust. So I guess I've become more tolerant and accepting in general."

Greg can see his new "tolerance" before his very eyes every time he looks around his immediate surroundings. "This place always looks like a disaster area," he told me. "There's not even time to do the kind of normal cleaning we used to do. But you have a choice. You can either vacuum the cobwebs or read a book to the kids."

Joanne Marks said, "I keep hearing that as a working mother I should lower my standards for housework and so forth if I want to stay sane, but I sometimes think my standards couldn't possibly get any lower. When I come home from work I just sit and hold the baby by the hour. And that's okay. The laundry, if we don't get it done, will still be there tomorrow. I just enjoy my children so much; I want to be with them as much as I can now, every day. It's amazing to look at Cara and think what she was like a short time ago and see what she can do now and imagine where she'll be next year. It all moves along so quickly; the laundry can wait. I think one of the biggest things you learn as a parent is not to sweat some of the less important things in life."

Becka Moldover, whose primary job for the last seventeen years has been motherhood, says that she thinks "nothing but parenthood can make you feel so complete and totally inadequate all at the same time. Scaling down aspirations to a realistic level is a continuous process. I started out wanting to be perfect in every way for my kids, and probably hoping my kids would be perfect for me. Now my goal is simply to achieve an appreciation of our various strengths along with the ability to take our various weaknesses more lightly. That's hard enough!"

LEARNING PATIENCE

Among the areas in which parents told me their behavior had improved or is in the process of improving (they hope), anger control is in a class by itself. And not just controlling anger but practicing forbearance—which, in the case of parenting, begins with gracefully accepting the fact that nobody has invented a device to move children from point A to point B like their beloved battery-operated toys, and ends with being able to deal gracefully with the consequences of that fact. Which takes time. Lots of time. Which in turn, given our national propensity for instant gratification (even when it comes to toilet training, even when it comes to shoelace tying), means that through teaching our children virtually anything, through putting in all that time, we can learn patience.

Tanya Landau can summon a Buddha-like calm during her two-year-old daughter's worst moments; I've seen her do this several times. If there is one word that sums up Tanya's personality, it is "tranquil." Her impressive self-control is, in part, innate. But it has been enhanced, she says, through mothering, through weathering all the bad moments, which she regards as "challenges," not crises.

I visited Tanya one afternoon when she had just come back from a walk to the park with her daughter and a little girlfriend, also two. The outing had seemed interminable to Tanya. At no point was she able to get one toddler to sit in the stroller while the other walked or helped push. For the most part, neither one of them wanted to be in the stroller or walk or help push. "I felt really challenged," Tanya said with a laugh. "How am I going to stay patient? How do I not scold them? How do I not become like these mothers I hear screaming at their kids in the park?"

Tanya is, of course, not always as successful in controlling her temper as she was that afternoon. She does slip up. "I hear my daughter scolding her dolls," she told me, "and I realize that she must've gotten it from me!" But Tanya does feel that through parenting she has become a more patient person.

Other parents I interviewed found it more of a struggle not to fall apart when the kids do. "I haven't been able to completely control my anger, unfortunately," Ruth Sack told me. But her conscious effort to do so is an accomplishment in itself, she thinks. And the effort springs directly from seeing her own temper flare up in her younger son from time to time and not liking what she saw.

"I was really thinking about this the other day," she said, "about where my anger and bad temper came from. I know it came from my father, and he had a real reason for it. He was a Holocaust survivor. And he incorporated that anger into his life. But then I adopted it into my life; and this is where it has to stop. There's no real reason for it now. It's learned behavior. It's not a response anymore. And I don't want it to go to Matt, though, unfortunately, I think it may have already."

It is striking and entirely noncoincidental that almost all the parents who told me that childrearing had taught them patience, or provided a forum in which to learn patience, also said that their anger problem had come from their parents. Parental rage is one of the most frequent "ghosts in the nursery."

"My father was a real authoritarian and quite a disciplinarian," Rich Garner told me. "In the heat of my own frustration, it's as if my father's right inside my brain, manipulating my thoughts into my mouth, and I hear thoughts I've buried for years coming out like that and I'm . . . bite my tongue! I don't want to make my father sound like a bully; he was a great dad. He just wasn't too enlightened in some areas."

"Lots of times now, especially if I lose my temper, I hear my father's voice saying the same things," Greg Weber said. "And my wife, too. She has a temper. As quiet as she seems, she'll scream at the kids if she gets annoyed. Her mother used to scream at her, and her mother is the quietest, gentlest person, an elegant hostess. But her kids remember that when they were growing up, she was a screamer. And my father was short-tempered. If you didn't jump when he asked something, he'd lose his temper."

The idea of hand-me-down anger is hardly news, of course, but usually we hear about what happens when parents are unable to deal with it. We don't often hear about the parents who, having borne parental anger that falls anywhere along the continuum one therapist described as "losing it, *losing* it, and LOSING it," become determined never to inflict it on their children.

"I've tried hard to make sure I'm more broad-minded in raising my children than my dad was," Rich Garner said. And Greg Weber told me, "I'm very conscious of trying not to be like my father. I do have a little bit of his temper and I've had to work on controlling it. But every once in a while the kids catch me off guard and I'll go through my ups and downs, particularly when I'm tired and they do something that really ticks me off. I lose it."

Kevin Marks, who was raised by his mother after his father's death, said, "I consciously try not to do some of the things she did. I don't use demeaning nicknames. I don't believe in hitting. My rule is: not under any circumstances. Some of the ways my mother would put me down, call me stupid or something like that—I don't do those things."

Stephanie Hickson's "hot temper" is not, as far as she knows, a reflection of her parents' behavior toward her. But controlling it has always been a problem. Stephanie's two-year-old son's tantrums have brought this problem into sharper focus, and by trying to help him learn self-control, Stephanie has furthered her own maturation in two ways. First, in order to help him she's had to get a grip on her own temper. She is proud that she's become far more patient. Second, "when I show him that's not the way to act and he changes, that makes me feel good because he's learning self-control at a young age. It took me so long to make that transition. Helping him do that makes me feel good."

SELF-ESTEEM

Feeling good is a large part of what Therese Benedek meant by achieving "a new level of integration" in our personalities. When we succeed in resolving a dormant (or, in the case of those short-tempered parents, not so dormant!) conflict from our childhood that our children revive in us, our self-esteem moves up a notch. The process of confidence building that begins with the successful mothering and fathering of our infants can continue throughout the course of parenthood.[3] And each improvement in our outlook or behavior or mental health can, as we've seen, contribute to our confidence in parenting and to our overall confidence.

But our children can enhance our self-esteem in another way, Benedek pointed out—at least when they are very young—and that is through the esteem they have for us. Children, until they are old enough to know better—to separate reality from fantasy—tend to see their parents as the only things standing between them and dragons, witches, monsters, wars, belligerent bigger kids, and any number of other threats and dangers, real, imagined, or as seen on television.

Very young children look up to their parents and see not only their defenders, but menders, healers. "The normal parent," Benedek wrote, "in spite of his insight into his realistic limitations, embraces the gratifying role of omnipotence . . . As long as the fantasies of his child do not become hostile against him, the parent derives . . . the reassurance that he is a good parent and, even more, the hope that he is or can be better than his own parent was."[4]

But, of course, even in the best of parent-child relationships, children's "fantasies" do become "hostile" toward parents from time to time. And furthermore, as Benedek explained, parents "anticipate that the child's independent activities will expose their [own] mistakes [and] inferiority, and diminish their self-esteem. The spiral of negative transactions can be activated at any time. This hazard increases with the growing self-differentiation of the child."[5]

Predictably, while all the parents I interviewed could point to an area in which interacting with their children boosted their self-esteem, when I asked about parenthood as a source of general self-esteem, it was the awareness of their own "realistic limitations," as well as their children's talent for exposing them, that held sway. Self-esteem, for people in the throes of parenting, can be hard to come by—or to recognize.

"I know what you're saying," Rich Garner told me. "I see it all the time. Dad can fix this. Dad's a hero. But there's going to come a day when they'll bring something and Dad won't be able to fix it. When the cat dies, that's it, baby. I can't fix the cat.

"I think it's neat that they look up to us that way, but I try to tell them I'm not Superman. I tell little Rick, 'Look, if you take this piece here and you put this piece on there and turn it this way, you can fix it, too. I'll just show you how.' And he'll say, 'Okay.' That way I try to build up his confidence and self-esteem. But my own confidence? I don't think their thinking I'm great has built me up, no."

Melinda Stern also has found that her older daughter's belief in her "omniscience" reminds her mainly of all she doesn't know, of all her imperfections.

Sometimes, despite Melinda's insecurities, she manages to accept, even to "cherish," her daughter's admiration—"when she draws pictures of me and says, 'This is my mommy,' or the time she said to me, 'When I grow up I'm going to have two babies in my tummy, like Mommy.' "

But even more gratifying to Melinda is the affirmation, through things her daughter says or does, that she is doing a good job as a mother, that she's instilling lessons she feels are very important to her child. "The other day, Amanda said, 'I love you, Daddy, I love you, Mommy, I love baby Libby, and I love myself,' " Melinda said, illustrating how Amanda's budding self-esteem had boosted her own—for the moment. And there have been other moments. When Amanda went up to another child who was upset and said, "It's okay," Melinda thought: "She's got a heart; she's got compassion. I *am* getting through to her."

Rich Garner, too, periodically feels his confidence rise when he sees he's "getting through" to his children. "I realize now we do have such a permanent effect on our children, positive and negative. I never thought about how much of an effect my parents had on me, but now I do. So I've gained much more respect for the influence we have on our kids, much more respect for parenthood . . ."

"Much more respect for yourself as a parent?"

"Well, when I'm having a positive effect—yes."

Sheila Weber told me, "The thing is, self-esteem can change from moment to moment in parenting. Intellectually, yes, I know I've done well. Then the next moment, one of my sons can fall apart over the smallest little thing, and I think, 'Where did I fail?' There are enough of those moments that I don't spend too much energy thinking about how competent I am."

Kate Robicheau said, "The cynical way Ben, my thirteen-year-old, sometimes talks or when he's narrow or mean or not coping, makes me think, 'What have I raised?' And then he can make the loveliest comments, and I think, 'My Lord, this is great! Something has come through, and maybe the love or appreciation he expresses comes partly from me and all our talking together and reading. I won't take credit for it all, but there must be some connection, and it does make me feel wonderful."

Only three parents, all fathers, told me they felt that parenthood has, across the board, made them more self-assured, more convinced of their own worth. Greg Weber qualified this observation, reminding me that he had started out with such low expectations of himself—since his father had been virtually a missing person throughout most of his childhood—that he had nowhere to go but up. "I guess I still have low expectations as to how I'm going to score," he said. "I don't expect the A's. But any time I feel I've done at least an okay job with my kids, I count it a success; I think parenting *has* given me more confidence in myself."

Kevin Marks said that he has gained as much as his daughter from the imaginative hours the two of them have spent playing together, from the "projects," as his daughter calls them, that they've done. "Play is a way of becoming unstructured and uninhibited and of having somebody accept you," he told me, "and not only accept you but think that you're a nice person, a great person."

John Petaway, who has raised his son and daughter by himself, feels that the experience has raised his opinion of himself. He takes pride in having resisted what he views as a natural male inclination toward the Great Santini school of childrearing —"you know, the handshake and the rub on the head instead of grabbing the kid and saying, 'I love you.' " And he's proud, as a single father, that he's remained unfazed by jibes from "the guys," some of whom have been known to send him Mother's Day cards. His years of parenting, he says, have strengthened his confidence in his own masculinity, and this has made him a better parent, as he realizes each time he kisses and hugs his son good night. "This is easier with a daughter, but with a son it's difficult if you're not sure of yourself, you know."

An exchange between Roberta and Stanley Friedman, whose children are both grown and living two thousand miles away from them, clarified my perspective on how, when, and if parenthood can enhance one's self-esteem.

"Well," said Stan, "maybe I could take part credit for their turning out well in that I provided some guidance, and my self-esteem would be boosted by that. But I think what we learned was that you never have full control. And therefore you shouldn't take credit or blame for how they turn out. You shouldn't pat yourself on the back too readily if they turn out fine."

"Wait a minute," said Roberta. "There is one thing that does make me feel good about our parenting and does give me more self-esteem. At different times both our kids, having gone away to college and met all sorts of kids, and sharing with them their family experiences—both our kids independently came back to talk about our family and how we raised them and how good they felt about the home they came from."

"That's something I forgot," said Stan. "You're right. And when I think of that, it is pretty satisfying."

Even in retrospect, even when the prime time of parenting

is over and we look back and reflect on it, the realization that our self-esteem has risen through parenthood does not surface and is not sustained too easily.

Staying Young

"Parents are said to stay young with their children," Freud wrote, "and that is indeed one of the most precious psychological gains that parents derive from their children."[6] Freud, of course, was quick to mention the possible downside of this happy state of affairs, and others have embellished his observations. We're all familiar (and not just from reading psychological literature) with the mother-in-law who wages a pathetic battle with the ravages of time in order to compete with her daughter-in-law for her son's affections. Or the father who, threatened by his son's flourishing sexuality, embarks on some sexual adventures of his own. Or the mother who, seeing herself wither as her daughter blooms, becomes obsessed with trying to look like her daughter's sister.

But for many parents, Freud's "precious psychological gain" is just that. It comes from a healthy identification with our children that keeps us learning, in sync with the times and what is going on around us, more fully alive. Some parents tend to dress youthfully, often at their children's suggestion. "I was always aware of dressing appropriately," said one father whose son and daughter are grown now. "I did want to look more cool and with-it. I didn't want them to think of me as old. That was important."

Some parents pick up their children's language (like, I mean, y'know . . . Yeah, *right!* . . . chill) not so much as a means of facilitating intergenerational communication—although it helps—but as a way of remaining . . . well, "fresh." Some parents find themselves enjoying the same music their children do, often because, as Stan Friedman pointed out, "a lot of what they thought was their music was actually our music when we were their age!" Nevertheless, Stan credits his sons with keeping him up to date musically and in other ways.

Now that his sons have left home, Stan says he suddenly

feels older. "When you tell people you have a kid of twenty-four, you feel old, anyway. But it's also because there's no one around to keep us up with the slang and the dress and the new music. We find out ourselves from TV or magazines—or from them when they come home to visit—but it's not the same thing. Having them around all the time was invigorating."

Many parents discover that through playing with their children they can recover something of their lost childhood. Or, as in the case of Kevin Marks, for whom playing with his daughter provides reassuring self-esteem, it can mean the chance to be childlike for the first time. "I was alone a lot as a child," he said. "After my father died, my mother had to work until late at night. My younger sister was seven years younger than I was—too young to play with. So one of the nicest things about children for me is that I finally get a playmate."

Through play, parents often find a new or renewed capacity to invent and imagine, to let down their guard and be a pirate, a cowboy, an astronaut, or merely themselves as they were before they had to do things like pay the mortgage. Kevin Marks's wife, Joanne, sometimes feels old when she sees how young the mothers of Zoe's day care buddies are. But, for the most part, Zoe and her baby sister make Joanne forget her age.

"Being with my children gives me an excuse to play, to go outside, run around, play hopscotch, enjoy. It's very liberating. A lot of the time I just stay outside in the yard instead of going in and starting dinner. And if we have to open another can of ravioli, so what? They say that play is the work of childhood, but sometimes I think it's really the work of life. To me, it's maybe the most fulfilling part of life."

Helene Sapadin, the single mother of two-year-old Molly, said that "there are a lot of things, duties, adult things, I used to put first that I now put off because I'd rather be rolling around on the floor playing with Molly. I was always playful in my classrooms but it's different at home, more special. I'm just doing things in the style of a much younger woman now. And I feel myself to be much younger. I'm tired a lot, but I've got a lot more energy, too."

Sheila Weber, who is forty but feels twenty-five, partly because she has become "more playful" since becoming a mother, remembers watching Jeremy, who is now seven years old, roller-skating on the sidewalk and suddenly deciding to join him. "There was a pair of old skates that the people who lived in this house before us had left. You know, those metal ones that you wear over your shoes? They're just like the ones I used when I was young, so I put them on. They vibrate; they're really weird. And I went up and down the sidewalk with them. And now Jeremy's been playing baseball. I was thinking, I'm a lefty, so I can't use anybody else's mitt; maybe I really want to get my own mitt because I enjoy this."

Changes in How We Relate to the World

INTO THE RABBIT HOLE

Another way of looking at it would be "into the tornado." The point is that, just as Alice's tumble down the rabbit hole led to adventure after adventure and just as the tornado zapped Dorothy into the wonder-filled land of Oz, our plunge into parenthood can dramatically expand our own curiosity and interests.

"Parenthood has, I think, made me be more involved in life," Stephanie Hickson told me. "I don't just sit back and watch it go by; now I have to participate. Before, things didn't seem too exciting. Now, the world's become exciting. Before, I didn't look around the corner and see the place that was full of fun. I walked by it every day and I've even been in it. But I didn't see it."

It occurred to me that Stephanie was not speaking figuratively. "What place?" I asked her.

"The Peabody Museum. You know, I'd been there, but Earl never had. When I took him there, all of a sudden I started seeing little things. He'll go, 'Oh, look at that bird, you know, the bird with the yellow beak!' All these things I never paid any attention to—and now I pay attention."

In New York City, it's the American Museum of Natural History. In Washington, it's the Smithsonian. In London, it's the Natural History Museum. In Philadelphia, it's the Academy of Natural Sciences Museum and the Franklin Institute. In Toronto, it's the Royal Ontario Museum. In San Francisco, it's the California Academy of Sciences and the Exploratorium. But since my research was conducted in and around New Haven, I heard repeatedly from parents about Yale's Peabody Museum of Natural History. For parents, it is much more than a repository of dinosaur remains, geological treasures, lovingly preserved specimens of marine, bird, plant, and animal life, and at least two dead ancient Egyptians and artifacts of primitive cultures from all over the Americas; it is the leading local symbol of the amazing way that our children can lead us into intimate, rewarding, and lasting relationships with all of the above.

Rich Garner, for example, has rediscovered his inner geologist. "I was always interested in rocks and minerals as a child," he said, "but I lost interest as I got older. I don't know why. Then I took Ricky to the Peabody. I wasn't too enthusiastic. But you know how there are times you do things you think will be boring but that the kids will find interesting—and they turn out to be very interesting for you? Well, Ricky and I both got interested in the mineral display. And I dug up my stuff at my mom's house from when I was a kid." And the rest is natural history.

I identified strongly with Rich, and with all the other parents who mentioned the chemistry between their children and the Peabody as vital to their own cognitive development. Although I've always had more than a passing interest in pre-Columbian artifacts, I had never been moved much by fish, birds, mammals, or reptiles, or by the remains of creatures who lived millions of years before there were any people. Now, as the mother of a six-year-old and a regular at the Peabody, I am.

I've found that, as Greg Weber explained, "You become blasé about things, but then you take your child to an aquarium and he says, 'Oh, Dad, look! A fish!' And you get caught up in the excitement of learning."

Sheila Weber has discovered birdwatching via Jeremy's first-grade birdwatching "unit." "I take him on bird walks. I never would have done anything like that if I didn't have him. I go out, I see a bird, and right away I want to know what kind it is.

"You know, Greg and I never went camping. It's not my cup of tea. I'd rather stay in a hotel with a bathroom any time. But Greg's been saying maybe we'll get a tent and go for the whole weekend, and that's something we'll do for the kids and I'll end up learning about all sorts of things and I'll enjoy it.

"Also, because the kids need me to help them sometimes on the computer, I've gotten into it, and that's something I ordinarily would have had no interest in whatsoever."

"What sums it all up," Ruth Sack said, "is my experience with kids' soccer. Here I am, a nonathlete. I like dance, ballet. I don't like football and basketball. But all of a sudden, my son has to be on a team, so I take him to the park for his soccer practice. Before I signed him up in the first grade, I thought, 'Oh, my God, I'm going to have to sit for two hours without working? Without reading? Can I bring a book with me? I'll sit there and read a book. And I'll use the time because every minute has to be used.'

"When I get to the soccer field, I'm up there shouting and screaming and rooting for my kid. And I never thought it would be that way; I thought I would be completely bored. Now I watch everything and make sure things are fair. I make sure he's okay. And I watch the games with great enthusiasm. So this is one of those changes that are happening, you know, all these new things bumping out all the things that used to be so important to me."

HOW PARENTHOOD CAN RESHAPE OUR SOCIAL LIVES

Not too many people remember Eva Le Gallienne's *Flossie and Bossie*. Although it is just as captivating as *Stuart Little* or *Charlotte's Web* (and, like both of E. B. White's books, just as whimsically illustrated by Garth Williams), it's been out of print for a long time. It should be back in print.

Flossie is a shy, dowdy hen, and Bossie is the Barnyard glamour girl. They don't get along with each other, (more haughty Bossie's doing than poor, bedraggled Flossie's). And neither of them, because of her own particular quirks, mixes well in Barnyard society. Then they become mothers. Things heat up between them, then warm up. They become friends (more Flossie's doing than Bossie's). Bossie helps Flossie become more polished. Flossie helps Bossie become a *mensch*. And through nurturing each other and each other's chicks, they form their own little neighborhood and become cherished members of Barnyard society.

Now, there's much more to the story than this, making it as relevant in many ways to today's parents and children as it was in 1949, when it was published. But at the moment I'm concerned with only one way in which it's still relevant. It shows that the popular view of parenthood as isolating, particularly for parents of newborns, particularly for the parent who stays home with the children, may be somewhat short-sighted.

In fact, many parents find that having children gives them the opportunity to connect with new people and groups and to form new and lasting relationships. It's true that for many of us the huge dollops of time swallowed by work and by simply being with our children do not leave much room for cultivating our social lives—not as we used to, anyway. "We don't entertain much anymore," Ruth Sack told me. "It's funny—a lot of the things that used to mean a lot, like my old friendships, have been bumped out of their once very significant places and replaced by my children. I would much rather stay home all weekend, hanging out with my kids, with no particular plans, than go to a party. And I used to be very social."

Stephanie Hickson knows that most "experts" would probably say that, as a single mother, she should go on a date occasionally. But she too prefers her son's companionship to anyone else's. "I can be with my child and not think about being with grown-ups," she says, "but there's no way I could be with grown-ups and not think about being with my child!" So Stephanie finds herself with grown-ups who also have children. And although her social life has contracted in one respect—no dates—she feels that it's actually expanded. She has made friendships at work that carry over outside.

Ruth's social network has also grown (even as some old

relationships and activities have fallen by the wayside) through her involvement in her sons' day care, then school.

Most of the parents I interviewed found that, as Becka Moldover put it, "some of my closest friendships have been established through the context of common experiences in parenting." In Becka's case, this included "a reforging of relationships with my siblings."

Stephanie told me that her new friendships with her supervisor at work and with several co-workers wouldn't exist if not for her son, "because their lives revolve around their children, too. They'll invite me to parties; most of the functions we go to are for the kids. And we share stories. Sometimes we don't know what to do, but we have someone to go to, because we trust each other's judgment. I know their concerns for their children are just like mine, so I say to them, 'What do you do in this situation?' or 'What did you do when your daughter or your son did this?' And they'll tell me it's not abnormal for a little kid to talk to himself the way my kid does. Or if they read a book they like, they'll tell me about it."

When Helene Sapadin was going through the process of adopting Molly, she met a couple who were also waiting. "They became like family. We waited together and then we traveled together to pick up our children, and the intensity of that experience, and the fact that we have similar values, has made us very close. Molly and I go there every Tuesday night for dinner; it's like a ritual. Last year around this time my back went out, and I ended up spending two weeks recovering in their living room. They took care of Molly."

Rich Garner told me that before he became a father, "I just had a core group of friends and I was satisfied with that; I could've just gotten stuck in a rut and stayed there. But my kids have forced me to get out of that and meet their friends, and their friends' parents."

"Before the kids came along," said Greg Weber, "I wouldn't say we were socially withdrawn, but we were much more isolated. Neither one of us had many connections here; we're not from this immediate area. We knew a few couples, and maybe once a month we'd get together with them. But

mostly we'd go out to dinner ourselves or go to a movie ourselves or sit around and read. And both of us were working.

"I think for many people what anchors them to the community is the activities they get into through the children.
We've made connections now through the school, the PTA activities. We've met the children who live in the neighborhood
and their parents. And we've done the same thing through the
YMCA. And baseball. And then you find somebody you met at
the PTA who is also at the Y. And someone you met at baseball
is also in PTA. You start seeing the same people in multiple
places. And you do become connected."

Our outward mobility may also be enhanced by seeing how
our children greet and drink in each new discovery as their
worlds open outward.

"Before, I used to think people were into themselves,
cold," Stephanie told me. "But now I see people, especially
older people, who take time, talk to my son. Sometimes he just
sits on the stoop and goes, 'Hi, hi!' to the people walking by,
and a lot of them will stop and talk to him, and I see how
excited he gets about meeting new people and different kinds of
people. It's contagious.

"We go to a park, and there are kids from all over; one
kid's from Israel. And they all play the same game. They don't
talk, but they're all playing the games together with no problem. And you wonder, How do they know? Then you realize
you did that when you were a child—and all of a sudden you
lost it. You lost communicating so easily with another person.
Something got in the way of your seeing this person as being a
lot like you. You sit back and say, 'How can I make this stay in
him? How can I make him be like this for the rest of his life,
open-minded and not prejudiced against anyone?' "

Stephanie has answered her own question by acting on
what she has absorbed through her son's embrace of the world.
By trying to emulate his sociability, responsiveness, and tolerance, she plays back for him the values and qualities she wants
him to develop and retain.

Some of the most important things we teach our children
come not from our own adult experience but from the wisdom

they themselves have given us by being the way they are, simply because they are children.

ALTRUISM REVISITED: PARENTHOOD AND SOCIAL ACTION

Even as our children can amplify our personal and social ties, they can deepen our understanding of the problems that plague other individuals and groups—and make us want to help solve those problems.

More than one parent I spoke with likened parenting to being a missionary, and not just in the sense that in dealing with children we are dealing with members of "an unusual, partly savage tribe," as Alison Lurie wrote, with its "customs, manners, and rituals, its folklore and sacred texts."[7]

These parents, one of whom mentioned Dr. Schweitzer rather than Dr. Spock as a source of inspiration, were half joking—but only half. The fact is, missionaries, whether or not they are parents, personify the unselfishness that is supposed to be a hallmark of parenting. They are acting outside the home (often way outside the home) on an impulse that, for many people, begins at home with nurturing the infant, then the growing child, and then by identifying in various ways with this vulnerable being whom we consider part of ourselves but who is becoming more his or her own person every day.

For mothers of sons and fathers of daughters this can mean a greater understanding of the opposite sex. "Through the process of identification," wrote Theodore Lidz, "the child can . . . provide one of the two parents with the opportunity to experience intimately the way in which a person of the opposite sex grows up. The sharing of the vicissitudes in the life of a child of the opposite sex, almost as if they pertained to the self, provides a broadening perspective."[8]

"You see the world through their eyes, and you see what they're subjected to," according to Jeffrey Lustman. "When I see my daughter, who is fourteen, cope with all the subtle and not so subtle prejudicial attitudes she faces, I get furious and very involved. A teacher who steers her into certain activities and not others just because she's a girl, that stuff drives me up the wall."

A friend of mine, whose twelve-year-old son was beaten up when he tried to stop a group of boys from picking on a girl, told me that this experience gave her first-hand knowledge of part of what it's like to grow up male. She said, "My first impulse, to tell you the truth, was to go grab those kids. I was surprised by the violence I felt in myself because of this outrage, that these kids had pounded on Sam. And I realized how hard it is, being a boy. Sam wants to be tough and strong and not a sissy. He wants to stick up for himself and other people. At the same time, he doesn't want to hurt other people or get hurt."

This new empathy for the conflicts inherent in growing up female or growing up male almost always makes us attentive to the messages we're giving our children about sex roles. (Sam, for instance, is now taking Tae Kwan Do classes; his mother says he's learning pacifism but also the techniques he needs, should pacifism fail, to take care of himself.)

Sometimes this concern spreads outward. Some parents gain, through their deeper understanding of their sons and daughters, more compassion for the opposite sex. And some of them act on this compassion.

Susan Molinari of New York, who holds the seat her father, Guy Molinari, once held in the House of Representatives, says that her father, who "comes from a very traditional background . . . now goes out of his way to work with women, to give them credit. To a large extent that might have started happening the day he had a baby girl instead of a baby boy."[9]

Our children can provide the impetus for political involvement or social activism simply because their presence is a constant reminder of how much needs to be done to protect or ameliorate their lives. "My interest in other aspects of the world awoke from total dormancy once I had kids," Becka Moldover told me. "Especially political, social, and environmental issues. I lost my sense of being a transient on earth. What didn't mean much to me when I was living here on my own mattered a lot because my kids were now living here, and once it mattered for my kids, I found it mattered for everyone else's. Now you're really stuck; you care about what happens in the world. This is a lot to worry about. But every time you see a picture of a hungry or lost or abused child, you sense your own child's potential pain. Indifference is gone forever."

"Having children makes you think more about a lot of things you took for granted," said Stephanie Hickson. "Like human rights, political issues. They'll matter to your kid. The government cuts school budgets but builds roads. That kind of thing is important to me now because my kid will be affected by such decisions. It's my responsibility to get more involved; it's like going from passive to active."

Kate Robicheau found herself getting interested in school board politics when her older son was two years old, "because I foresaw that in five years it would matter to him. There was a lot on the line, and I've stayed involved. That way, I have a stake in the future and my children have a stake in the future. I've been involved in elections. I was on the town committee.

"When you have kids, you suddenly realize that it matters who's on the school board and who your mayor and police chief are and things like having SLOW: CHILDREN PLAYING signs on the streets. You never even noticed them before, but suddenly you realize *you* can make those signs happen!"

When Melinda Stern was explaining how she considers raising her children as well as she can to be her major contribution to the world, she mentioned a few other contributions she has made or intends to make through citizens' action groups. "They're lobbying for some legislation to control lead levels in the water, and I'm interested in getting involved in that effort. They want to do annual lead checks on kids. Recycling is another big issue with me. And I just called Literacy Volunteers to help teach people how to read.

Melinda has found that her altruism redounds to enhance the way she is raising her children. "I want my kids to actively care about the environment and society," she says, "and there's no better way than setting the example."

The Reverend Jerry Streets, chaplain of Yale University and a psychiatric social worker, told me that fatherhood and grandfatherhood reinforced his advocacy efforts—but not so much with the thought of improving the world his children and grandchildren *someday* will enter or with the hope that they'll follow in his footsteps.

What they have taught him is the extent to which children enter the world outside their homes and the world enters them even before they've left their parents' sphere of influence. "Peer pressure," he says, "the school environment, the street environment, can permeate walls that even the strongest family builds up."

The world, as the Reverend Streets sees it, is inevitably our accomplice in raising our children. Through lobbying, voting, campaigning, joining or forming groups to promote our goals and ideals, and supporting organizations that exist to support us (such as Parent Action and the Children's Defense Fund), we can exert more control than we may think over the world and over its impact on our developing children.

Activism is, to the Reverend Streets, a way to make the world our ally, not our foe, in childrearing. It is a logical extension of parenthood, which begins as we bond with our children and optimally leads to bonding through them with other children, other parents, our neighbors, our communities, and our world—and which, therefore, should not end at our front doors.

VIII

How Parenthood Can Make a Marriage Grow

Greg would probably not say to me, "Let's go out and have a catch" without the kids. But with the kids he'll do that. And then sometimes they lose interest—and then Greg and I will be out there, playing.
—SHEILA WEBER

SALLY AND PETER TENZER have moved to a new home in a nearly rural area, where the schools are far better than in their former neighborhood. Sally is eager to show me around. The wide-open design makes each room seem a continuation of the last one; everywhere, picture windows and sliding glass doors bring the outdoors in, along with plenty of light and an illusion of even more spaciousness. "If you had been here a few days ago," Sally says, as I admire one view of the woods beyond the back yard, "you would have seen me planting azaleas and rhododendrons. I was out there on Saturday from nine till it got dark, blowing leaves."

The newly cleared back yard—only weeks ago the forest came right up to the back deck—looks somewhat barren on this chilly fall day. But soon it will be as lavishly landscaped as the Tenzers' old yard, where Sally had been planting annuals the day she told me about the tornado that knocked a live telephone wire into the street, endangering her two daughters and bringing home for her the feeling that her job away from home was also, albeit less dramatically, endangering them.

She had quit her job. Her daughters' "miserable" behavior had improved dramatically. She had felt great satisfaction in "coming to the rescue" of her children by opting, at least temporarily, for full-time motherhood. And she had found an outlet for her need to do more by engaging in a variety of volunteer projects. Like Melinda Stern, she felt that setting an example of altruism in action was important for her children.

Peter agreed with her; the children were his top priority, too. Sally's volunteer work not only would inspire the children but took place mostly in their various milieus. She was the treasurer of the PTA, for instance, and did computer programming for their younger daughter's swim team. Peter's career as a business consultant involved a lot of traveling and left little time for outside activities like the PTA. But Peter soon found that his appreciation of his wife's good work was diluted by the letdown of coming home to an empty house or competing for her attention with a stack of bills she had to pay for the PTA. Her activities, like his, involved a lot of traveling (she was logging over fifty miles a day on the car without even leaving town) and left little time for him.

So Sally and Peter faced another crisis in a marriage of over two decades that had been threatened and—they both agreed, sitting at the kitchen table in their new home—strengthened by many similar crises. The children, they said—as Sally served the blueberry muffins she had just baked and poured tea, exhibiting the hospitality, the homeliness, that had always made her so attractive to Peter—had put a constant strain on their marriage.

Yet when I asked what they thought their marriage would be like had they not had children, they answered immediately, and practically in unison, "We wouldn't still be married."

. . . .

The concept of children giving cohesion (if not always coherence) to a marital or romantic relationship, the idea that collaborating in childrearing can nourish that relationship, is no more evident in the literature about parenthood than it is in the daily outlook of most parents. It may be acknowledged here and there, but that's about it.

One such acknowledgment appeared recently in a *Redbook* magazine report on its national survey of a thousand parents about the ways that having children had changed their marriages. The results? "Sixty-five percent of fathers and 64 percent of mothers say the reality of family life is better than they imagined; 54 percent of fathers and 56 percent of mothers say they became closer after they had children," *and* "despite the energy drain kids place on a couple, two out of three men and women feel they get enough emotional attention from their spouse."[1]

Encouraging news! All the more so because it indicates two facts that the *Redbook* report is quick to emphasize. First of all, fathers, despite the stereotypes, seem as positively motivated by parenthood as mothers. And second, these figures represent quite a shift—almost a revolutionary one—from the reading Ann Landers got when she tested the parental waters in 1976 and discovered that 70 percent of her respondents thought parenthood "interfered with their lifestyle."

But acknowledging that children can and do contribute to the success of the parental relationship is not the same as explaining how this happens, what those contributions are. In reading the summary of the *Redbook* survey, I felt the same frustration I had when reading Bruno Bettelheim's observation, in *A Good Enough Parent*, that nothing short of good genes can make a child flourish more than the confidence he gets from the certain knowledge that his parents' marriage is enriched by his presence.

But how, exactly, does the child contribute to the parents' marriage? How has the child's presence furthered their relationship? Bettelheim, true to his own statement that "books on childrearing (such as this one)" gloss over "the great impact that children . . . have on the development of their parents" both individually and "as individuals who are married," does not explain this process in detail.

Nor does Therese Benedek, for all her insistence that "under fortunate circumstances" (that is, if the parents' response to a given external or internal conflict does not take a pathological turn) childrearing "deepens the meaning of marriage" and provides the psychological wherewithal for patching up an immature or shaky relationship.

In other words, although I kept stumbling on indications that children can be catalysts to the growth of couplehood, I was not turning up much to explain how this process of mutual development works—until, that is, I broached the subject with Sally Tenzer and, a little later, with Peter. Through getting to know them—as a team, as two people who have suffered and exulted together over their joint upbringing of two daughters for fifteen of their twenty-one years of marriage—I began to learn how raising children can help two people move forward together and develop in tandem.

A New Us

Peter Tenzer remembers the first six years of his marriage as "a piece of cake." His high school romance with Sally had waned when Peter, who was three years ahead of her, left for college, but during her junior year she got a "remember me?" letter from him. He was at business school nearby. They got together and were married soon after her graduation. "Marriage was simple," Peter recalls. "Going to graduate school was simple. Moving to a new town, getting a good job. It was all simple."

Sally's memories of that period are somewhat less rosy. "I don't think we realized before we got married how much of our families we brought to our marriage. It wasn't two of us in that bed; it was all those other people in there, too. And our families are totally opposite. We had a lot of issues to work out."

But dealing with this historical residue was, indeed, "a piece of cake" for the Tenzers compared with what happened after their first daughter, Amy, was born. Sally had a difficult delivery and was physically and emotionally drained for months. Peter found out he needed back surgery. But those were the least of their problems. Their baby was born with a hole between the bottom two chambers of her heart, and when she was a little over a year old, Amy underwent major surgery.

"They put a Dacron patch on her heart," Sally said, "but some of the stitches holding the patch in place peeled loose during the surgery. We lived the whole second year of Amy's life with the potential of her having to have more surgery. But by the end of that year they did a catheterization, and the hole had closed up. So that nightmare was over. But now we had a new one. Our marriage fell apart."

According to Peter, they had gone—overnight, it seemed—from being like two kids playing husband and wife to being adults who were really married and confronting a real crisis. "This was the first time either of us had had to face up to the possible death of someone close to us," Peter told me. Sally, who came from a family where everything was always laid out on the table, needed to talk. Peter, whose family's style of coping was combative but noncommunicative, couldn't—or wouldn't.

Peter moved out. His apartment was only a block away; he continued supporting Sally and Amy; he visited almost daily and sometimes sat for Amy, but Sally knew he was involved with another woman. "He had a lot of integrity about it," Sally told me. "He couldn't see this other woman and stay home, so he left." Sally was "devastated" by Peter's affair and by the stress of coping alone, for the most part, with a baby who was now physically fine but "psychologically damaged" from her ordeal.

"I don't think I ever truly faced up to the possibility of Amy's dying," Peter said. "I think Sally did. As a result, she grew a lot, but I probably repressed the hell out of it. I always had the point of view that it's going to be okay, it's not a big deal. Sally's point of view was that we were facing a major crisis in the life of our child. I didn't want to approach it that way. But, to tell you the truth, I don't know what really happened during that period. Everything was so convoluted. Everything."

Now, looking back, both Peter and Sally agree that the

reasons for being unable to deal with the crisis are not as important as the reasons that Peter came back. On that subject he's absolutely clear, although he doesn't find it easy to articulate.

In his explanation I found my first clue to the mysterious process by which children can bring their parents closer. Peter's decision to return was prompted in part by his love for Sally and in part by his sense of responsibility for his child. But the major reason that Peter came back was his discovery that he and Sally plus their child equalled something new, something larger, something he was drawn to and found essential. "I realized that there's a sort of evolution from a marriage to a family that is really hard to put a finger on, and that dimension became extremely important to me. When you're married, you have a relationship and that's all you have. When you add a child, you add more than a third person. What you're adding is the concept of family, and it doesn't exist without that third person, that child. And that's the dimension that for me was critical.

"When I look back on that period I would say that our splitting and coming back together probably did more than anything to ensure we would stay together no matter what happened. I think we both discovered that what had been just a relationship, a marriage, was now considerably enlarged."

The old song that goes "Just Molly and me and baby makes three" doesn't begin to tell the story of what children bring to a relationship or where children can take a relationship. When psychologists speak of a dyad becoming a triad, the numerical composition of the unit is not nearly as significant as its chemistry, including the changes the new element triggers in the composition of the original two elements. The triad is bigger, weightier, fuller, loaded with far more potential for joy, sorrow, learning, growing. This is the "more" that Peter sensed. This was what drew him home to his family, which, he realized, meant far more than being an extended couple.

A New You

We've seen how children cast new light on our individual lives, how we come to see ourselves, now that we are parents, almost as different people. Something of the same phenomenon underlies the transformation that takes place in a couple on their first becoming parents. Bruno Bettelheim, despite his observation that parental development is given short shrift in childrearing books (including his), does mention the fresh view of our mate that often follows the arrival of the first child. Suddenly, we see our partner as different. He or she is no longer only our mate but is somebody's parent, our child's parent.

This is what Peter was getting at when he mentioned Sally's having faced up to the seriousness of their baby's illness as he could not, and his impression that she "grew a lot" as a result of her willingness to confront their crisis. He immediately saw her almost as a new person, Amy's mother, not just his wife. Bettelheim wrote that the experience of the revised edition of our mate can inspire "stronger and different feelings of tenderness." Or it can work the other way, stirring up "feelings of resentment . . . even jealousy."

Peter had the latter reaction. It wasn't until he recognized the value of what he and Sally and the baby had together that his "tenderness" overcame his "resentment" and he was able to appreciate the new Sally.

In fact, he found the blossoming of the nurturing qualities she had undoubtedly absorbed from her childhood deeply attractive, all the more because they had been notably absent from his own childhood. Sally as a mother offered hope that he and she together could create what he had never had and always missed, a sense of family, the reality of being a family.

But, as Sally is quick to point out, though he may have come back to her, he did not, as far as she could see, undergo an instant transition from husband to husband *and* father.

Roberta and Stanley Friedman arrived more quickly at a mutual appreciation of what they viewed as the new and improved models of each other that emerged when they became parents.

Stan was finishing his first year of internship, twenty-five years ago, when David was born. He was working constantly, often overnight or for days on end, and was exhausted. The trepidation that Roberta felt as her due date approached came partly from her awareness that she would be left alone much of the time with a tiny infant. But she also feared that even when Stan was there, he wouldn't be there in the way she hoped.

"He was a very reserved person," Roberta says, "much more closed than he is now. And he was programmed to his profession, completely involved in it. I wasn't sure how he'd be as a father. I didn't know what he had to give as a father or whether he'd have anything left over to give."

It immediately turned out that he had a lot to give. Roberta was thrilled to see a side of Stan that, despite the length and depth of their relationship (which had begun in high school), she hadn't known existed. "It was unbelievably exciting," she recalls, to see her husband in love with their baby, thoroughly involved with the baby during those precious, and precious few, hours he was home. Her love for Stan was immeasurably enriched, she feels, by the qualities their baby brought out in him.

The miracle of seeing one's partner reborn as a parent can be as rewarding as sensing the transformation in oneself. As Melinda Stern put it, using nearly the same words as Therese Benedek, such revelations "imbue the marriage with meaning." And they continue to add meaning over the years. Stan's "pouring out" to David continued, Roberta says, and continues even now, with David in law school and his younger brother, Mark, in college.

Stan, for his part, was as moved by Roberta's emergence as a "wonderful mother" and the continuing development of that side of her as she was by his transformation. "The challenges that have occurred from year to year as the children's problems and as life in general dictate, the way she's handled everything, have given me a great amount of admiration for her. I've always been proud of her as my mate, but my love for her was continually enhanced by the way she dealt with our children. I think it's been a very strong factor."

Roberta and Stan are several years removed from the daily hurly-burly that tosses up plenty of "challenges" which may refresh our appreciation for our spouses as parents and renew our love for them. They had trouble recalling such incidents, although Roberta did say that her love for Stan swelled once

again at his recent "extraordinary, very loving" way of helping
David with a crisis that had stymied her—which indicates that
David, at twenty-four, together with his twenty-two-year-old
brother, Mark, is still busy imbuing his parents' relationship
with meaning.

But Melinda Stern, speaking from the midst of the hurly-
burly (with one kindergartner and one toddler), was able to spell
out exactly how a mundane event rekindled the light that
showed the parental side of her husband, Jerry. "Just this week
Amanda told me a little girl on the school bus had said to her,
'You're stupid and your daddy's stupid.' My first reaction was to
reassure her—'You're a very smart girl! And she doesn't even
know Daddy!' But then she told me that Jerry had already heard
about this. 'Daddy said maybe there's something wrong in this
little girl's family and she feels bad so it makes her feel better to
make me feel bad.'

"And, although I didn't quite agree with Jerry's approach,
it did make me feel very good about him. He showed such concern for her, and thoughtfulness; he didn't just brush this incident off. That's what I would have expected, but he took the
time to explain things to her in his own way. When something
like this happens and I see him as a good father, I do think this
is the good stuff! This is nice! This makes everything worth it!"

It can even be romantic in the same sense that seeing one's
spouse elegantly dressed for an evening out is romantic. All of a
sudden, the same person one is accustomed to seeing in sweats,
in pajamas, unadorned, uncombed, laid back, just being his or
her self, appears radiant, freshly scrubbed, all decked out—and
one falls in love all over again. Is this, I asked Melinda, what it
feels like when you discover, or rediscover, Jerry as a nurturer,
as a caring, creative father?

"Definitely, yes!" she said. "It's invigorating—it gives me a
kind of rush—each time it happens."

Peter Tenzer remembers that Sally's motherliness sparked
such feelings in him early on. But while Sally recalls moments
of savoring Peter in his paternal role, once he came home and
accepted it, she didn't really experience until later the heightened emotion and closeness that come with seeing one's
spouse's continued development through parenthood.

"The new Peter" did not really materialize for years, not until Amy was ten years old and Samantha was four and a half. Sally was then immersed in getting her master's degree.

Until that time, Peter's paternal role had been just that—a role, the traditional one of father as provider. He had excelled at it. His career as an organizational consultant to large corporations provided more than enough financial support to his family. His success, however, hinged on his being on the road much of the time, which considerably limited the amount of emotional support he was able to give Sally or contribute to the family as a whole.

So Sally continued to see him pretty much as she always had—a bright, inventive, energetic professional; a husband who was "never boring" but who, unfortunately, was also almost never home. Since she was doing nearly all the parenting, while also holding down a succession of jobs, her perceptions of Peter were unleavened by signs of his fatherliness, of those new and endearing nurturing qualities that invigorate and cement a relationship. She often felt angry with him, in those days, as they went their separate ways, leading the parallel lives that so many commuter marriages become. Her determination to get a business degree was spurred on by her desire to become self-supporting. The Tenzers' marriage was in trouble again—but this time it was Sally who wanted out.

And Peter did not want her to leave. It was partly to preserve their marriage and partly because, with Sally's hectic graduate school schedule, there was simply no other way to keep their home from collapsing into chaos that he took a plunge into homemaking and childrearing. Peter, while consulting full tilt, was now also fathering full time when he was home, finding baby sitters, doctors, dentists; chauffering and cleaning up after the kids and helping them with schoolwork. Every weekend he would cook a week's worth of meals so that when Sally came home from school each day she had only to take that night's dinner out of the freezer.

And, along with the hands-on management of what Peter likes to call "the taxi and feeding service we run here," he consistently tried to give his daughters the attention, tenderness, and everything else that goes into moment-to-moment parenting. "The kids and I got a lot closer," he says. Sally's recognition that this was taking place reawakened her faith in their marriage, renewed her love for Peter, brought them closer. "I finally felt that we were really in this together and he was trying to understand some of the things that had irritated and upset me for so long. He was providing emotional support, and he hadn't been very good at that before." The new Peter had emerged—and new hope for their marriage.

"That whole period was good for me, too," Peter says, "because I began to understand how crazy parenting is. Managing children and a household is endless, and you keep having to do things all over again. It frustrated me, because I spend my professional life trying to help people make things systematic, and here we have a system that's totally random. The complexity of what women go through in managing a household, that became clear to me in those three years. In some ways it's more complex than a business. You have randomness in business, but you have some sense of control. You know if the economy's going up or down or if some of your customers are getting in trouble or if suppliers are out on strike. You can see that. But at three o'clock in the afternoon when someone's supposed to pick your child up at three-ten and they call and say they're not coming? It was that kind of thing that helped me understand how crazy the whole thing is."

And so just as Sally felt her commitment to Peter strengthened by his efforts to achieve this understanding, Peter found that his new insights enhanced his appreciation of and devotion to her.

No Strain, No Gain?

Let's return for a moment with Roberta Friedman to her first hours, days, weeks of motherhood. The presence of the new baby in the life she and Stan had shared shattered forever the exclusivity of their marital relationship. But at the same time, as Roberta immediately became aware, David added to their potential as a couple, because he brought out, right before

Roberta's eyes, Stan's passion for fathering, a paternal instinct that astonished her because she had seen no sign of it before in her "reserved" husband.

Her exhilaration at watching portrait after living portrait of father and child, seeing the new side of her husband emerge and flourish, recharged her love for him. But at the same time she felt "sort of cheated."

"The two things were mutually exclusive, almost," she recalled. "I was thrilled that he was involved and demonstrative and affectionate and so clearly overjoyed to have this child. But I was jealous, because I really needed him then. I was home with the child all day and a lot of nights when he was working, and when he did come home he was absolutely exhausted; all the attention he could work up went to the baby. I was thrilled to see this, but I wasn't thrilled that he had almost zero energy and attention left over for me."

Roberta no longer remembers exactly how she got over feeling like an outsider, looking in on the little father-son club that, even as it excluded her, made Stan all the more attractive to her. "But I do remember," she says, "immediately having to talk about how I felt. To Stan. And somehow things got worked out, because things changed for the better after that. Obviously, Stan's behavior must have changed. He must have consciously included me, asking me to come over. It may have been as simple as that, but it was fine, because I knew he was making an effort to respond to me. And we became a unit, the three of us, rather than them over there and me over here."

The baby's arrival had created a small hurdle in the Friedmans' relationship, but instead of becoming a roadblock, it helped them move closer together, strengthening their bond. It was, as Stan put it, the first of the thousands of "episodes" a couple with children encounter that "provide a common experience which either cements or breaks apart your relationship. And you know you're not alone in this event or this emotional state, whatever it is, good or bad, so that builds up; it's like a brick in the wall of your relationship each time you have something like that."

It seems, from the Friedmans' experience, that just as the conflicts within each parent can lead to individual growth, the conflicts that arise *between* two people through childrearing can cause their relationship to mature. But is it scientifically sound to say that couple development is propelled by the same process as individual development? The psychologist Philip A. Cowan, in an essay entitled "Becoming a Father: A Time for Change, An Opportunity for Development," wrote that, although the behavioral sciences have not yet come up with "a specialized language" for spelling out how two people can grow together, "it seems perfectly appropriate to describe a mature couple . . . in much the same terms we would use to describe an individual."[2]

Through the Becoming a Family Project, a longitudinal study of the effects on couples of having a first child, and the book based on the study, *When Parents Become Partners*, Philip Cowan and his wife, Carolyn Pape Cowan, have become perhaps the leading authorities on the ways in which parenthood makes or breaks relationships. In his essay, Cowan expressed his regret that research reveals far more about the "breaking" end of the spectrum than the "making" end, and he offered an explanation for the omission. Although "there are reasonably good instruments for assessing problems and stress . . . we lack clear concepts of what developmental change should look like, and we lack instruments for assessing when that change has occurred."

And then—as if to say, "Instruments, shminstruments, here's what I know in my guts"—he theorized (building on foundations laid by Piaget, among others) that "disequilibrium" of the sort generated by childrearing may, in fact, be a prerequisite to their maturing as a couple.

"Although we tend to assume that even short-term increases in internal or interpersonal conflict are undesirable," he wrote, "perhaps these conflicts serve a function of helping to reorganize the family to cope with the needs of both children and parents."

Furthermore, the frustration that parents may feel at having to invest in childrearing so much of the energy that used to go into the couple relationship may itself enrich the relationship. Parents who are able to assuage this frustration by taking the long view, recognizing that their marital needs (the need for privacy, for uninterrupted time together) will not forever be usurped by their children's needs, tend to experience a palliative "change in their expectations and a redefinition of what is necessary for a satisfactory marriage at this time of life."

(Humor appears to be essential in both acquiring and maintaining this perspective. One couple, for instance, jokes about nicknaming their baby C.I.—for coitus interruptus.)

Cowan, while "not trying . . . to turn every disaster into a triumph," clearly feels that "stress can lead to growth" and that "using the disequilibration of the transition as an opportunity for development" can go a long way toward preventing that other outcome of stress, "family dissolution."

But since "disequilibration" hardly stops at the end of the first three years, known as "transition to parenthood," the opportunities for growth through stress go on throughout the far less frequently investigated years of parenting that follow, as Terry Eicher confirmed in his dissertation on fathers of daughters.

Many of the fathers Terry interviewed, like the mothers and fathers I interviewed, have children who are teenagers or older, so their experiences expand on those documented in "transition to parenthood" studies. They describe both the transforming effects of becoming parents and the transformations that occur throughout the entire course of parenthood.

Terry's research, then, provides a partial response to Cowan's proposal that there should be studies of developmental changes in parents "as their children proceed through the explorations of toddlerhood, the anxieties of entering school, the agonies of adolescence, and the uncertainties of beginning families of their own."

Terry's subjects provided ample evidence of the long-range applicability of Cowan's theory. Father after father described to Terry the "mixed bag" effect of parenthood on marriage. "It's as if they bring us together *and* pull us apart," one of his subjects said,[3] echoing the Tenzers' contention that their children put pressure on their relationship but at the same time were responsible for its survival, and Melinda Stern's observation that parenthood has "brought friction" to her marriage even as it gives her and her husband "something to share."

"The simultaneous centrifugal and centripetal forces at work over the course of . . . marriage (and in the course of any one moment)" can themselves, Terry suggested, push a relationship forward through time and over time, solidifying it, helping it survive, "in defiance of the laws of physics, which do not appear to bear on human relationships."[4]

Melinda Stern showed me exactly how this phenomenon occurs when she described a recent children-related "crisis" in her marriage. "Jerry always gets to do what he has to do, and I'm here. There are so many women who say the same thing; I have a conversation with my friend and we say, Wouldn't it be nice if you could get your teeth cleaned without having to figure out what to do with the kids? I mean, Jerry just goes and gets his teeth cleaned. But for me it's a big thing. What do I do with the kids?

"There are plenty of meetings I've wanted to go to that I skipped, but when I got elected to the board of our temple, I told Jerry, 'This is the deal. The meeting's the second Monday of every month.' And he said, 'I think I have something the second Monday.' But he checked and it was the third Monday, so I said, 'Good. I'll be here for you on the third Monday, and you'll be here for me on the second Monday. Deal?' He said okay.

"All last week I kept reminding him, but on Sunday night he said, 'I'm on call tomorrow.' I reminded him of my meeting. And he said, 'Well, when I'm on call, I'm on call. Sorry.' I was furious. He had screwed up! I had given him ample notice.

"And then he said something that just made me out of my mind. He said, 'If it was really important to you, you should've called my secretary to check my schedule.' I said, 'Excuse me? I'm your wife. I'm not a patient.' And I really let him have it.

"I guess I got through to him, because this morning he was sitting here with his calendar and he said, 'When are your meetings?' It seems he got the message, and I consider that a real victory. He's trying to accommodate me. And that's great!"

Melinda recognizes that this one resolution does not, of

course, a great relationship make. Development as a couple is cumulative, the product of resolving incidents and issues that never stop arising.

As Roberta Friedman put it, "Having kids forces you to face issues you wouldn't otherwise have faced. Methods of discipline and the best way to bring the world to these people you've brought into the world. Who drops off, who picks up? Who does just about everything? Issues of time and space. There's never enough of either."

And, as Melinda Stern suggested in a postscript to her story, what we learn about dealing with each other through weathering conflicts *with* our children can be as constructive as the conflicts that arise because of them. "When I saw that Jerry was trying to accommodate my schedule," she said, "I thought, 'Now I have to reward that.' Just as I do with the kids. I've learned in dealing with the kids that the way to success is praising what they do that's good instead of dwelling on what's bad. That probably works the same way with grown-ups you have to deal with, especially the grown-up you're married to!"

Maybe, Melinda joked, there should be a book called *Bringing Up Your Spouse.*

Another Take on Altruism

Of everything we learn from childrearing that could be directly translatable into what we might call relationship-rearing, putting someone else first is the most significant. It is undeniable that parenting can, like no other pursuit, awaken the other-centeredness in us. As Peter Tenzer put it, "On the whole, kids pull the egoism away from you and you can become less egoistic in general." And Sally jumped right into the discussion with "I think it goes another step. It moves out into society. You nurture them and then you want to nurture others, to give of yourself, to make donations, volunteer . . ."

"But does this altruism," I asked, "rub off onto your relationship with each other? Have your children contributed to your relationship by making you as generous, giving, nurturing *of each other* as you are of them and of society?"

Silence.

The Tenzers, remember, had faced a crisis on this very issue. Sally, once she decided to quit her job and "stay home" with her children, had become what could only be called hyperactive in her community.

The problem was that Sally's altruism did not, in fact, spill over into her relationship with Peter. On the contrary, her concern and involvement with both her children's and the world's well-being left her little time, energy, or willingness to be as concerned and involved with the well-being of Peter or of their marriage.

"I began feeling neglected," Peter said. "There was a period when her volunteerism was taking probably forty hours a week. And then there were the kids. Basically, I felt a lot of the time I was coming home to nothing."

At this point I mentioned something that had particularly impressed me in Philip Cowan's essay. His measure of the success of a relationship harked back to Freud's view of individual growth as the progression toward balancing the egoistic and altruistic sides of the personality. A relationship can be said to develop positively, or to mature, when it helps to promote each partner's ability to be autonomous and to connect with the other partner. This "challenge of coordinating individuality and mutuality" is, as Cowan put it, "the overarching issue for couples."

The Tenzers couldn't have agreed more. Peter, they both thought, had managed the balancing act better than Sally. His years of being the involved parent while Sally went to school and then took a job that required a long commute had made him more nurturing. He brought this nurturing to the relationship, giving of himself, satisfying Sally's emotional needs even as Sally devoted more of herself to satisfying the children's and the community's needs. Peter sustained Sally while she sustained the kids and her organizations.

Now that the volunteerism crisis has let up somewhat—as Sally's terms of office in several organizations ran out, she did not renew them—she is "there more" for Peter. "I made him lunch the other day," she jokes. "He almost fell over."

The fact that he was around at lunchtime indicates another way in which they are attempting to balance their give-and-take. Peter's frustration at his wife's absenteeism was undoubtedly exacerbated by his own absenteeism. His job left him so little time at home that when he did manage to be there, he wanted Sally to be there, too. It could even be said that Sally exaggerated her community roles because she resented that Peter was away so much.

Recently, Peter has been cutting down on his traveling, finding clients closer to home, arranging to work more from his home office than from his clients' offices. "This has been really important to us," he said, "as a couple. I mean, here I am today. Other fathers are gone."

And he and Sally have found mutual outlets for the remarkable energy and need for self-expression they have always had in common. Sally has become enamored of potting, originally Peter's hobby. Everywhere in their house are Peter's high-fired stoneware and the bowls and plates on which Sally has painted flowers from their gardens.

The Tenzers have vacationed periodically without their daughters because, as Peter explained, "there's so much of a focus on the family relationship that you have to go back and sort of renew a relationship without all that. And that's been important."

But it is the family relationship, both he and Sally emphasized, that is the primary source of their increasing cohesion—and, yes, even coherence—as a couple. Most of their time together does include their two daughters, and how it is spent is determined largely by the children's needs and interests, not their own.

It could be said that the Tenzers are the perfect example of "the family that plays together, stays together." But their wholeness is more than the sum of their family activities, and has grown from more than investing in their relationship the altruistic outlook and behavior they've each acquired from the parenting process. The bottom line is Peter's observation that "no matter what the issues are between the two of us, I think both of our concerns always, above all, have to do with providing the best for the kids."

It's as if each one, in getting into the children, has found the other in the process. Peter may not always feel that Sally is fulfilling his emotional needs; she may not always feel "happily married" for any number of reasons. But their relationship derives sustenance from what they've created together through their mutual giving of themselves to their children.

I was struck that the word "sacrifice" never came up in my discussions with the Tenzers. Although on a micro-level, as Peter might say, "giving" might be construed as giving up things, they're both clearly focused on the macro-level, which, from Peter's point of view, the last time I spoke with him, was symbolized by the imminent arrival of twenty-five of his older daughter's summer camp friends for a Thanksgiving weekend reunion.

"My first thought was, twenty-five? Why couldn't it be fifteen? How are we going to handle a mob like that?" he said. But he knew that he and Sally would pull out all the stops because it was important to their daughter. They always pull out all the stops; Sally has taught him how to do that. Sally may not gratify his every need at any given moment, but he feels consistently gratified in a larger sense by having been drawn into the nurturing environment she has built around them in response to the kids' requirements. He has been sustained by the creativity and hospitality she expends on cultivating their common ground, their family—from serving not just tea to an afternoon visitor, but tea with homemade blueberry muffins served on their best china at a beautifully laid-out table, to their lavish holiday celebrations (sometimes the two of them spend days in the kitchen, cooking and preparing), to the impending house party for twenty-five teenagers.

This particular conversation with Peter ended because he had to run out and meet Sally. They were going to a parent-teacher meeting at Amy's school.

I remembered a word Sally had once used for parenthood —the "crucible." It has certainly been that for the Tenzers. But now I understood a lot better why their children have also been their salvation.

IX

Everlasting Impressions

The love between parents and children is unceasing, never ceases, but everything changes and takes on new forms.
—KÄTHE KOLLWITZ

WE RECEIVE CLUES from the very beginning. There I was, basking in the early light of parenthood, so caught up in the moment that the first clue was meaningless to me, the sadness in the response of elderly people to my baby, to me and my baby. "Enjoy it!" was the counsel, followed by the inevitable warning: "It all goes by so fast."

One evening when Jonathan was not quite a year old I brought him with me to a lecture by the Reverend William Sloane Coffin, who noticed the baby immediately. (This was not surprising, since Jonathan was the only one in the crowd wearing diapers.) "Ah!" the minister said, stooping to admire my son, "nothing makes you feel your own decline like the sunny ripening of a young child!" He said this with a merry grin and a half chuckle. There was no trace of sadness in his voice or on his face, but there was sorrow in his words, and truth as well.

At the time, I was so taken with Reverend Coffin's eloquence—"sunny ripening"—in capturing the charm of a healthy baby that I didn't think beyond it. But the remark stuck with me as I considered the process of parenthood, its development over time.

My husband and I, latecomers to the early parenthood scene, used to joke that when Jonathan began losing his teeth, we'd probably be losing ours, too. This has not happened so far, although Jonathan just did a thorough job of losing his first tooth. (It went down with his tuna fish sandwich. The Tooth Fairy found this note under his pillow: "Der Toth Fare, You wil find my toth in my stummek.")

But all parents, even those who are far younger than we are, sometimes think of their own aging as their children come of age, of their "decline" paralleling the "ripening" of their children. All parents occasionally feel the weight of their "paradoxical goal." We bond with our babies so that within the trusting relationship they can absorb from us all that they need to leave us and survive on their own. We try to give them, in their state of dependence, the means to be independent. Our love, from the beginning, is tinged with the knowledge and fear of impending loss, because our ultimate ambition as parents is to send an autonomous human being into the world, bearing more of us than our name, perhaps, but an individual in his own right, his own person.

We know from the start that just as our child will separate from us, we will separate from our child and stand on our own, be ourselves alone again. We know that for a child this process is never complete. Our children will leave home, but home will never leave them. (Do any of us, after all, ever totally shed our own parents' presence? I'm haunted by the image that closes *Anna Freud*, by Elizabeth Young-Bruehl: the old, ailing Anna Freud sitting in her wheelchair in a London park, huddled in, embraced by, the carefully preserved greatcoat of her father, who had been dead for forty-three years.)

And some of us sense that for us as parents it's the same

story. No matter where our children are, they will always remain part of who we are. Kate Robicheau recalls never having had a firm vision of where her life was heading until the birth of her first son. "And then," she says, "I knew for the first time who I would be in ten years, in fifteen years. In ten years I would be the mother of a ten-year-old, in fifteen years I would be the mother of a fifteen-year-old . . ." I remember having similar thoughts even before Jonathan was born. Early in my pregnancy, I realized, and kept telling myself, that I would never really be alone again.

Stephen Spender crystallized what Kate and I presaged in his poem "To My Daughter":

> Bright clasp of her whole hand around my finger
> My daughter, as we walk together now.
> All my life I'll feel a ring invisibly
> Circle this bone with shining: when she is grown
> Far from today as her eyes are far already.

Nothing could capture more beautifully the miracle, the weight, and the permanence of parenthood than that symbol of the ring shining invisibly. And yet this image is incomplete as, indeed, are our projections into our future as parents. What does never *really* being alone again *really* mean? Who will this future mother of a ten-year-old and then of a fifteen-year-old be?

What we don't understand, not for a long time at least, is that the ring does not just "circle this bone"; it is part of it. Even as our children absorb our parenting, we absorb parenting them. Just as they internalize our values, tastes, habits, and interests, we internalize whatever wisdom we've gleaned from guiding them and from our attempts to resolve the conflicts that rearing them has produced within us and around us. Each period of their development is an interplay of progress and regression for them and for us. As they grow, so do we. And although we may anticipate the sense of loss we'll experience later, envisioning our children's independence, when that moment actually arrives we may find ourselves contemplating how much we've gained and still stand to gain.

It may well be true, in a physical sense and even psychologically, that "nothing makes you feel your own decline like the sunny ripening of a young child." But perhaps, over the long haul, "ripening" describes what happens to parents as well as children. It can mitigate the signs of decline we anticipate or do, in fact, experience.

In his dissertation on fathers of daughters, Terry Eicher expanded on Bruno Bettelheim's observation that it may take years for parents to know what has hit them. "The full meaning of [having children]," Terry wrote, "develops over time and does not erupt full-formed upon or even soon after . . . birth, which has been until now the major node of interest in [research on] fathers."[1]And, of course, in research on mothers.

Nothing in our entire life experience quite matches the drama of the early years of parenthood, when we are still close to the line of demarcation between our former selves and our parental selves and are keenly attuned to both the positive and negative changes our new role has wrought. But perhaps it is only later, when insight is enriched by hindsight, during what we've been conditioned to think of as the waning years of parenthood that we come to know the full extent to which our children have helped us expand our selves.

The Myth of the Empty Nest

Sally and Peter Tenzer see their efforts to travel together without their children and to collaborate on non-child-related projects—gardening, making pottery—as an investment in their future as a couple, the behavioral equivalent of money in the bank. "We're creating options for us when the kids are gone," Peter said. "I mean, we're not kidding when we talk about moving to Hawaii or something . . ."

"Not that we're sure we'll have enough income by then to do it," Sally added, "but our vision is to take advantage of that freedom when the kids are out of the house. Because now we're not really as free as we'd like to be sometimes. But when we're fifty-two, fifty-three, when Samantha's gone, I'm hoping we can do that. It's important. But at the same time I think they'll still need us and we'll need them and I just hope we'll have enough money or be close enough that we'll be able to make that happen."

What Sally intuits—that this two-way need will outlive their children's separation from them and in many ways lessen its impact—Roberta and Stan Friedman have experienced now that twenty-four-year-old David and twenty-two-year-old Mark are living half a continent away. Yes, there is the "freedom" Sally anticipates. "There's so much more time for each other," Roberta said. "In the evening you don't have kids with the TV on, you don't have kids with homework to do, you're not picking up from soccer and delivering to whatever. When we're home at night, even when we're absorbed in our own things, there is a sense of our own bond that's less fragmented. We're aware of that. We happen to be very physical, so if I'm painting up in my studio and Stan's downstairs, I'll walk down, give him a hug, and walk back up again. And he'll do the same thing. We didn't do that as much when the kids were around, although we were demonstrative."

But along with the liberating aspects of postdeparture parenthood came "the big surprise," as Roberta put it, of finding "how much of your time you're still spending on them, how they're still present in one form or another on a daily basis even if it's passive."

When Stan disagreed, maintaining that he's not as preoccupied with his sons as he was when they were home—"I don't, for instance, find it as unsettling as Roberta does that the kids haven't found mates, because when they do come up with women, that could be even more unsettling"—Roberta became slightly indignant, pointing out that at this very moment, for instance, Stan had on his desk "this little pile of stuff for Mark, this little pile of stuff for David." And what about the fact that every time he sees a good buy at the music store, he snaps it up for one of the boys? And what about his calling one or the other of them three times a day when that son is having a problem? "I rest my case," she said.

"But that doesn't mean I'm still defining myself as a parent," Stan insisted. "I'm acting that way, but I'm not thinking about it as such. I'm just doing what comes naturally."

"That's the whole point," Roberta said. "You just are that way. You've become that way." She went on to define what "that way" implies, comparing her situation with that of her sister, who is in a far earlier stage of parenthood. It is a period reputed to be more intense—and it is, Roberta thinks, but only in the sense that the action is unremitting. "My sister calls me up and she's worried about where she's going to put her kid in seventh grade, but I'm just as worried about my kids—whether they're going to have jobs for the rest of their lives and who they're going to marry and are they going to have kids? These are serious issues. Things get more and more difficult. Nothing is resolved. We're not out of the woods. There's a potential for more serious conflicts. I do feel settled with the two of us, but there's something in the background, as if I'm waiting for the other shoe to fall. That's how I feel all the time—as if I'm still parenting, and pretty actively, because I really am."

In some ways, Roberta looks back on her sons' earliest years as easier years. Not that there weren't problems—the problem in week one, for instance, of being simultaneously enamored by and jealous of Stan's rapture with the new baby. No point along the parental continuum could be said to be trouble-free. And no two parents (even ones who are a team) experience a given stage with any of their children in exactly the same way.

But from the vantage point of late parenthood, the earlier years often do seem to have posed, if not fewer dilemmas, at least less onerous ones. From this vantage point it is particularly difficult to understand why so much that is written on parenthood concerns the early years as opposed to all the other ones, a bias that has created a lacuna in the literature the size of the Grand Canyon.

One exception is Therese Benedek, who observed that, although one may think that a child's acquisition of language would facilitate the parent-child interaction, in fact it works the other way around. The ability to verbalize does not necessarily bring with it a willingness to communicate. The child's growing independence often compromises the growing ability to communicate, especially with the parents.

To Roberta—and she is far from alone in this observation —there are never happy endings to any parent-child story, at least not for long. The plot just thickens as parents and children grow older. And older. Roberta described, for example, the recent travails of a friend, the grandmother of six, who was "a wreck" over having to deal with her two children going through divorces at the same time.

Adding to the complexity of the issues we face as we and our children struggle toward maturity is the corollary of our children's having declared their independence. "Now," Roberta said, "even if the kids consult with us, they don't necessarily follow our advice!"

But there is an upside to this increasing pressure. Roberta hit on it when I asked what she and Stan would be like without children. "Stale is the word that comes to my mind," she said. "It's the difference between: Can you lie in bed all day, or do you have to keep getting up every five minutes? With children, you keep getting up every five minutes. You have one thing after another, a school thing or a sports thing or some sort of emotional trauma or whatever that keeps you from that staleness. Children stimulate, they provoke, they keep things perking."

"And now that they're not right there in the house?" I asked, remembering a comment Stan once made about feeling "older" without the daily, invigorating presence of his sons.

"It's very common for me to call my children in the middle of the day, from work," Roberta said. "And I think about them all the time. So does Stan. Don't you?"

"Yes," said Stan, "but I don't call them from work."

It turned out that the children's ability to "stimulate, provoke, keep things perking" sometimes may even be greater at long distance. When Mark was in a hockey accident two years ago—the day after his parents got home from one of their visits with him and his brother—"it made me crazy," Roberta said. "We didn't know anything about it till it was all over."

"Till we got the bill for the CAT scan of his brain," Stan added.

"That's a weird feeling for a parent," Roberta said. "If you think of your little Jonathan—I'm not sure it's all that different if it happens when your child's grown and living somewhere else."

In fact, she thinks, it may be harder. Once our children are living on their own, we're not right there with them. We're not in control—or not as much as we once were. We can't kiss it and make it better. But we still want to.

And therein lies the poignancy and the pain of late parenthood and its power over us.

There's more. There's a sense, Roberta told me, of still watching grown kids grow. "It's a very funny feeling," she said. "It's not as if they're getting taller, but I see changes in them, in their faces. They're getting to look more like men; they're becoming men. It's very touching. I'm very moved, seeing this."

That the Friedmans are still, in the wonderful words of the single mother Laura Cerciello, "present for the parenting," even in their children's absence, comes from more than force of habit, more than the weight of parental responsibility, more than the impulses of love.

What is going on was suggested in a casually delivered but loaded comment from the mother of two "off-the-wall" teenagers: "If it weren't for the Bond," she said, "I would've killed them by now."

She meant, of course, the much-researched miracle that occurs between parent and infant in their first moments and days and months together, the transaction by which they become fused, each gratifying the needs of the other, each building trust (the child becoming confident of being cared for, the parent becoming confident of being able to care for the child).

But it is not as if this magical connection just happens—and then sits there, grand, rich, immutable, and available as the one source of solace and strength to draw from every time our relations with our children resemble detachment more than attachment. There is not just the Bond and then the rest of parenthood for which the Bond is the balm.

There is no doubt that the initial magic lasts. "The Krazy Glue effect," one of my friends calls it. But it is not the be-all and end-all. It is followed and, optimally, enriched by all the interactions between parents and children through which they attempt to resolve the kinks in their relationship created by internal and external events and through which they progress, growing closer.

The Bond is negotiated throughout the course of parenthood. And it is the innumerable subsequent bonding experiences or incidents (which reflect, as Benedek reminds us, that original big bond), some of them so swift and minute that we hardly notice them, that in their aggregate form the core of our constantly evolving parental selves.

The accumulation of all that the Friedmans have gained from parenthood, all that they have internalized and added to their individual and mutual selves through parenting—what Spender evoked in the ring that shines invisibly—motivates their continuing responsiveness to their children.

This psychological lodestar makes long-distance parenting as formative as any previous period in their history with their children. They're still feeding their children's confidence, if only by their children's awareness of their undiminished attachment and interest. And their children, in signaling back their successes and failures, tell their parents that they still matter, nourishing their self-esteem, even though their advice may go unheeded, even though they may feel powerless to heal and soothe as they could long ago. They are still valued. They have not become obsolete. That's what counts. That's what "keeps things perking."

A few years from now, Sally and Peter Tenzer will find that their pottery and travel plans, the options they're creating "for us when the kids are gone," will not be their sole or primary source of development as individuals or as a couple. It will not be only the interests they've cultivated apart from their children that will keep them psychologically alive, but all that they've gleaned through cultivating their children. Their separate undertakings may contribute to their sense of fulfillment, but it's what they've done and will continue to do together as parents that will keep them from feeling that their nest has emptied.

The emotional wealth they've earned and stored up

through parenting is, by their own admission, what has brought them to the point that they're still here, together, planning their future. It may also ensure that their future remains as formative for them as their past.

Grandparenthood

"It all goes by so fast." And parents tend, with each passing stage, to look back on previous ones with growing nostalgia. Jeffrey Lustman, reminiscing from his vantage point as the father of a ten-year-old and a fourteen-year-old, says, "What I miss is the physicality of it. When I would hold them I had a sense of well-being that I wished would never end; like, I don't want this hug to ever stop. And I can remember in the middle of the night when my daughter was a newborn and I'd have the TV on because she'd fallen asleep on me and I couldn't go back to sleep. I could put her back down, but I put it off because it just felt so good."

As the gap between then and now widens, we struggle to retain such memories. And should our memory falter, suggests Susan Millen, whose son and daughter are now young adults, we might turn to the family albums or turn on the home movies and videos. "I know how much I enjoyed my children," she says, "how observant I was, how amazed I was by the things they were doing. And it's interesting how certain pictures bring back the exact sense of all that, how it felt. We have a wonderful picture of Todd sitting on a balcony with a butterfly and I remember watching the wonder in his eyes as he held the butterfly. I have a lot of those kinds of memories. I can remember sitting outside when he was doing high jumps and just looking at his body—he must have been about seven—and marveling at his development, at his muscles working.

"That's why pictures are really important. That's why I go back often and look at early pictures. And movies. We have a movie of our kids and about four other kids at the beach, and I was dancing with them. The kids must have been about four, five. I was getting great joy out of them, and I watch this and say to myself, 'I really did do fun stuff with them and I was happy and they were happy.' I enjoy watching those scenes and remembering."

Then Susan exclaims, "I can't wait to be a grandmother!"

Grandparenthood, Susan thinks, will enhance her memories by providing a new and appreciative audience for the family photos and films—"Oh, look! Here's your mom when she was just your age!"—as well as all the stories that form our unwritten treasure troves of family history, folklore, and, often enough, myth. But Susan suspects that there will be more to grandparenthood than that. She looks forward to reliving, not merely remembering, many aspects and moments of active parenting.

This romantic notion, shared by millions of would-be grandparents, does reflect reality. The standard line from grandparents is something like "It's just like being a parent again!" "But," the observer inevitably adds, "without all the responsibility." Many a rapturous description of a day with the grandchildren ends on a relieved note (as in "And then they go home!"). In a *New York Times* piece, Morris Wessel (until his recent retirement one of the few pediatricians in America who still made house calls) recalled being awakened at two A.M. by his infant granddaughter's cries and then falling asleep again to the reassuring sounds of his son and daughter-in-law soothing the baby.

"Reassuring" is the key word here—and not just in the sense that sleepless nights are not usually among the aspects of parenthood that grandparents relive. More important—vital, in fact, to the psychology of grandparenthood—is the reassurance of seeing one's children be good parents. "It's their problem, not mine!" Wessel wrote of his granddaughter's parents. "And," he might have added, "I know they can handle it."

Personal essays like Wessel's constitute the bulk of the literature on grandparenthood. Research on grandparenthood's influence on personality development is almost nonexistent. Yet grandparents who have been moved to write about their feelings offer evidence that the effects of grandparenthood go far beyond making our nostalgia tangible. Grandparenthood, in reconnecting us with our parental roots, revives parenthood's potential to make us become, as Jeffrey Lustman put it, more truly who we are. It is not a mere postscript to parenthood. It can be a significant source of fresh opportunities for developmental progress.

"I place a high priority on being a parent," Morris Wessel wrote, "and seeing my son repeating this role with obvious pleasure is particularly satisfying." Why? Because the new father's paternal competence tells the new grandfather that he himself must have been a pretty competent parent.

Sidney J. Blatt, chief of psychiatry and psychology at the Yale School of Medicine, was speaking as a devoted grandfather when he said, "I always knew I'd enjoy having grandchildren. But I hadn't anticipated how much pleasure I'd get from seeing my daughters be good mothers. That for me was an incredible experience and still is. What it does is confirm that my wife and I did good jobs as parents. It consolidated a sense that what we had done with our daughters was reasonably successful and worthwhile, that we had communicated our love and concern for them—because they are able to communicate that to their children."

Grandparenthood, therefore, echoes and amplifies parenthood's potential of building self-esteem, and not only by proving the success of our childrearing. "They think we can do everything and anything," Annette Streets, a social worker, says of her four granddaughters. And the consequent "gratification" she and her husband feel revives something of their earliest years of childrearing. "I think it was Bennett," Annette says, "who thought, when he was four years old, that we never slept. Well, he'd go to bed and we'd be awake. And he'd wake up and we'd be awake. He thought we were always up and doing things.

"And when he was eight or nine, he'd see someone and think they were having trouble and he'd say, 'Call my daddy; he could help you.' In fact, at some point, he was handing out Jerry's business cards. In those days he and his sisters thought we were capable of all things. And I feel it's even more so with the grandchildren, because to a certain degree it's unearned. We don't have the daily responsibility for them."

Therese Benedek (who, once again, trod where few researchers have gone in recognizing grandparenthood as a developmental opportunity) evoked her vision of the two-way nature of the bonding process as a model for the psychodynamics of grandparenthood. The response of the grandchild to the nurturing grandmother or grandfather—"a loving glance . . . a trusting hand, an actual appeal for help, a warm, feverish body clinging—whatever it is, for better or for worse . . . is a message conveyed to the grandparent that he or she is needed, wanted, and loved."[2]

And through various responses to this "message," through the ongoing interaction with this new generation, the parent, "newly hatched," as Morris Wessel put it, as a grandparent, continues to grow creatively, spiritually, in any number of ways. Our children, their children, and—if we're really lucky—*their* children continually offer us chances for self-expansion and self-fulfillment right up until, in Benedek's words, "memory is lost and intrapsychic images fade out."

X

From Parent Development to Parent Empowerment

Only the empathic understanding of the ongoing process (be-tween himself and the child) can guide the parent's interaction with the child toward a successful end.
—THERESE BENEDEK, "The Family as a Psychologic Field"

IN ONE of the earliest parenting morality tales on record—a fable dating from the end of the fourth century—a young crab answers his mother's admonition to stop walking so "un-gracefully," to walk "straight forward without twisting from side to side," with this advice: "Pray, mother . . . do but set the example yourself, and I will follow you."

The moral of the story—"Example is the best precept"—is not the only lesson contained in it.

It is striking that the author of this fable had the advice come from the mouth of the baby crab and not from the mother or another grown-up crab.

So one of the oldest aphorisms concerning parenthood—

indeed, one of the biggest clichés in the parenting books—origi-
nated with a child, not a parent. That's something to think
about.

The little crab might well have said—but fabulists can go
only so far—"Because of me, Mom, you're going to become the
first crab in history to walk straight, and then I'll walk straight,
too. Because of me, you will change. You'll improve yourself
and then I'll be able to improve myself. If you learn to walk
gracefully without twisting your body from side to side, so will
I. You'll become a better parent because of me—because listening to me will tell you how to become a better parent."

We've seen how listening to our children—in the broadest
possible sense—can put us in touch with our own childhood
(the better to understand and help them deal with what they are
going through), spark or renew our spiritual selves (the better to
help them retain and cultivate theirs), stir our creativity (the
better to encourage their inventiveness and to be more inventive in parenting them), inspire us to drop bad habits and personality traits and adopt good ones (the better to set that all-
important example in innumerable ways), help us to recover
from loss and trauma (the better to participate fully in each
day's living—and parenting), awaken or reawaken our curiosity
and urge to learn (the better to guide our children intellectually), and, in general, expand our selves (the better to enlarge
our capacity for doing all the things parents have to do in the
average day to make it through to the next day). And so forth.

But above and beyond these special effects—or maybe it
would be better to say within and beneath them—is another
element that, if in place, becomes our personal and familial in-
frastructure. And that is our wholehearted awareness that we are
walking straighter, so to speak, and more gracefully, because of
having children. Simply—although sometimes it's not so simple
—realizing how our children can help us reach our full potential
as people puts us well on the way to realizing our full potential
as parents.

It is, finally, through acknowledging everything we gain
from bringing up our children, through articulating (to ourselves, at least) just how our children enhance our lives, that we

empower ourselves to be more effective parents. Because this appreciation permeates each interaction with our children. It makes us truly "present for the parenting."

"With the single exception of the child's natural endowment," Bruno Bettelheim wrote in *A Good Enough Parent*, "nothing shapes a child's personality more than the experience of family living—the feelings it arouses and the attitudes it inculcates . . . If his parents—despite . . . the real difficulties that are part of everybody's life—are essentially well satisfied . . . their contentment will form the firm basis for a deeply satisfying relation to their child . . . As his parents rejoice . . . in his well-being, or share their worries about it, the child becomes convinced of his importance and great value to them; on this basis, he develops his convictions about his own value as a person."

In February 1994 the whole world was treated to a heart-stopping image of what the "essentially well-satisfied" parent looks like: the speed skater Dan Jansen, moments after accepting his Olympic gold medal in the 1000-meter race, gliding euphorically around that rink in Lillehammer, Norway, with his nine-month-old daughter, Jane, in his arms.

Winning the gold medal was of almost unimaginable importance to Jansen; he had promised his dying sister that he would win it. He had competed in seven Olympic speed skating races since 1984, but never won the gold medal. And as recently as three days before this victory—when he lost the 500-meter race—he thought the gold would elude him again, for good. This was his final Olympics. And then he won the 1000-meter —the last race in his last Olympics. His joy was palpable in his every move, his every look. And it was shared by everyone who watched.

But by including his daughter (who is named after his sister) in his moment of victory, by holding up his baby, and not just his medal, for all the world to see, Jansen alluded to something surpassing even this enormous personal and professional triumph, something with which most of the people who watched could identify even more. Here, Jansen seemed to be saying as he skated around with "the new Jane," as his wife called their baby, is something of infinite value. Compared with this, the value of everything else, including the gold medal, is finite.

And the following week, Jansen came right out with it. In an interview with Tom Brokaw he described his feelings the morning after he lost the 500-meter. He and his wife woke up, he said, and "the way we were situated, Jane had to sleep in a crib right next to us and—we watched her wake up. And she peeks her little head up and looks over and gives us a big smile." Jansen thought about losing the race—in the light of being here with his wife, sharing their enchantment with their daughter— "And I said, 'You know, who cares?' "

As I write, I'm interrupted by a call from the parent-volunteer coordinator at my son's school. She is reminding me that this Wednesday is my day to spend the hours from eleven to three helping out during recess or gym or in a classroom or in the office (as I had agreed to do at the beginning of the year, five long months ago).

It occurs to me that I need this opportunity to bond with my child's school as much as I need another snow day. (This winter, Connecticut has become a suburb of Siberia.) I have a lot of work to do.

Wednesday rolls around. I drive to the school, buoying my spirits by playing my "Billboard Top R&B Hits of 1965" tape. Loudly. (Ironically, the first thing I hear is "Rescue Me.")

I report for duty at the office. My worst fear—that I will spend four hours stuffing envelopes or stapling—is dispelled. The science teacher needs help. Jonathan is crazy about this woman and, consequently, about science, so I am pleased with my assignment: going through a large box of lesson plans and filing them according to subject—fish, birds, rocks, weather . . . This is fun, although the decibel level in the room, populated at the moment by about a dozen seventh-graders badly in need of an exercise break, exceeds that of my rhythm-and-blues blast and is giving me a headache.

The class is over. The room empties. The teacher throws on her coat and scarf and rushes out to supervise recess. A few minutes later the door creaks open. Jonathan, bundled in his snowsuit, tiptoes in and gives me an is-this-all-there-is? look. "Where's the class?" he wants to know.

"They left. I'm just here, working."

"What're you doing?" Apparently he expected something more exciting—like his mother the parent volunteer leading a battalion of students on an adventure with Bunsen burners. I explain what I'm doing, and then—remembering the day he got a bathroom pass in order to sneak into the day care room to see his baby cousin—ask whether his teacher knows where he is.

"Yup. She knows."

"Well, shouldn't you be going to recess now?"

"Yup." He stands there grinning, then runs up and gives me a big hug before racing out of the room.

And I go back to sorting out the lesson plans and my thoughts. As it turns out, these hours of doing someone else's work instead of my own are more rewarding than I would have imagined. Above all, I've made Jonathan's day, as well as a major contribution to his self-esteem. There he is right now, outside the window, pressing his nose to it, steaming it up, pointing me out to several other Munchkins in snowsuits. He can hardly contain his glee. Mommy's here. She cares.

She's also learning a lot. That there exists, for instance, a classification of tiny life forms that are crustaceans, not insects, and that do not live in water. Incredible! Because of Jonathan I'm here in a place where I can absorb all sorts of facts and ideas that I'll be able to pass along to him. This is like a trip to the Peabody Museum.

And there's something else. Last night when I told Jonathan I'd be working at his school, his "Oh, goody" was followed by a question. "Mommy, if you're out on the playground when we're having recess and somebody hits me, what would you do?"

"Well, I'd tell the kid not to do that, for sure. And—I don't know; maybe I'd even send him to the principal's office."

"It was a bigger boy."

"Oh? You mean this already happened?" (As if I hadn't guessed.) "Somebody hit you during recess?"

"Yes. He hit me hard. I was crying."

"And what did the teacher do?"

"The teacher just told me to tell him not to do that."

This incident happened "a long time ago," Jonathan told me. Why hadn't he mentioned it before? For the same reason he probably doesn't mention a lot of things that happen at school. No particular reason. He doesn't know why. He guesses he "just forgot."

But now that his mother has said she's going to be at school, he digs up the incident from his memory. He really hadn't forgotten it—because he was bothered, not comforted, by the way the teacher handled it. He was afraid to confront the "bigger boy" who hit him hard enough to make him cry. Jonathan is only six. I believe six-year-olds need a little more help in a situation like this than the teacher offered. And I tell him so—to his obvious relief.

Why did Jonathan bring up this incident now? Simply because I was going to be there. I suppose that by his reasoning, which is so different from my reasoning, he arrived at the hope that if some kid punched him and I was there, I would take a stronger stance than the teacher had taken. Or maybe he simply hoped I'd yell at the boy.

Of course, these hopes didn't pan out. I didn't "do" recess, for one thing. Nor can I set right what happened weeks or months ago. I can't defend Jonathan in retrospect. But I can— and did—bolster his confidence that he was right. He deserved more help than the teacher gave him, and perhaps my backing him up will give him the gumption to demand more help from the nearest available grown-up should any child pick on him again.

If I hadn't agreed to come in to school today, Jonathan might never have let me in on his secret. I wouldn't have had this particular chance to feed his faith in himself. Not to mention this particular chance to show, and not just tell him, how important he is to me. And the chance to pique my curiosity about the natural world, the better to encourage his curiosity.

•   •   •   •

Over my desk hangs a huge bulletin board. I put it up as an organizer for notes, quotes, outlines, all that goes into my writing. But it has become, instead, a catch-all (decidedly disorganized) for everything. Jonathan's drawings and stories. The four-leaf clover I found on our lawn on his first birthday. Shopping lists. A note scribbled by my mother-in-law, who has Alzheimer's disease, that was found among her papers after she was moved to a home for the aged. "I love my sons' pictures," it says, "because photographs Never Grow Old."

There are, of course, plenty of family photos on my bulletin board. And photos of other people's families from magazines and newspapers, including G. Paul Burnett's magical shot of Dan Jansen's triumphant lap around the Olympic rink, a bouquet in one hand, his baby snug in the crook of his other arm, his hair and the child's haloed with gold by the spotlight.

Jansen said later that he was wishing, at the time, that he could take another lap. He wanted to keep that moment going. He wished it would never end. In a way, of course, it will never end. The photographs of it will never grow old. There it is on my bulletin board. The man and his medal, the father and his daughter, are one and the same. Jansen's private life is right up there with his public triumph. He put it there. And in his Olympic moment we see all the millions of other moments, his and ours, that may not glitter but are gold, nonetheless. We see that every one of them is equally worthy of celebration. Because in each of them we can find the means to keep on growing.

Notes

Introduction

1. Erikson, Erik H., *Identity and the Life Cycle* (New York: W. W. Norton, 1980), p. 103.

2. Ibid.

3. Spock, Benjamin, "What We Know About the Development of Healthy Personalities in Children," in *Proceedings of the Midcentury White House Conference on Children and Youth* (Raleigh, N.C.: Health Publications Institute, Inc.), 1951, p. 69.

4. Maslow, Abraham H., *Toward a Psychology of Being* (New York: D. Van Nostrand, 1968), p. 136.

5. Hoffman, Edward, "The Last Interview of Abraham Maslow," *Psychology Today*, January–February 1992, p. 73.

6. Heschel, Abraham Joshua, "The Earth Is the Lord's," in *The Earth Is the Lord's and the Sabbath* (New York: Harper & Row, 1966), p. 9.

I Beyond Jonathan's Lunchbox

1. Eicher, Terry Boyd, "Understanding Fathers of Daughters," unpublished dissertation, Yale University, 1991, p. 368.

2. Ibid., p. 21.

3. Eicher, Terry, and Jesse D. Geller, eds., *Fathers and Daughters: Portraits in Fiction* (New York: Plume, 1991), p. 15.

4. I used the most recent edition of this correspondence as my source: *The Complete Letters of Sigmund Freud to Wilhelm Fliess, 1887–1904*, trans. and ed. by Jeffrey Moussaeieff Masson

(Cambridge: The Belknap Press of Harvard University Press, 1985).

5. Gay, Peter, *Freud: A Life for Our Time* (New York: W. W. Norton, 1988), p. 162.

6. Updike, John, "Grandparenting," *The New Yorker*, February 21, 1994, p. 92.

7. Pruett, Kyle, *The Nurturing Father* (New York: Warner Books, 1987), p. 162.

8. Benedek, Therese, "Parenthood as a Developmental Phase: A Contribution to the Libido Theory," *Journal of the American Psychoanalytic Association*, 1959, 7, pp. 400–1.

II Not Just from Caterpillar to Butterfly

1. Blatt, Sidney J., and Rachel B. Blass, "Relatedness & Self-Definition: A dialectic model of personality development," in G. G. Noam and K. Fischer, eds., *Development and Vulnerability in Relationships* (Hillsdale, N.J.: Lawrence Earlbaum Associates, in press).

2. Benedek, Therese, "The Family as a Psychologic Field," in *Parenthood: Its Psychology and Psychopathology*, p. 114.

3. Blatt and Blass.

4. Erikson, *Identity and the Life Cycle*, p. 102.

5. Ibid., p. 103.

6. Benedek, "The Family as a Psychologic Field," p. 114.

7. Benedek, Therese, "Parenthood as a Developmental Phase: A Contribution to the Libido Theory," *Journal of the American Psychoanalytic Association*, 1959, 7, pp. 400–1.

8. Ibid., p. 399.

9. Eicher, Terry, "Understanding Fathers of Daughters," p. 77.

10. Benedek, "Parenthood as a Developmental Phase," p. 397.

11. Ibid., p. 400.

12. Eicher, Terry, "Understanding Fathers of Daughters," p. 185.

13. Ibid., p. 185.

14. Ibid., p. 193.

III The Spiritual Nature of Parenthood

1. Young-Bruehl, Elisabeth, *Anna Freud: A Biography* (New York: Summit Books, 1988), p. 18.

2. Eicher, Terry, "Understanding Fathers of Daughters," p. 365.

3. Mailer, Norman, *The Prisoner of Sex* (Boston: Little, Brown & Co., 1971), pp. 10–12.

4. This material was suggested by lists of factors affecting paternal behavior in "Historical Perspectives in the Father's Role," by Jonathan Bloom-Feshbach (in *The Father's Role in Child Development*, Michael Lamb, ed. [New York: John Wiley & Sons, 1981]), and in "Understanding Fathers of Daughters" by Terry Eicher.

5. Lewis, Sinclair, *The Job* (New York and London: Harper & Brothers 1917), p. 43.

6. The year 5753 in the Hebrew calendar, which is reckoned according to lunar and solar cycles, began on October 28, 1992, and ended on September 15, 1993.

IV The Healing Nature of Parenthood

1. Fraiberg, Selma, "Ghosts in the Nursery: A Psychoanalytic Approach to the Problems of Impaired Infant-Mother Relationships," *Journal of the American Academy of Child Psychiatry*, 14, 1975, pp. 387–424.

2. Anthony, E. James, "Afterword," in Cath, Stanley H., Alan R. Gurwitt and John Munder Ross, eds., *Father and Child: Developmental and Clinical Perspectives* (Boston: Little, Brown, 1982), p. 571.

3. Fraiberg, pp. 397, 398.

V Creativity

1. I am indebted for this material to Professor William W. Hallo. For a more detailed analysis of Enheduanna's blending of literal with literary conception, see *The Exaltation of Inanna*,

William W. Hallo and J. J. A. van Dijk (New Haven: Yale University Press, 1968), p. 61.

2. Freud, Sigmund, *The Interpretation of Dreams* (New York: Basic Books, 1958), p. 455.

3. Ibid., p. 487.

4. Heschel, Abraham Joshua, "The Earth Is the Lord's," in *The Earth Is the Lord's & The Sabbath*, p. 9.

5. Alicia Ostriker, *Writing Like a Woman*, Michigan Poets on Poetry series (Ann Arbor: University of Michigan Press, 1983), p. 126, quoted in LeGuin, Ursula K., "The Fisherwoman's Daughter," in *Dancing at the Edge of the World: Thoughts on Women, Words, Places* (New York: Grove Press, 1989), p. 229.

6. Pareles, Jon, "Springsteen, 42, Leans Toward Family Values," *New York Times*, July 25, 1992, and Holden, Stephen, "When the Boss Fell to Earth, He Hit Paradise," *New York Times*, August 9, 1992.

7. Preston, John Hyde, "A Conversation with Gertrude Stein," in Ghiselin, Brewster, *The Creative Process: A Symposium* (Berkeley and Los Angeles: University of California Press, 1954), p. 171.

8. Quoted by Tillie Olsen in "One Out of Twelve: Women Who Are Writers in Our Century," in Ruddick, Sara, and Pamela Daniels, eds., *Working It Out* (New York: Pantheon, 1977), p. 332.

9. Ibid., p. 331.

10. Ibid., p. 335.

11. Woodward, Richard B., "The Intensely Imagined Life of Daniel Day-Lewis," *New York Times Magazine*, July 5, 1992.

12. Carver, Raymond, "Fires," in *Fires: Essays, Poems, Stories* (New York: Vintage Books, 1984), pp. 19–30.

13. Spender, Stephen, *The Making of a Poem* (New York: W. W. Norton & Company, 1962), pp. 54–55.

14. Bernhard, Emery, "Painting, Writing, and Parenting: Can Art Survive Children?," *Mothering*, Spring 1993, p 104.

15. All Ursula K. LeGuin and Margaret Oliphant references are from: LeGuin's "The Fisherwoman's Daughter," in *Dancing at the Edge of the World: Thoughts on Women, Words, Places* (New York: Grove Press, 1989), pp. 212–37.

16. Canfield, Dorothy, "How Flint and Fire Started and Grew," in Ghiselin, Brewster, *The Creative Process: A Symposium*, p. 176.

17. Kollwitz, Käthe, in Hans Kollwitz, ed., *The Diary and Letters of Käthe Kollwitz* (Evanston: Northwestern University Press, 1988), p. 53.

VI How Our Children Can Improve Our Work and the Way We Work

1. Bernhard, Emery, "Painting, Writing, and Parenting: Can Art Survive Children?," p. 101.

2. Gay, Peter, pp. 108–9.

3. Mahl, George F., "Father-Son Themes in Freud's Self-Analysis," in *Father and Child Developmental and Clinical Perspectives*, p. 63.

4. The relevance of Freud's observation of his little grandson to his thoughts about the meaning of repetitive behavior are discussed in: Erikson, Eric H., *Childhood and Society* (New York: W. W. Norton, 1950), pp. 188–91, and Gay, Peter, pp. 399–401.

5. Elkind, David, "Piaget—Giant in the Nursery," *New York Times Magazine*, May 24, 1968.

6. Singer, Dorothy G., and Tracey A. Revenson, *A Piaget Primer: How A Child Thinks* (New York: New American Library, 1978), p. 7.

7. Demos, John, "The Changing Faces of Fatherhood: A New Exploration in American Family History," in *Father and Child Developmental and Clinical Perspectives*, p. 436.

8. Dowd, Maureen, "Growing Sorority in Congress Edges into the Ol' Boys Club," *New York Times*, March 5, 1993.

VII "I Can't Fix the Cat!"

1. Benedek, Therese, "Parenthood As a Developmental Phase," *Journal of the American Psychoanalytic Association*, 7, 1959, p. 415.

2. Kestenberg, Judith, "The Effect on Parents of the

Child's Latency," in Anthony, E. James, and Therese Benedek, *Parenthood: Its Psychology and Psychopathology*, p. 300.

3. Benedek, Therese, "Parenthood as a Developmental Phase," p. 393.

4. Ibid., pp. 409–10.

5. Ibid., p. 410.

6. Freud, Sigmund, *Totem and Taboo* (New York and London: W. W. Norton, 1950), p. 20.

7. Lurie, Alison, *Don't Tell the Grown-Ups: Subversive Children's Literature* (Boston: Little, Brown, 1990), p. ix.

8. Lidz, Theodore, *The Person: His or Her Development Throughout the Life Cycle* (New York: Basic Books, 1983), p. 480.

9. Collins, Gail, "The Age of the Smart Woman," *The Ladies Home Journal*, April 1993, p. 146.

VIII   How Parenthood Can Make a Marriage Grow

1. Harris, Marlys, "Love After Parenthood," *Redbook*, January 1994, p. 128.

2. Cowan, Philip A., "Becoming a Father: A Time for Change, An Opportunity for Development," in Bronstein, Phyllis, and Carolyn Pape Cowan, eds., *Fatherhood Today: Men's Changing Role in the Family*, New York: John Wiley & Sons, 1988, pp. 13–35.

3. Eicher, Terry Boyd, "Understanding Fathers of Daughters," p. 337.

4. Ibid.

IX   Everlasting Impressions

1. Eicher, Terry, "Understanding Fathers of Daughters," p. 358.

2. Benedek, Therese, "Parenthood During the Life Cycle," p. 201.

Bibliography

ANTHONY, E. JAMES. "Afterword," in Cath, Stanley H., Alan R. Gurwitt, and John Munder Ross, eds. *Father and Child: Developmental and Clinical Perspectives.* Boston: Little, Brown and Co., 1982.

ANTHONY, E. JAMES, and THERESE BENEDEK, eds. *Parenthood: Its Psychology and Psychopathology.* Boston: Little, Brown and Co., 1970.

BARRY, DAVE. "How to Talk to New Parents." *Glamour*, May 1987.

BENEDEK, THERESE. "The Family As a Psychologic Field," "Motherhood and Nurturing," "Fatherhood and Providing," "Parenthood During the Life Cycle" in E. James Anthony and Therese Benedek, eds. *Parenthood: Its Psychology and Psychopathology.*

BENEDEK, THERESE. "Parenthood As a Developmental Phase." *Journal of the American Psychoanalytic Association*, 1959, 7.

BERNHARD, EMERY. "Painting, Writing, and Parenting: Can Art Survive Children?" *Mothering*, Spring 1993.

BETTELHEIM, BRUNO. *A Good Enough Parent: A Book on Childrearing.* New York: Alfred A. Knopf, 1987.

BLATT, SIDNEY J., and RACHEL B. BLASS. "Relatedness & Self-Definition: A dialectic model of personality development," in G. G. Noam and K. Fischer, eds. *Development and Vulnerability in Relationships.* Hillsdale, NJ: Lawrence Earlbaum Associates, in press.

BURNETT, FRANCES HODGSON. *The Secret Garden.* Philadelphia and New York: J. B. Lippincott Co., 1949.

———. *Editha's Burglar.* Boston: Jordan Marsh and Co., 1888.

CANFIELD, DOROTHY. "How Flint and Fire Started and Grew," in Ghiselin, Brewster, *The Creative Process: A Symposium.* Berkeley and Los Angeles: University of California Press, 1954.

CARVER, RAYMOND. "Fires," in *Fires: Essays, Poems, Stories.* New York: Vintage Books, 1984.

COLES, ROBERT. *Erik H. Erikson: The Growth of His Work.* Boston: Little, Brown and Co., 1970.

———. *The Moral Life of Children.* Boston: Houghton Mifflin Co., 1986.

COLLINS, GAIL. "The Age of the Smart Woman." *The Ladies Home Journal*, April 1993.

COLWIN, LAURIE. *Family Happiness.* New York: Alfred A. Knopf, 1982.

CORMAN, AVERY. *Kramer versus Kramer*. New York: New American Library, 1977.

COWAN, PHILIP A. "Becoming a Father: A Time for Change, An Opportunity for Development," in Bronstein, Phyllis and Carolyn Pape Cowan, eds. *Fatherhood Today: Men's Changing Role in the Family*. New York: John Wiley and Sons, 1988, p. 13.

DEMOS, JOHN. "The Changing Faces of Fatherhood: A New Exploration in American Family History," in Cath, Stanley H., Alan R. Gurwitt, John Munder Ross, eds. *Father and Child: Developmental and Clinical Perspectives*.

DOWD, MAUREEN. "Growing Sorority in Congress Edges into the Ol' Boys Club," *New York Times*, March 5, 1993.

EICHER, TERRY, and JESSE GELLER, eds. *Fathers and Daughters: Portraits in Fiction*. New York: Plume, 1991.

EICHER, TERRY BOYD. "Understanding Fathers of Daughters." Unpublished dissertation, Yale University, 1991. Available through University Microfilms International, 300 N. Zeeb Road, Ann Arbor, MI 48106.

ELKIND, DAVID. "Piaget—Giant in the Nursery," *New York Times Magazine*, May 26, 1968.

ERIKSON, ERIC H. *Childhood and Society*. New York: W. W. Norton and Co., 1950.

———. *Identity and the Life Cycle*. New York: W. W. Norton and Co., 1980.

FRAIBERG, SELMA. "Ghosts in the Nursery: A Psychoanalytic Approach to the Problems of Impaired Infant-Mother Relationships." *Journal of the American Academy of Child Psychiatry*, 14:387–424, 1975.

———. *The Magic Years*. New York: Charles Scribner's Sons, 1959.

FREUD, SIGMUND. *The Complete Letters of Sigmund Freud to Wilhelm Fliess: 1887–1904*, edited by Jeffrey Moussaieff Masson. Cambridge and London: Belknap Press of Harvard University Press, 1985.

———. "On Narcissism," in *A General Selection from the Works of Sigmund Freud*, ed. by John Rickman. New York: Anchor Books, 1989.

———. *The Interpretation of Dreams*. New York: Basic Books, Inc., 1958.

———. *Totem and Taboo*. New York and London: W. W. Norton & Co., 1950.

FRIEDAN, BETTY. *The Feminine Mystique*. New York: Dell Publishing, 1984.

GAY, PETER. *Freud: A Life for Our Time*. New York: W. W. Norton and Co., 1988.

HALLO, WILLIAM W., and J. J. A. VAN DIJK. *The Exaltation of Inanna*. New Haven–London: Yale University Press, 1968.

HARRIS, MARLYS. "Love After Parenthood." *Redbook*, January 1994.

HESCHEL, ABRAHAM JOSHUA. *The Earth Is the Lord's and The Sabbath*. New York: Harper & Row, 1966.

HEWLETT, SYLVIA ANN. *When the Bough Breaks*. New York: Basic Books, 1991.

HOFFMAN, EDWARD. "The Last Interview of Abraham Maslow," *Psychology Today*, January–February 1992.

HOFFMAN, MIRIAM, and EVA SAMUELS. *Authors and Illustrators of Children's Books: Writings on Their Lives and Works*. New York: R. R. Bowker Co., 1972.

HOLDEN, STEPHEN. "When the Boss Fell to Earth, He Hit Paradise," *New York Times*, August 9, 1992.

JACOBS, JOSEPH, ed. *The Fables of Aesop*. New York: Schocken Books, 1966.

KALINS, DOROTHY. "New Parents' Style: Bunny Modern," *New York Times*, October 21, 1993.

KESTENBERG, JUDITH. "The Effect on Parents of the Child's Latency," in Anthony, E. James, and Therese Benedek, *Parenthood: Its Psychology and Psychopathology*.

KOLLWITZ, KÄTHE. *The Diary and Letters of Käthe Kollwitz*, Hans Kollwitz, ed. Evanston, IL.: Northwestern University Press, 1988.

KOTZWINKLE, WILLIAM. *The World Is Big and I'm So Small*. New York: Crown Publishers, 1986.

LEGALLIENNE, EVA. *Flossie and Bossie*. New York: Harper & Brothers, 1949.

LEGUIN, URSULA K. *Dancing at the Edge of the World: Thoughts on Women, Words, Places*. New York: Grove Press, 1989.

LEE, HARPER. *To Kill a Mockingbird*. New York: Warner Books, Inc., 1980.

LEWIS, SINCLAIR. *The Job*, New York and London: Harper & Brothers, 1917.

LIDZ, THEODORE. *The Person: His or Her Development Throughout the Life Cycle*. New York: Basic Books, 1983.

LURIE, ALISON. *Don't Tell the Grown-ups: Subversive Children's Literature*. Boston: Little, Brown and Co., 1990.

MAILER, NORMAN. *The Prisoner of Sex*. Boston: Little, Brown & Co., 1971.

MAHL, GEORGE F., "Father-Son Themes in Freud's Self-Analysis," in Cath, Stanley H., Alan R. Gurwitt, John Munder Ross, eds., *Father and Child: Developmental and Clinical Perspectives*.

MASLOW, ABRAHAM H. *Toward a Psychology of Being*. New York: D. Van Nostrand Co., 1968.

OLSEN, TILLIE. "One Out of Twelve: Women Who Are Writers in Our Century," In Ruddick, Sara, and Pamela Daniels, eds. *Working It Out*. New York: Pantheon, 1977.

PARELES, JON. "SPRINGSTEEN, 42, LEANS TOWARD FAMILY VALUES," *New York Times*, July 25, 1992.

PRESTON, JOHN HYDE. "A Conversation with Gertrude Stein," in Ghiselin, Brewster. *The Creative Process: A Symposium*.

PRUETT, KYLE. *The Nurturing Father*. New York: Warner Books, 1987.

RAWLINGS, MARJORIE KINNAN. *The Yearling*, New York: Collier Macmillan Publishers, 1988.

SINGER, DOROTHY G., and TRACEY A. REVENSON. *A Piaget Primer: How a Child Thinks*. New York: New American Library, 1978.

SPENDER, STEPHEN. *The Collected Poems*. New York: Random House, 1955.

———. *The Making of a Poem*, New York: W. W. Norton and Co., 1961.

SPOCK, BENJAMIN. "What We Know About the Development of Healthy Personalities in Children," in *Proceedings of the Midcentury White House Conference on Children and Youth*. Raleigh, N.C.: Health Publications Institute, Inc., 1951.

STEVENS, MAY. "My Work and My Working-Class Father," in Ruddick, Sara and Pamela Daniels, eds., *Working It Out.*

UPDIKE, JOHN. "Grandparenting," *The New Yorker*, February 21, 1994.

WESSEL, MORRIS. "The Liberation of Being a Grandparent," *New York Times*, April 26, 1987.

WOODWARD, RICHARD B. "The Intensely Imagined Life of Daniel Day-Lewis." *New York Times Magazine*, July 5, 1992.

YOUNG-BRUEHL, ELISABETH. *Anna Freud.* New York: Summit Books, 1988.

About the Author

Elin Schoen is a journalist and photographer whose work has appeared in the *New York Times, Family Circle, Parents* magazine, *New York* magazine, *Life, Redbook, Glamour, The Ladies' Home Journal, Mademoiselle,* and many other national publications. She is the author of several books of nonfiction, including *Tales of an All-Night Town* and *Widower.* In 1992, while researching this book, she was made a fellow at the Bush Center in Child Development and Social Policy at Yale University. She lives in Connecticut with her family.